In this interdisciplinary study, Professor Clyne examines the impact of cultural values on discourse. Through an exploration of the role of verbal communication patterns in successful and unsuccessful communication, he sets out to integrate and develop a framework for a linguistics of inter-cultural communication. Professor Clyne draws on data derived from recordings of spontaneous communication in the Australian workplace between people of vastly differing backgrounds, notably European and Asian, who use English as a lingua franca.

This study offers both a pragmatics and a discourse perspective, not simply analysing data, but seeking to extend the theoretical model. The rapidly increasing use of English as a language of inter-cultural communication between non-native speakers means that the issues raised here will be of interest not only to linguists, but also to those involved in education, business, and industry.

Inter-cultural communication at work

Inter-cultural communication at work

Cultural values in discourse

Michael Clyne
Monash University

CAMBRIDGE
UNIVERSITY PRESS

Published by the Press Syndicate of the University of Cambridge
The Pitt Building, Trumpington Street, Cambridge CB2 1RP
40 West 20th Street, New York, NY 10011-4211, USA
10 Stamford Road, Oakleigh, Melbourne 3166, Australia

First published 1994
Reprinted 1996
First paperback edition 1996

Printed in Great Britain at the University Press, Cambridge

A catalogue record for this book is available from the British Library

Library of Congress cataloguing in publication data

Clyne, Michael G., 1939–
    Inter-cultural communication at work: cultural values in discourse/
Michael Clyne.
        p.   cm.
    Includes bibliographical references and index.
    ISBN 0 521 46137 5 hardback
1. Inter-cultural communication.   2. Discourse analysis.   3. Speech acts
(Linguistics).   4. Language and culture.   I. Title.   II. Title: Inter-cultural
communication at work.
P94.6.C59   1994
306.4'4–dc20   93-44673   CIP

ISBN 0 521 46137 5 hardback
ISBN 0 521 57509 5 paperback

Contents

Figures

Tables

Acknowledgements

This project was carried out with the help of a grant from the Australian Research Council (1989–91) and some supplementary assistance from the National Languages and Literacy Institute of Australia as part of the budget for the Language and Society Centre. I thank both these organizations. I am indebted to Martin Ball, Connie Giannicos, and Deborah Neil who collected, transcribed and analyzed the factory data and provided many insights, and also to Margaret Carew and Youle Bottomley for collecting and transcribing office and catering data and to Adult Migration Education Services (especially Susan Allender) for releasing them fractionally to undertake this work. My thanks are due also to Martin Ball for assistance with the technical production of the final draft, to Lona Gottschalk for technical advice, and to Sandra Kipp for compiling the index.

I express my gratitude to all those who made the data collection possible – the informants, management of the companies, shop stewards, and trades union representatives. I thank Millicent Vladiv-Glover, Nguyên Xuân Thu, and Burusutama Bilimoria for advice on communication patterns. My thanks are due also to Konrad Ehlich for his helpful and constructive comments on an earlier version of the manuscript and to Robert Kaplan, Keith Allan and Leslie Bodi for theirs on sections. The responsibility for this rather imperfect product is, of course, mine. Finally, many thanks to Judith Ayling and her colleagues at Cambridge University Press for their kind co-operation at all stages of the development of this monograph.

1 Introducing the field

1.0 Scope of this book

This book intends to examine cultural variation in discourse, to explore the role of verbal communication patterns in successful and unsuccessful inter-cultural communication, and to integrate and develop frameworks for a linguistics of inter-cultural communication incorporating cultural values systems. It should be seen as a small contribution to the ongoing research on the development of a typology of communication patterns across languages and cultures and their relation to cultural values systems. To facilitate this process, it will modify some categories and features of the theoretical frameworks of pragmatics and discourse/conversational analysis, particularly the interface between these areas. It is hoped that this monograph will be of some interest not only to linguists, but also to teachers of English, education policy planners, and to those practising inter-cultural communication in any context.

Immigration patterns, rapid international transport, new technologies of communication (fax, E-mail, satellites, cable TV, computers), and opportunities for working in international teams and networks are all contributing to the importance of inter-cultural communication in the developed world. That is not to say that inter-cultural communication is a new phenomenon, but that the above factors are requiring a different kind of understanding of it. The assumption is often made that all that is needed for inter-cultural communication to be successful is for one of the parties to learn the other's language or for both (or all) parties to adopt a lingua franca, a common language which is the first language of neither. I will not dispute the value of second or foreign language learning but argue that this is only the first step. Language represents the deepest manifestation of a culture, and people's values systems, including those taken over from the group of which they are part, play a substantial role in the way they use not only their first language(s) but also subsequently acquired ones. I will be focussing on the discourse level – that is, the level of language beyond that of the sentence, considered in its context.

Spoken discourse is also temporal and presupposes a speech situation requiring the co-presence of a speaker and hearer, and common perceptual access to the discourse. In European work in this field, discourse is sometimes contrasted with text (see Chapter 5) which is passed on either through literary production, whether it be a novel, a letter, or a piece of academic discourse, or remembered through its form (e.g. parallelism, cf. 4.4).[1] Text is also used for a passage that forms a unified whole (Kallmeyer and Meyer-Hermann 1980). Kinesics (the study of gestures) and proxemics (the study of how people position themselves in relation to one other) will be outside the scope of this study.

It is true, the 'new world order' will, on the whole, bring together nations and cultures with similar communication patterns within a region. But each region will be interacting with other regions on a global scale. English is already emerging as the most significant inter-regional lingua franca, but it is at the inter-regional level that communication patterns in English will be most divergent. Present-day Australia is a microcosm of such cultural diversity.

In a consideration of the role of cultural values in discourse, the level of language beyond the sentence, it is important to bear in mind the various major functions of language:

(i)   It is the most important medium of human communication. Through language, we express information, ideas, emotions, attitudes, and prejudices, among other things.
(ii) It is a means of identification. Through language, we indicate group membership and mark group boundaries, whether at the national, regional or local, ethnic, political, or religious level.
(iii) It is a means of cognitive development for children and of conceptual development for adults. The way in which we use language enables children to experience the reality of the world around them, and facilitates the development of new concepts by adults.
(iv) It is an instrument of action. As Austin (1962, 1963) has shown, certain important acts are performed purely linguistically. These include promises and apologies.

It is because language fulfils *all* these functions in human beings and human societies, that it is so crucial. Characteristically, the scope of this monograph includes all the four functions of language.

Culture is the 'whole way of life of a distinct people...' (Williams 1981: 11), its 'total set of beliefs, attitudes, customs, behaviour, social habits' (Richards et al. 1985: 70). Kluckhohn (1951: 86) sees culture as

[1] I thank Konrad Ehlich for drawing my attention to the dichotomy.

'patterned ways of thinking, feeling and reacting, acquired and trans-mitted mainly by symbols, consitituting the distinctive achievements of human groups, including their embodiments in artifacts; the essential core of culture consists of traditional (i.e. historically derived and selected) ideas and especially their attached values'. Redder and Rehbein (1987), tracing the development of the notion of 'culture', suggest that Williams investigates the forms of emotional structures as their ex-pression side, drawing meanings from the practice of the life style of an epoch, thereby showing indifference to surface linguistic forms. Redder and Rehbein (1987: 20) opt for a pragmatic notion of culture – an 'ensemble' of social experiences, thought structures, expectations, and practices of action, which has the quality of a 'mental apparatus'. This is the kind of definition which underlies the use of 'culture' in the chapters to come. A useful 'shorthand definition' is that of Hofstede (1991:4) who views culture (except in the narrow 'high-culture' sense) as 'collective programming of the mind which distinguishes the members of one group or category of people from another'.

Values are, in Rokeach's (1968: 160) words, 'internalized... stan-dard(s) for guiding action ... an enduring belief that a specific mode of conduct or end-state of existence is personally and socially preferable to alternative modes of conduct or end-states of existence'. Kluckhohn and Strodtbeck (1961: 4) see value orientations as 'complex but definitely patterned ... principles ... which give order and direction to the ever-flowing stream of human acts and thoughts as these relate to the solution of "common human" problems'.

In this context, I refer to Halliday's (1978: 139) statement: 'In its most general significance, a text is a sociological encounter through which the meanings that constitute the social system are exchanged.' As I will attempt to show in this monograph, cultural values constitute 'hidden' meaning underlying discourse structures.

1.1   Approaches to inter-cultural communication

Inter-cultural communication, like any kind of communication, takes place both orally and in writing. There are three main ways in which the role of culture in discourse can be, and has been, studied – by comparing native discourse across cultures (the Contrastive Approach), by exa-mining the discourse of non-native speakers in a second language (the Interlanguage Approach), and by examining and comparing the discourse of people of different cultural and linguistic backgrounds interacting either in a lingua franca or in one of the interlocutors' languages (the Interactive Inter-cultural Approach). Although the three approaches are not always clearly differentiated, the third approach is the one which so far has been the least developed and investigated, especially interaction in a lingua franca (see 1.3, also Clyne, Ball, and Neil 1991)).// One reason for this is that applicable contrastive pragmatics databases are available only for a limited range of languages. Such a database would facilitate the pin-pointing of 'interference' from the first language and culture, convergence towards norms in the target language, and convergence between the participants in inter-cultural communication situations. Nevertheless, there is a need for a dynamic interactive model which takes us well beyond the necessarily limited confines of the contrastive approach.

I will be basing the monograph on an interactive inter-cultural study of spontaneous workplace communication of immigrants from diverse backgrounds using English as a lingua franca (see Chapter 2).

1.2   The study and the data

Our main study is concerned with communication, mainly in work situations, in a lingua franca which is the national language. The speakers are people who migrated to Australia as adults and whose first language is a language other than English, or a 'New English' from Asia or the Pacific: 'a (semi-) institutionalized variety which came into being in a country in which English was originally not the main native language' (Newbrook, 1991).

The corpus consists of audio-tapes of typical spontaneous workplace communication, supplemented by video- and audio-tapes of formal meetings. It is intended to comprise interaction between dyads and between larger groups of people representing a wide diversity of cultural communication patterns in contact and capable of isolating cultural from other differences (individual, gender, class/status) as well as identifying relationships between these variables. The data are derived from different companies in diverse industries and different work situations within them so that industry- and situation-specific phenomena can be identified. The corpus should facilitate the description of the nature of, and factors in, successful and unsuccessful inter-cultural communication as well as inter-cultural factors in the negotiation of meaning and the resolution of inter-cultural communication breakdown. The nature and purpose of the corpus will be discussed in Section 2.4 after the context of the research sites has been introduced.

This research is supplemented by a small inter-cultural study of attitudes to specific instances of communication breakdown based on videos of reactions to videoed role-play (see 2.6). In later sections of the book, relating cultural values to discourse structures, I will also refer to some previously collected data on written academic discourse produced in English by English native speakers and in German and/or English by German native speakers, supplemented by an inter-cultural study of the attitudes of Australian and German scholars to academic discourse structures that, in the corpus, tend to be employed by one or the other group (see 5.1, 7.3). Reference will also be made to a small corpus of letters written in English by students from the Middle East and the Indian sub-continent. This provides a diverse range of sociolinguistic research contexts and represents the social extremes that language teachers and language planners have to contend with.

1.2.1   *The models*

The extension of the 'linguistic model' to include the social setting and to recognize variation as central made it (Labov e.g. 1970, 1972, Hymes 1972, Gumperz 1982) possible for wider questions of communication to be treated in 'mainstream linguistics'. On the other hand, communication rules also have a wider (non-linguistic) context and an existence of their own.

Under 1.1, I mentioned three approaches that linguists work with in the study of inter-cultural communication. In terms of linguistic theory, this field is informed by pragmatics and speech act theory (e.g. Searle 1969, Wunderlich 1972), the ethnography of communication (e.g. Hymes 1974), discourse analysis (e.g. Brown and Yule 1983, Stubbs 1983), conversation analysis/verbal strategies (e.g. Gumperz 1982, Schiffrin 1987, Button and Lee 1987), and neo-Prague School post-structural linguistics (e.g. Neustupný 1974). A brief account of the most relevant literature will be offered in the sections under 1.3. I believe in the fruitful interplay between theoretical frameworks and empirical research advocated in the papers in Tomić and Shuy (1987). Most of the papers in that book make the point that, apart from the application of theoretical linguistics, there is also the opposite type of interaction – research on language which is based in real-life situations leads to good theory. It is therefore not surprising that many of the linguistic studies of inter-cultural communication have been driven by the exigencies of language teaching (e.g. Edmondson 1981, House and Kasper 1981, Kasper 1981, Færch and Kasper 1983).

In relation to contrastive analysis, the reader is reminded of a much earlier debate on contrastive analysis (Selinker 1972, Corder 1981, Schumann 1978) following the great predictive and explanatory power it was afforded in phonology, morphosyntax, and semantics around the

1960s (e.g. Lado 1957, Moulton 1962, Kufner 1962, Stockwell and Bowen 1965, Stockwell, Bowen, and Martin 1975, di Pietro 1971, Leisi 1952). Interference proved to be only one of several sources of errors, and a positive response based on the notion of an interlanguage which is developing towards the target language was found more productive. This should, however, not detract from the intrinsic value of contrastive studies or the reality of transference phenomena. In fact, contrastive studies (without extravagant predictive claims) have made a comeback at the pragmatic and discourse levels (e.g. Sajavaara 1977, James 1980, Blum-Kulka, House, and Kasper 1989, Olesky 1989).

There is a well-known tradition in linguistics which has presupposed and supported the pre-eminence of language in culture. It began with Humboldt (1903–18) and Herder (1877–1913) who demonstrated that each language had its own way of looking at the world (linguistic relativity) and that consequently speakers of different languages had different ways of seeing the world (linguistic determinism). This has led to both the Weisgerber thesis (1962) that lexical fields in the 'mother tongue' play a crucial role in conceptual development, and the strong form of the Sapir–Whorf hypothesis (arising from Whorf 1956), based on the study of the syntax and semantics of Hopi, an American Indian language, that people are at the mercy of the language that they speak. Janney and Arndt (1993) refer to Urban's (1939) view of the cyclical alternation of intellectual history between attitudes favouring universality and ones favouring relativity. While these excesses have been discarded in recent years and a more moderate perspective of the relation between culture and language has been developed (e.g. Cole and Scribner 1974, Fishman 1960, Fishman 1985: 473–87, Mathiot 1979, and cf. Lucy 1992), new forms of linguistic determinism have emerged (e.g. the language and class, language and gender, language and war, language and racism, language and environment controversies – e.g. Bernstein, 1962, Spender 1980, Coates 1986, Chilton 1985, Clyne 1986, Mühlhäusler 1983, Halliday 1993a,b, and the 1993 AILA Symposium on language and the environment). This is not the place to discuss determinist, relativist, and interactionist points of view. In this monograph, I will argue not that language determines culture, but rather that the discourse level of language is inseparable from cultural behaviour and that, except in individuals with a high degree of biculturalism as well as bilingualism, this will determine a great deal of inter-lingual transfer at the discourse level.

1.3 Literature survey

The literature on pragmatics and discourse analysis is vast. This is not the place to offer a critical summary of it. I will restrict myself to a discussion of a limited number of topics drawn from a few sources particularly relevant to the issues to be treated in this monograph.

1.3.1 *Discourse analysis and conversational analysis*

Discourse analysis, a branch of linguistics (in fact, an extension of the linguistics model), deals with language in context beyond the level of the sentence, enabling us to follow the implications of a given utterance. It contributes towards an understanding of cognitive processes. It is conceived variously as a grammar of discourse (Sinclair and Coulthard 1975), as a socially oriented analysis demonstrating how people make sense of one another's communications (e.g. Van Dijk 1980, Halliday 1978), and the linguistic application of critical theory (e.g. Kress and Hodge 1979). The second of these links with the 'grammar of discourse' in the Hallidayan emphasis on cohesion and coherence. The Prague School linguists had introduced discourse into the agenda of mainstream linguistics through the (functional) linguistic study of written texts.

Discourse analysis has benefited a great deal from psycholinguistic research on language and cognition, which has given rise to categories such as schemata, frames, and scripts. Schemata (Rumelhart 1975, Van Dijk 1977) are socially constructed patterns of communicative behaviour available to the interlocutors from the experience and knowledge they bring to the encounter, e.g. how to make (and sequence) a complaint to subordinates at work. Frames (Bateson 1972, Goffman 1983) describe the speaker's intention and the hearer's interpretation of it, e.g. explaining a work procedure. Scripts (Schank and Abelson 1977) are episodes remembered in terms of a standardized generalized episode, e.g. restaurant visit, by recalling what was significantly different. Scripts facilitate the representation of plans and stories.

A sociological counterpart of discourse analysis whose practisers give it autonomous status is conversational analysis, a branch of ethnomethodology (Garfinkel 1967, Sacks, Schegloff and Jefferson 1974: for its background, see Button and Lee 1987: 20–1). Here talk, which is rule governed, becomes the object of an investigation of social structures and relations, and the structure of a conversation is identified, focussing on the devices for managing the interaction and constructing joint meaning (Schiffrin 1987). Wardhaugh (1985: 21) describes conversation as 'coping behaviour'. 'Relationships are made, maintained and broken through talk', writes Tannen (1986: vii), 'so linguistics provides a concrete way of understanding how relationships are made, maintained and broken.' The principal conversational mechanisms examined are turn taking and adjacency pairs. Tannen (1986: vii) refers to conversation as a 'turn-taking game'. As Wardhaugh (1985: 150) points out, 'once you have acquired the turn to speak, you have a strong right to continue speaking until you voluntarily give up the turn'. As interruption is usually a 'violation of another's territory or rights', speakers will organize their discourse to prevent interruption. In some cases, interruption is intended to promote co-operation (e.g. request for clarification or repetition or to help the other person express themselves, Wardhaugh 1985: 151).

Usually one speaker is speaking at a time with some overlap and interruption as well as silences. In adjacency pairs, which are the two-part exchanges, where the first speaker initiates the first of the pair and, having been the hearer, responds with the second part of the pair Sacks, Schegloff, and Jefferson (1974). Examples of adjacency pairs are:

> Invitation or request – acceptance or refusal.
> Accusation – denial or admission.
> Greeting – greeting.
> Farewell – farewell.
> Summons – answer.
> Trouble indicator – trouble clarification (Deen and Van Hout
> 1991).

The discourse analysts, Sinclair and Coulthard (1975), in their analysis of classroom discourse, work with three-part exchanges: Initiation – response – follow on. Fox (1987) works with more flexible combinations involving two or three categories, e.g. issue – elaboration – background, or issue – elaboration – (elaboration).

The analysis of conversations received impetus from Gumperz's (1982) work that gives central importance to the background knowledge and assumptions that participants draw on to interpret the social meanings of others. This approach attaches importance to contextualization cues which help channel interpretations in a particular way. They can be any features of linguistic form, e.g. syntactic ones, and especially intonation. Where communication rules are not shared, the wrong inferences can be drawn. For instance, Gumperz (1982: 149) shows that, in developing an argument, Indian speakers 'take great care to formulate the background for what they are going to say', increase stress to mark the background information, and then shift to low pitch and amplitude.

Dorval (1990) sees conversation as organized from the perspective of what is talked about, as turn-for-turn interplay of speech acts and reactions, reflection of expectations determining a whole series of turns, and a reflection of expectations organizing whole conversation engagements. A turn is defined by Markel (1975: 190) as 'begin[ning] when an interlocutor starts solo talking and end[ing] when a different interlocutor starts solo talking'. This is essentially the sense in which I will use 'turn'. There is some lack of clarity as to whether back-channelling terminates another's turn. I do not take it to do so.

In his analysis of English conversations, Bublitz (1988) pays much attention to coherence, 'ascribed by participants in a conversation (or by observing participants or analyzers) to a sequence of utterances in relation to their surroundings' (1988: 32). In his desire to achieve a balance between the autonomy of participants and consideration of fellow speakers, he focusses on topic change and topic continuity, their relation to conversational control, and how and by whom they are determined. His account deals especially with the role of the secondary interlocutor in conversations. From a cross-cultural point of view, I find Bublitz's discussion of his 'original erroneous hypotheses' very significant. He writes (Bublitz 1988: 3): 'I had...assumed that each conversation of the type analysed in this work, requires a dialectic structure ...it appeared to be inevitable that each participant was compelled to expose his own deviant interests at least some of the time and to impress them on the interlocutor, lest the conversation should be "marking time" or even "reach a deadlock"...It turned out, however, not to be realized in the particular type of everyday conversation at hand. Instead of a structure of thesis and anti-thesis...what is in fact preferred is the pattern "thesis and confirmation or support of the thesis".' I would venture the speculation that this hypothesis would have been prompted by everyday conversations in German, Bublitz's native language (cf. 1.3.4, 5.1) and might have been supported in German data.

Hatch (1978) uses conversational analysis as a means of understanding second language acquisition of communication strategies (cf. Færch and Kasper 1983), including the negotiation of meaning and the compensatory strategies non-native speakers utilize when they have an incomplete knowledge of L2. Pica (1992, Pica, Doughty, and Young (1986)) have investigated the role of negotiation of meaning in the acquisition of a second language.

Conversational analysts have argued (Button and Lee 1987, Sharrock and Anderson 1987) that there is incompatibility between conversational analysis and discourse analysis because of their conflicting frameworks. I hope to employ gainfully all the above-mentioned approaches to discourse because they all enable us to illuminate the interrelation of language in use with culture, taking into account social and cognitive structures. Like many others, I shall employ 'discourse' and 'discourse analysis' as the superordinate terms.

There is potentially a close interrelation between discourse and conversation analysis and pragmatics (Austin 1962, Searle 1969), which concerns itself with language in use, in particular with communicative intent and communicative function, the role of speech acts – i.e. language as an instrument of action. In fact, conversational analysis with its sociological origins and its emphasis on social interaction, regards all its work as concerned with social action (Sharrock and Anderson 1987). Ethnography of communication (Hymes 1972), which is seen as an approach to sociolinguistics, considers the function of language choices in interaction and by examining social processes through language use. An emphasis on discourse has been part of Systemic Linguistics with its strong emphasis on meaning and social semiotics (e.g. Halliday 1973, 1978, Halliday and Hasan 1976). Just one example of the application of a combination of conversational analysis and pragmatics is Neu (1985). She examines (monocultural) business negotiation as a model speech event with the speech act as the unit of *langue* and the turn as the unit of *parole*. Episodes (conversational units, such as planning, bargaining) are shown to be predictors of negotiation outcomes. The analysis indicates the importance of structural variables such as repair, pause, simultaneous start-up, acknowledgement, and prosodics.

An example of discourse analysis with a strong objectivity in relation to the social context, Watts (1991) demonstrates the value of discourse analysis to investigate politic (co-operative) behaviour and power in a close-knit group, namely in an extended family. There are two main concepts in the investigation – interruption and the 'emergent' social network. This is the actual group involved in a communication, whose power is measurable according to floor occupation and topic control. Watts contrasts it with the 'latent' social network, the potential network based on existing social relations. Network structures are examined through three main forms of statistical analysis: density (i.e. degree of co-operation/sharing the floor); degree of connection between members; and centrality of individual members. The latter forms 'a power base from which members can impose on others their own conceptions of the role and function they assume in the ongoing discourse' (Watts 1991: 244). The model is tested on radio phone-in discourse.

1.3.2 *Speech acts, Cooperative Principle, and extensions to this*

The extension of linguistics to include the communicative intent, function, and effects of utterances (in Austin's (1962) terms 'how to do things with words') paved the way for the linguistic study of cross-cultural communication. Austin established a dichotomy of: Constatives, which have truth values; and Performatives, which he claims have no truth values but perform actions whose successful completion rests on felicity conditions (see Allan 1986, 1994).

Austin (1962) and Searle (1969) conceptualize speech acts as comprising:

Locution –   the actual form of an utterance;
Illocution –   the communicative force of the utterance; and
Perlocution –   the communicative effect of the utterance.

Searle summarizes Austin's speech acts – divided into verdictives, commissives, exercitives, behabitives, and expositives – under five categories:

Assertives –   stating: where S is committed to the truth of P;
Directives –   commanding, requesting: where the onus is
                placed on H to do something;
Commissives –   promising and offering: where S is committed
                to a future act A;
Expressives –   thinking, forgiving, blaming: where S makes
                known his/her attitude to H; and
Declaratives – baptizing, naming, appointing, sacking: which
                bring about correspondence between the pro-
                positional content and reality.

Grice's (1967) Cooperative Principle, formulated as a universal to help account for the high degree of implicitness in conversation and the required relation between (rule-governed) meaning and force (Leech 1983), comprises four categories of maxims (quantity, quality, relation, and manner). Allan (1991) cautions us to regard the maxims as 'reference points for language interchange', not as 'laws to be obeyed'. The two maxims of Quantity are:

1. Make yourself as informative as is required (for the current purposes of the exchange).
2. Do not make your contribution more informative than is required.
                                                    (Grice 1967: 45)

The supermaxim of Quality asserts that the speaker 'try to make [their] contribution one that is true' (p. 46).
There are two maxims in this category:

1. Do not say what you believe to be false; and
2. Do not say that for which you lack adequate evidence.   (p. 46)

I shall discuss some misgivings about this in 5.2.7. Grice's specific maxims of Manner are:

1. Avoid obscurity of expression.
2. Avoid ambiguity.
3. Be brief.
4. Be orderly.   (p. 46)

The last two of these maxims – as well as that of *Relation*: 'Be relevant' – are symptomatic of a form-boundness that assumes that such considerations are important, measurable and determinable outside a social context. In common with researchers in other fields of theoretical linguistics, those exploring pragmatics strove to establish universals, but often presupposed universals through assumptions based on English. This applies to some extent to Grice and his Cooperative Principle (see below, also 6.5), but not to Sperber and Wilson (1986) whose theory deals with how people make assumptions and inferences from the context. Their theory is more explicit than Grice's conversational implicatures which, assuming a greater degree of co-operation, clash with some cultural values systems. Sperber and Wilson regard successful communication as the only common purpose of communication. This is inherent in their principle of relevance: 'Each act of ostensible communication communicates the presupposition of its own optimal relevance' (p. 158).

   The work done so far on contrasts in discourse structures (see below, and Chapter 5) indicates an anglocentric element in the maxims of the Cooperative Principle as worded by Grice and their inapplicability or limited relevance to cultures where content and knowledge are core values. The very notion of Co-operation needs to be developed with caution to allow for cultural variation. As Schiffrin (1984), Kochman (1981), and Wierzbicka (1991) have shown, in some cultures (e.g. Jewish, Israeli, Black American), contrariness (and therefore saying a lot) and immodesty are ways in which to be co-operative, while (as I shall discuss in 6.2.7), in Chinese and Vietnamese, being co-operative means saying little enough to avoid (causing) a conflict. Watts (1989) suggests that

English people tend to 'share' a text, that is, they negotiate about the choice and development of the topic whereas German-speaking Swiss (and, I believe Germans and Central Europeans in general), simply put forward their point of view.

While Wierzbicka rejects the Gricean maxims as monocentric (see below), Allan (1991) insists that the Cooperative Principle is motivated by conventions that pertain to face effects and are sensitive to situations and communities. In 6.5, an attempt will be made to reformulate Grice's maxims in the spirit of his intentions but with more regard for the communication patterns of non-English cultures.

Ehlich (1987) subjects the Cooperative Principle to theoretical scrutiny in relation to the German concept of *Sprachliches Handeln* (linguistic action). He distinguishes between three types of co-operation: materiell (material as opposed to spiritual – in the process of production); material (any form of co-operation involving interactants with a common purpose); and formal (any kind of *Sprachliches Handeln* usually involving more than one actant with elementary characteristics of co-operation). The methodological consequences of formal co- operation in *Sprachliches Handeln* are: there is immediate co-operation, including face-to-face communication, co-presence in space and time is a requirement, and formal co-operation is a basis for interaction. It involves in principle a speaker and hearer, translates into a system of purposes (illocution), and is formed into a linguistic system. It results in a system of expectations in relation to the realization of formal co-operation.

Leech (1983) extends Grice's framework in an attempt to explain why people often convey their meaning indirectly. He complements the Cooperative Principle by a Politeness Principle with maxims of tact, generosity, approbation, modesty, agreement, and sympathy, and an Irony Principle. At the end of the book, Leech (1983: 231) alludes to cross-cultural comparisons of communicative behaviour, but implies that the differences are due to strategies, not principles.

The pragmatic parallel to the psycholinguistic concept of the schema is the *Handlungsmuster* (pattern of action), devised by Ehlich and Rehbein (1986). Taking classroom discourse as an example, they view communication as the reconstruction of the concrete, actual phenomena which are the expression of their underlying governing rules. A pattern is a complex of activites manifested in surface realizations comprising a number of pragmatic units called pragmemes, which are sequenced in a particular order (e.g. S says something startling, H is startled, S expresses confirmation). A single surface succession may be the expression of the pattern, it may be a multiple realization of a pattern, two surface utterances may realize successive pattern positions, or one surface utterance may realize positions from two patterns at the same time. An understanding of patterns underlying communication practice can form the basis of social criticism of institutions such as schools.

Speech act research, whether inter- or intracultural, has been enriched by drawing on Goffman's (1955) notion of 'face' – 'positive social value a person claims for himself by the line others assure he has taken during a particular contact' (1955: 213), i.e. sensitivity to the rights of others. This applies especially to Brown and Levinson's (1978, 1987) pragmatic theory, based on the premise that speakers share assumptions about politeness, which inform their choice of communicative strategies. The three major tenets of the model are the degree of relative power, social distance, and relative ranking of impositions in the particular culture. Brown and Levinson differentiate between negative face, the 'want' not to be imposed on by others, and positive face, the 'want' to be approved. Similarly, they develop a dichotomy between negative politeness in which a conflict is avoided through modesty, formality, and restraint, and positive politeness where a closer relation with the interactant is established through frankness. Brown and Levinson propose five categories of politeness strategies, offering a degree of security and avoiding a face threatening action – bald on-record, positive politeness, negative politeness, and being silent. Brown and Levinson's model is based on three unrelated languages and cultures – English, Tamil (a Dravidian language), and Tzeltal (a Mayan language). As Allan (1986: 10) points out, speakers need to take care constantly that they 'will either maintain, enhance or threaten H's face' in accordance with their intention.

Bayrataroglu (1991) extends the framework to develop the notion of interactional imbalance, categorized as:

Boosting face of self –	Face Boosting Act/self: e.g. boasting;
Threatening face of self –	Face Threatening Act/self: e.g. self-degradation;
Boosting face of self –	Face Boosting Act/other: e.g. compliments; and
Threatening face of self –	Face Threatening Act/other: e.g. accusation/criticism.

She creates a base for the analysis of politeness in stretches of conversation. Speakers attend to interactional imbalance rather than just to face threatening acts with the possibility of precautionary error correction.

A criticism of Brown and Levinson's model comes from Ide (1989) who considers it incapable of dealing with politeness in languages with honorific systems in which social conventions do not permit interactional choice. Ide refers to the Japanese concept of *wakimae* (sometimes translated as 'discernment') where language use is predetermined by the person's place in society. This contrasts with interactional choice of strategies which Brown and Levinson can address by concentrating on the weight rather than the content of 'face'. Hill et al. (1986: 348) create the dichotomy of 'volition' (where the speaker has an active choice) vs. 'discernment' (where the ascribed roles of the participants have to be acknowledged). Watts (1991) contends that 'discernment' is operative in European cultures too, though not as automatic as the grammaticalized and lexicalized honorifics of Japanese. Based on Weber and Habermas, Ide proposes a model contrasting the instrumental-rational, strategic, success oriented with the value-rational communicative. A review of psychological and anthropological studies by Markus and Kitayama (1991) supports the non-universality of 'face'. They distinguish between a western independent construal and a largely non-western interdependent one (see also Kasper 1994). Janney and Arndt (1993) project Brown and Levinson's framework within the historical context of western individualistic cultures and consider it in need of extension. Kwarciak (1993) argues that early development of linguistic politeness in young children could supply insights in the debate on universals in this field.

The European notion of 'politeness', where particular linguistic formulations are employed in order to avoid conflicts, dates back to the eighteenth century (Watts 1991: 49). The development of 'polite' behaviour in the Middle Eastern, Graeco-Roman, medieval courtly, and European bourgeois traditions is traced historically in Ehlich (1992) (cf. also Elias 1936/1969). Watts (1989, 1991) introduces the concept of 'politic behaviour' which aims at establishing and/or maintaining 'in a state of equilibrium the personal relationships between the individuals of a social group ... during the ongoing interaction' (Watts 1991: 50, also Held 1992). 'Non-politic' behaviour leads to communication breakdown and 'polite behaviour', according to Watts, to 'an enhancement of *ego*'s standing with respect to *alter*' (Watts 1991: 51) – linguistic means of 'masking less altruistic ends'. Held (1992: 136) sees politeness as both 'status conscious behaviour' and 'more deportment and [bourgeois] decency which shows concern for general human decency and the maintenance of one's personal sphere'. Held takes 'indirectness' beyond the traditional politeness aspect to argue that it lowers the interlocutors' obligations, relieving them of indirect responsibility (p. 141). Fraser (1990) conceives politeness as part of a conversational contract determined by participants' rights and obligations which are flexible enough to change during the conversation.

Wierzbicka (1991: 454) rejects what she calls the 'anglocentric' bias of mainstream modern pragmatics, a field which developed largely under the influence of British and American philosophers of language who drew their examples almost exclusively from English and postulated all sorts of 'universal maxims' or 'universal principles' of human interaction on the basis of Anglo-Saxon or Anglo-American cultural norms and expectations. This applies also to the classic works of pragmatics, Austin (1962) and Searle (1969) and their whole notion of speech acts. By focussing on the word rather than the philosophical construct, Wierzbicka shows that there are, in fact, speech acts in individual cultures that have no equivalent in other cultures, e.g. Australian shout (to treat someone to a drink for companionship), Hebrew dugra talk ('straight talk'), Polish podanie (asking authorities for favours). The discussion started (Wierzbicka 1985) as a refutation of Fraser (1985), who claims that pragmatic strategies are essentially the same across languages and cultures, but that the appropriate use of the strategies may vary cross-culturally, even within the same (supranational) language. This is essentially the point of view taken in the Cross Cultural Speech Act Realization Project, where it is assumed that the speech acts can be realized – directly and indirectly – in all languages, even if the interpretation of what is polite and impolite may be vastly different between languages. The problem of inter-cultural comparison of speech acts is addressed by Coulmas (1978: 70) who argues that speech acts such as thanks and apologies, for instance, cannot be compared or translated across cultures.

Earlier in her book (1991: 9), Wierzbicka writes: 'It is impossible for a human being to study anything... from a totally extra-cultural point of view... We can find a point of view which is universal and cultural-independent, but we must look for such a point of view not outside all human cultures... but within our own culture, or within any other culture that we are intimately familiar with.' I agree with Wierzbicka's statements. She sees them as an argument in favour of her 'natural semantic metalanguage' (now termed 'cultural scripts', Wierzbicka 1992), based on a hypothetical system of universal semantic principles, i.e. expressed in terms of basic elements such as: I, you, want, don't, say, think, do, this, like this, good, bad, e.g.:

Chat (a) I want us to say many different things to one another
     (b) I think you want the same
     (c) I think we will feel something good because of this

(d) I don't think these things are important.

(Wierzbicka 1991: 172)

The advantage of this approach is that it avoids arbitrariness either in the formulation of absolutes or in the positioning of relatives. Although I will use cultural scripts a few times (3.1.2, 3.4), I will not be employing them extensively in this study – mainly because I am dealing not only with single speech acts, but also with discourse structures and patterns, because I am concerned with the total exchange between the inter-locutors, including the length of turns in relation to the discourse patterns. Incidentally, while strongly agreeing with Wierzbicka's criti-cisms of wrongly assumed 'universality', I believe that the primitives posited by Wierzbicka may not be as universal and culture-independent as she assumes, e.g. the meaning of think and feel, two of Wierzbicka's primitives, do not correspond completely in all languages. This applies particularly to distant languages and cultures. But even two languages as closely related as English and German, based on fairly similar cultures, exhibit substantial differences in the lexical fields (cf. Leisi 1952). In particular, there is a considerable overlap between feel and think (in the sense of 'consider') in English, but not in German. Natural language, being complex, requires complex resources, rather than simplified ones to describe it. I fear also that the 'absolute' categories in the components of the cultural scripts may weaken the relativist spirit of the approach which they are intended to propagate.

1.3.3   *Models of investigation*

1.3.3.1 *Methodology* The introductory chapter of Blum-Kulka, House and Kasper (1989) gives a comprehensive overview of research to date on contrastive and interlanguage pragmatics. More recently, Kasper and Dahl (1991) and Bardovi-Harlig and Hartford (1992) have produced critical surveys on research methods in the field, to which the reader is referred. It would be pointless to replicate such an exercise, suffice it to indicate the main types of procedures:

1. Data collection – rating tasks, multiple choice questions, interviews, observation of spontaneous authentic speech.
   (Unscripted non-experimental conversations in Bardovi-Harlig and
   Hartford 1992.)
2. Eliciting perception and comprehension data – comprehension and attitudes.
3. Methods eliciting production data – discourse completion in writing of specific given situations, role play.

(Scripted experimental conversations in Bardovi-Harlig and Hartford 1992.)
4. Eliciting conversations or tasks.
(Unscripted experimental conversations in Bardovi-Harlig and Hartford 1992.)

Kasper and Dahl refer to the great underrepresentation of authentic speech in contrastive and interlanguage pragmatics. Some exceptions are Wolfson et al. (1989) on compliments, and Bardovi-Harlig and Hartford (1990) on status preserving strategies in academic advising sessions, which falls under type 4 above. Despite the advantages of working with this type of data, the participants have fixed roles and status, the situation is domain-specific, there may be ethical problems, and the Observer's Paradox operates. The problem with data of type 1 is that it is very difficult to collect and is not always comparable material. As Bardovi-Harlig and Hartford (1992) point out, it may not yield any or enough of the items under consideration. The great advantage is that it is *real* data, spontaneous and unscripted. People are being themselves, saying what they actually say rather than what they think they would say. As has been pointed out in various places (e.g. Kasper and Dahl 1991: 245), tightly controlled data elicitation techniques 'might well preclude access to precisely the kind of conversational and interpersonal phenomena that might shed light on pragmatics'. This includes questionnaires because informants tend to indicate how they think they should behave under specific conditions, which is not necessarily the same as they do behave. As Wolfson, Marmor and Jones (1989: 181) put it: 'While questionnaires are useful ... we need to be careful not to conclude that findings from them represent the actual distribution of linguistic forms that occur in naturally occurring interactions.' This also applies to role-play, where stereotypes may be reinforced (cf. Clyne, Giannicos, and Neil 1993). Grießhaber (1987) compares attitudinal conversations in authentic and 'cited' speech action (role-plays). In the latter, the subjects can fall back on their knowledge and structural forms of the pattern. While the 'authentic' discourse proceeded without mental searching of the sche-mata, the respondents, speakers of German as a second language, had to ascertain the appropriate structure in 'cited' discourse. The teacher-interviewer was not sufficiently experienced in the discourse of the appropriate interaction. Wildner-Bassett (1989) claims that some of the 'errors' in cross-cultural pragmatics data elicited by role-play are the result of switching between the learners' 'coexisting discourse worlds'. Roberts, Davies, and Jupp (1992) use role-play for a different purpose – as stimuli, and as a means of encouraging participants to analyze their own communicative behaviour, thereby raising their awareness of potential intercultural communication breakdown.

The Heidelberger Forschungsprojekt Pidgin-Deutsch (1975: 45–9) compares the advantages and disadvantages of participant observation and interviews in studies of industrial communication (cf. Stubbs 1983: 218–46). Interviews are a well-established data gathering procedure which suffers from creating a formal, asymmetrical situation and the Observer's Paradox (cf. Labov 1972). Its advantages are in the well-definedness of the situation and the tasks and the opportunities for good-quality recordings. Participant observation offers supplementary data. Its problems relate to:

(a) the definition of the sample;
(b) the lack of a descriptive language of observation; and
(c) obtaining good-quality recordings of the situation being observed.

Senft (1982), in his research into the German of metal workers from Kaiserslautern, and Roche (1989), in his study of foreigner talk, both successfully gathered data by having their informants wear lapel microphones. The follow-up interview, developed by Neustupný (1985), enables the researcher to check up on the context of the communication and on sections that are difficult to decipher. Moreover, it makes it possible to obtain different perspectives on the communication. Wolfson's (1986) conclusion that no single means of data collection can provide all the answers is clearly still valid.

The question could be posed: should the data be recorded on audio- or videotape? Clearly there is a great deal that could be illuminated through videotapes ranging from turn taking to pauses, from the communication context and the order of the speakers to the relation between verbal and non-verbal communication. It is, however, hardly surprising that so little use has been made of video in linguistic research considering the difficulty of carrying around equipment and recording in an industrial situation with high electrical interference, classified information, and the likelihood of many respondents opting out. Moreover, video equipment is conspicuous and would probably affect communicative behaviour more than a lapel microphone, which people tend to take for granted after a brief period (see 2.4).

Clyne (1975) uses videotapes of people watching and commenting on videotapes of bilinguals employing 'mixed language' to study attitudes to different types of transference. So non-verbal phenomena can supplement the verbal comments.

1.3.4   *Cross-cultural pragmatics*

Jupp (1982) makes the observation that learners are thought either to 'know' or 'not to know' a language, so that inappropriate or unfamiliar language use is often misinterpreted as deliberately different behaviour. It is this problem that has motivated studies of cross-cultural pragmatics.

Ehlich (1986) has postulated six stages in the mastery of a language, four of which maintain the speaker's foreignness image and their out-group membership, and four options for the interlocutor who is a native speaker of the language: procedural ignoring of xenisms (foreignness markers in the speech); tolerance of errors; adopting a liking for the 'exotic' appeal of the xenisms; and correction.

Contrastive pragmatics has paid a great deal of attention to contrasts in levels of directness in the realization of speech acts as well as to culture-specific 'ways of speaking' and interlanguage pragmatics to the effects of this on the acquisition of second and later languages. The speech acts have tended to be promises, requests, and apologies, and in some cases compliments and closings. Most of the studies contrast English with other languages, especially German and Japanese (see literature survey in Blum-Kulka, House, and Kasper 1989: 1–34, also Kasper 1994). The levels of directness were developed in studies of the now dispersed 'Bochum School' appearing in the late 1970s and early 1980s (e.g. Edmondson, House, Kasper, and McKeown 1979, House and Kasper 1981, Kasper 1981). They form a substantial part of the basis for the C(ross) C(ultural) S(peech) A(ct) R(ealization) P(roject) which contrasted aspects of language use in Argentinian Spanish, Australian English, Canadian French, German German, and Israeli Hebrew.

House and Kasper (1981), for example, had twenty-four informal everyday situations – complaints and requests – acted out by two pairs of native speakers, one English and one German pair. Establishing eight levels of directness for each of the speech acts, they found a heavy concentration in the sixth (third most direct) level for the Germans and in the third level among the English, while the least direct level was far more frequent among the English than the Germans. Downgraders (e.g. please, kind of, I guess, or their German equivalents) were employed by English informants $1\frac{1}{2}$ times as frequently as by the Germans in the same situation, 2.7 times in the case of the complaints. Upgraders (e.g. absolutely, I'm sure, you must understand, and their German equivalents) were used 4.6 times as much by the Germans than by the English (who hardly employed them at all in complaints).

The House and Kasper investigation provided a frame of reference for Kasper's (1981) study of the English interlanguage pragmatics of

German learners in role-play dialogues with native speakers of English. Speech acts such as accept, apologize, complain, offer, and suggest are the object of the research. Kasper found many errors in modality. Some speech acts, such as complain and request, were realized more directly by the learners than by the English speakers or by the German speakers using German in House and Kasper's study. Suggestions were expressed more indirectly. There was an underuse of intensifiers other than very in thanking.

In CCSARP, Blum-Kulka (1989) found a variation in sub-strategies of 'conversational indirectness' in requests, with Hebrew speakers opting less than the others for can/could and most for possibility and willingness/readiness and the Argentinian Spanish speakers more than the others for prediction. While situations do account for some differences, Australian English speakers tend to opt for the least direct communicative behaviour, followed by Germans, French Canadians, Israelis, and Argentinians. However, Israelis and Australians use about the same proportion of 'hints', closely followed by Canadian French speakers, whereas Germans and Argentinians do not employ them much (Blum-Kulka and House 1989). For apologies, there was a large degree of inter-cultural agreement in the choice of strategies (Olshtain 1989). There were, however, subtle inter-group differences in the use of the expression of responsibility, according to situation.

In Cordella's (1991) role-play study of the apologies of Australian English speakers and recently arrived Chilean immigrants, positive politeness strategies (in the sense of Brown and Levinson, see above, 1.3.2) are employed more frequently by the Chileans. Women show the greatest use of intensification with an explanation regardless of whether they are speaking Spanish or English.

Béal (1990, 1992) expresses cross-cultural pragmatic variation between Anglo-Australians and French in a French company in Australia in terms of Brown and Levinson's dichotomy 'positive/negative politeness'. The French tend to make requests using the future, imperatives, and *il faut*, Anglo-Australians preferring conventionalized Would you mind? or softeners. The French strategies convey the impression of authoritarianism, disagreement, impatience, and assertiveness. Béal (1990) claims that the underlying premise of French is that all people have strong egos and that of Australians is that all people are vulnerable. In her analysis of small-talk based on weekend activities, Béal (1992) constructs rules contrasting French and Australian-English strategies. The Australian rules are: be positive without being over-enthusiastic, mention typical weekend activities, give facts, find common ground, use conversational style to show consideration. The French rules are: don't ask everyone around you, expect (or give) a definitive answer, be frank, be entertaining, mention relevant people and places in their lives, and use conversational style to show involvement (1992: 28–37). Béal's interpretation is that, while Australians preserve social harmony and protect the other's territory, the French are frank and committed, claiming their own territory.

Wierzbicka (1991) levels criticism against the whole notion of 'directness/indirectness' in earlier work on cross-cultural pragmatics. She shows how the dichotomy is often employed to project as absolute/ relative tendencies established on the basis of contrasts between two languages/cultures (e.g. American English and Japanese). So American English, being 'more direct than Japanese' is depicted as 'direct' when it is 'indirect' in comparison with, say, Israeli Hebrew. In the same or similar circumstances, Anglo-Americans need to say more than 'no', Israelis say 'no', and Japanese cannot say 'no'. Moreover, what constitutes 'directness' is an interpretation of certain aspects of the culture. Wierzbicka therefore goes on to describe pragmatic aspects of a language in relation to key characteristics of a culture. Another aspect that needs to be considered is the ambiguity of 'direct' – 'explicit', i.e. saying, not hinting, and expressing in terms of a direct speech act, e.g. through a performative verb.

Platt (1989) draws attention to areas such as engaging, disengaging, requesting, accepting or declining an offer or invitation, where different types of sensitivity between South-east Asians and Anglo-Australians could have a face threatening effect. He points out that in new communication sub-systems, e.g. Singapore, more direct rules may be applied than in L1 areas, e.g. China. In his research on communication in South Africa, Chick (1989) lists some barriers to effective inter-cultural communication: interlingual interference, different (socio-cultural) frames of reference, variation in the importance of face saving, different listening behaviour, different ways of regulating turn taking, and different politeness behaviour.

1.3.5   Cross-cultural spoken discourse

'Smooth-flowing conversational partners share considerable knowledge about the structure of the conversation itself', writes Reichman (1990: 29). It is differences in both the function and the structure of a conversation and written discourse that creates problems in inter-cultural communication. 'Discourse types and orders of discourse vary across cultures', states Fairclough (1989: 47). 'But', he claims, 'in (such) gatekeeping encounters, white middle-class gatekeepers are likely to constrain the discourse types which can be drawn upon to know those of the dominant group.'

Bremer et al. (1988) is an investigation of how 'understanding' is achieved by communicating in L2. It is also an extensive study of inter-cultural communication breakdown and its resolution based on the European Science Foundation Project on the acquisition of the national language – English, German, Dutch, French, or Swedish – by adult migrants using Punjabi, Italian, Arabic, Spanish, or Finnish. (Despite the cross-cultural and cross-linguistic comparative nature of the project, actual cultural variation is not dealt with explicitly in Bremer et al.). Bremer et al. show how the understanding of an utterance depends mainly on the native speaker's expectations. Expectations are global (schemata), triggered by the interaction context, or triggered by the 'immediate linguistic context'. Non-understanding occurs where there is minimal positive feedback (e.g. yes, mm, uh huh). This enables the speaker to retain face and stay in the conversation without any check on understanding. It may be marked by indicators (e.g. I didn't understand that) or symptoms, which convey indirectly that there is an under-standing problem (e.g. lack of reprise, minimal feedback, reprise of trouble source). Misunderstandings give the (surface) illusion of under-standing, which may be dispelled during the conversation, in post-encounter conversations, or by the researchers' interpretation of the data. They find very few instances of 'misunderstandings' in the data.

Bremer et al. are able to identify 'behaviours leading to greater understanding' (1988: 121): metalinguistic comment and reprise and (in later phases of development), hypothesis-forming and face saving of both speaker and hearer. They also identify behaviour which keeps learners at low levels of understanding – reliance on lack of uptake, formulaic responses, e.g. 'that's why' in reply to 'why?', laughter – and behaviour conducive to misunderstandings, such as 'overriding' by unresponsive native speakers. Such behaviour can be identified contextually. Bremer et al. show how communication breakdown can be prevented by the native speaker's 'metadiscursive' comments about the intention of the interaction, clear use of pauses and particles to make 'new topics salient and their content expectable' (p. 207) and left dislocation, e.g.:

and illnesses did you have any illnesses when you were a little girl?

Suggestions are also made as to how learner production could be facilitated – by inviting questions or comments and giving time for them, specific questions, and reformulating a minimal (one word or yes/no) answer. The need for resolution of communication breakdown is determined by the goal-driven nature of the encounter, the length of the interaction, and the type of communication breakdown problem. The main types of negotiation of meaning encountered in the ESF corpus are: topicalization of understanding by linking it to the context, reprises, reformulation, comprehension checks, and suggested answers. The main factors mediating success in managing understanding are speed of resolution and co-operation between the interactants.

In a subsequent summary of their data, Bremer et al. (1994) discuss three 'constellations' of the causes of problems of understanding – mishearings, the relative difficulty of the utterance or turn to be understood, and a pragmatic lack of understanding attributable to differences in cultural values. The markers of non-understanding are: metalinguistic comment, minimal questions, 'reprise' of trouble sources, lack of uptake, hypothesis forming ('best guessing'), and minimal feedback. Resolution may be achieved through collaborative discourse. 'The interactive nature of the understanding process requires that both sides negotiate to achieve sufficient shared inferences for a commonality of meaning to be established' (p. 193). However, such negotiation is risky for an adult immigrant worker prone to embarrassment, frustration, and judgment by gatekeepers. There is a need for native speakers to 'decentre' (p. 194) – to withdraw from their means of communicative behaviour to understand the others.

A collection of inter-cultural communication studies, Redder and Rehbein (1987), employs contrastive discourse analysis to study specific problems in native/non-native speaker interaction. The situations include a Japanese customer complaining to a German shop assistant about the quality of a product (Ohama), a Turk receiving advice at a citizen's advice bureau (Backa), classroom situations in Germany and Argentina (Lorf, Steinmetz), and Turkish migrants advising Germans on travel to Turkey (Wiesenhütter). Text segmentation, the role of particular segments, the role of each speaker or group of speakers, and problems in interpretation and negotiation of meaning are discussed. This is sometimes done with the help of a praxeogram – a diagram devised by Ehlich and Rehbein (1972) – showing each of the actions in which the interactants are involved. This enables the writers to comment on cultural variation and cultural roles, e.g. the Germans feel threatened by the Turks trying to help, misinterpreting it as a threat to their freedom (Wiesenhütter).

Tolerance of silence as opposed to filling silence with speech and 'thinking aloud' can be a factor in miscommunication, as has been pointed out by Scollon and Scollon (1981), working on communication between Athabaskan Indians and White Americans, Chick (1989: 152), contrasting the discourse of Zulus and South African English speakers, Watts (1991: 297), writing on speakers of English and Swiss-German, and Verschueren (1984) in a review article. Schröder (1989) refers to the Finnish tolerance for silent periods in contrast to the tendency of Germans to 'think aloud' and not to permit silences. Widén (1985: 168) goes as far as to describe Germans as 'more communicative and informative' than Finns. Lenz (1990), analyzing Finno-German business encounters, points to some specific causes of inter-cultural communication breakdown in this area – different rules for turn receiving (i.e. a Finn not recognizing the opportunity to take over the turn), non-back-channelling on the part of the Finn, different rules for terminating an exchange and therefore non-recognition by the Finn of the signals. Lenz finds that 'communicative restraint' by the Finnish partner is restricted to the first part of the exchange. Lenz suggests that the problem may be due to the Finn, unlike the German, communicating in a foreign language. However, Lenz's point about cultural variation in turn-taking rules is of underlying importance. In attitudinal testing of German speakers living in Finland, Yli-Renko (1993) finds that the Finns' slow tempo of speech and 'monotonous' intonation paralyzed communication. Halmari (1993) examines business telephone communication between native speakers of Finnish and of American English. The main structure of conversation is the same in both cultures, but while native speakers of English place most emphasis on the business matter, the non-topical (small-talk) element is important for the Finns. There are also differences in interruption behaviour. While native speakers of English initiate overlapping speech in the middle of the interlocutor's utterance or turn, the Finnish native speakers interrupt only close to the voluntary turn boundary.

Enninger (1987), who provides examples from the Amish, refers to the 'temporal management of transition relevant places' across cultures, or 'the cultural relativity of conversational chronematics'. 'Transition relevance places' are the points where speakers can change in conversation, i.e. they may choose to take a turn or not, or to do so with a delay. Carroll (1987) refers to the difference between Americans and French in coping with a small enclosed area – the Americans by talking and the French by being silent. In a study of turn taking in spontaneous speech and drama dialogue in Egyptian Arabic, Hafez (1991) concludes that, in Arabic, in contrast to English, there is an absence of competition between the parties, leading to minimal overlap and interruption, hesitation, and silence. There is also sub-cultural variation in turn-taking rules, as Keim and Schwitalla (1993) have shown from their Mannheim data. Members of a women's political group are far more likely to interrupt than members of a women's literary group, who wait for the previous speaker to complete her turn.

The importance of native speaker input in the development of L2 discourse has been demonstrated, e.g. by Hatch (1978), Pica and Long (1988), and Brock et al. (1988). Ferguson (1971) devised the term foreigner talk for a variety of a language employed to a person identified as a foreigner. Foreigner talk is subject to variation between speakers and to variation within one speaker according to interlocutor and the function of the discourse. Roche (1989) has postulated four levels of foreigner talk ranging from native-type (i.e. standard foreigner talk) to gross grammatical reduction and lexical simplification (i.e. non-standard foreigner talk) – including ellipsis, deletion of auxiliaries, copula, prepositions, pronouns, and grammatical endings – the level most frequently described in the speech of migrant workers in factories (see e.g. Hinnenkamp 1982, Klein and Dittmar 1979, Clahsen et al. 1983, Clyne 1977, Werkgroep Taal Buitenlandse Werknemers 1978). Foreigner talk can also be phonologically marked. Hinnenkamp (1987) shows that foreigner talk can act as a 'trouble prophylaxis' in inter-cultural communication. In their study of clarification sequences in native/non-native discourse in Dutch, Deen and Van Hout (1991) find that native speakers prefer to clarify through adjustments of linguistic input, non-native speakers prefer expansions or repetitions. Cooperation between native and non-native speakers in French-German language contact is the focus of Schmale's (1987) study based on the testimonies of students. He finds, not surprisingly, that the better the language competence of the non-native speaker, the less necessary is a consideration for the speaker's image (face) and the more the basis of co-operation 'being in conversation with each other' can be guaranteed.

Some of the basic terminological tools for the study of cross-cultural spoken discourse are provided by Gumperz (1982) and Thomas (1983). We are indebted to Gumperz, for example, for the distinction between the two types of communication breakdown:

Noncommunication –   where no message is communicated; and

Miscommunication –   where an unintended message is communicated.

Thomas (1983) distinguishes between two types of 'cross-cultural pragmatic failure':

Pragmalinguistic failure –   mistaken beliefs about the pragmatic force of an utterance (e.g.

                                        believing Bad luck! is the opposite
                                        to the wish Good luck!); and
Sociopragmatic failure –   caused by different cultural values
                                        (e.g. Directness/Indirectness).

The first is much easier to overcome than the second. Strtegic competence is the speaker's ability to solve communicative problems through strategies (Færch and Kasper 1983). These strategies compensate for insufficient communicative competence, and enhance the effectiveness of communication.

In their pioneering work in the now defunct National Centre for Industrial Training and in particular in the training programme *Crosstalk*, Gumperz, Jupp, and Roberts (1979) stress the point that South Asians in Britain tend to be unsuccessful in job interviews because they do not understand the assumptions behind the questions. Building on Gumperz (1982), they show that English speakers, e.g. pass judgment on interviewees because of differences in pragmatic formulae, intonation patterns, and ways of structuring information. This is disputed by Kandiah (1991) who claims that the instances of communication breakdown can rather be attributed to the South Asians' 'entrepreneurship' – intended to thwart any intended discrimination – which sometimes fails or is misinterpreted.

The most relevant publication so far in our area is Roberts, Davies, and Jupp (1992). As it appeared while I was already writing this monograph, it was unfortunately not possible to take it into account during the data collection and analysis stages. Based on the research and training activities of the National Centre for Industrial Language Training, it provides a framework for the study of communication between native and non-native speakers of English in a work environment and for ESL and cross-cultural training, with some data analysis. The major focus is on the discrimination that takes place as a result of a lack of sensitivity to cross-cultural variation in discourse and pragmatics. The discrimination is exemplified by interrogations, complaints, and other forms of discourse in job interviews and staff meetings. Suggestions are made for change. Programmes comprise three phases. In the first, the trainees are shown how to use learning strategies other than their customary ones. In the second, broad-based transferable workplace skills are presented (e.g. listening and reading for specific information, planning and problem solving). The individual autonomous development through transferable skills and strategies is the focus of the third phase.

1.3.6   *Intellectual styles and comparative cultural values*

On the basis of his experience in working with scholars from different cultural backgrounds, Galtung (1985) contrasts four 'intellectual styles' (ways of turning thoughts into language), which he designates as '*sachsonisch*', '*gallisch*', '*teutonisch*' and '*nipponisch*' as they are centered in, though not exclusive to Britain and the US, France, Germany and Japan respectively. Although the substance of Galtung's contrasts is relevant to written rather than spoken discourse (see Chapter 5), his framework is relevant to any work on discourse and cultural values (cf. Chapters 4 and 6). The 'Saxonic' style is very strong on the production of (hypo)theses and weak on theory formation and paradigm analysis. The 'Nipponic' style is described as similar to the 'Saxonic' but not quite as strong in theses. The 'Teutonic' and 'Gallic' styles are very strong on theory formation, strong on paradigm analysis, and weak on theses, with the 'Gallic' one attaching great importance also to elegance of expression. In 'Nipponic' style, the established order has to be preserved with respect shown to authority and a feeling of collectivity. 'Teutonic' intellectual style is more monologue-oriented, involving a test of strength and an attack on weak points, whereas 'Saxonic' style promotes dialogue and debate leading to a *rapprochement* between points of view among equals. 'Nipponic' and 'Saxonic' styles (especially the American variant of the latter) are characterized by Galtung as more tolerant and democratic and less elitist than the 'Teutonic' with its vertical, pyramid structure, and the 'Gallic' with the competition and individualism of the autocrat (where they are all irrelevant to each other). He associates the 'Nipponic' style with a need for modesty and the Buddhist emphasis on the inseparability of the basic elements, producing 'circular thinking'.

Galtung typifies 'Teutonic' as: vertical, individualistic, and polarized, 'Gallic' as: horizontal, individualistic, and polarized, 'Saxonic' as horizontal, individualistic, and non-polarized, and 'Nipponic' as vertical, collectivistic, and non-polarized. 'Peripheral' cultures which adhere to these styles less than the 'core' ones, and may be on the periphery of several cultures, may establish a balance of the features described above. Some 'peripheral' cultures shift towards a different 'core', eg. Dutch and Scandinavian cultures moving from the 'Teutonic' to the 'Saxonic' sphere of influence. While the above categories help account for some aspects of German academic discourse (see above), the 'democratic' characteristics of the 'Saxonic' are not necessarily accompanied by tolerance for variation, cultural or otherwise.

1.3.7   Kommunikationsbund (*communication union*)

Fundamental to our treatment of 'peripheral' and 'core' cultures is the notion of the *Sprechbund*. The term was coined by Neustupný (1969, 1971) by analogy with the Prague School term *Sprachbund* (linguistic union) denoting a group of languages in contact which influence one another whether they are genetically related or not. The *Sprechbund* (speech union) then is a group of languages/cultures that share communicative rules – what to say and when and how it is possible to say it in certain situations, how you can be ironical or humorous, and so on. This, for instance, is why it is easier for Czechs to learn German than to learn French. This is particularly appropriate for languages/cultures which share an area or are contiguous, e.g. the Balkans, Central Europe, The Caribbean, the Indian sub-continent (cf. Neustupný 1978).

The dichotomy *Sprachbund/Sprechbund* is inspired by Saussure's *langue/parole* (though *parole* is usually rendered in German as *Rede*). As this dichotomy is no longer central to linguistic theory, I am employing instead the more appropriate term *Kommunikationsbund* (communication union) (cf. Neustupný 1978: 108). This emphasizes the common communicative features of the languages/cultures concerned, which are used within an area.

1.3.8   *Comparative 'work-related values'*

Hofstede (1984, 1991) uses a survey among over 116,000 employees in a large multinational corporation in forty countries, verified by other empirical studies, to research cultural differences in value systems. The areas investigated are (Hofstede 1984, 1991):

(i)   Social inequality, including the relationship with authority;
(ii) The relationship between the individual and the group;
(iii) Concepts of masculinity and femininity; and
(iv) Ways of dealing with uncertainty (control of aggression, expression of emotions).

Four dimensions are postulated through 'human reasoning' and statistical analysis: Power distance, individualism, masculinity, and uncertainty avoidance. A high Power Distance Index (PDI) reflects, for instance, an acceptance of inequality in which the underdog is to blame, and a latent conflict between the powerful and the powerless. A low Power Distance Index, on the other hand, corresponds to a view supporting interdependence and equal rights with latent harmony between the powerful and the powerless and in which the 'system' is to blame. A high level of uncertainty avoidance has as its symptoms, e.g. anxiety and job stress, fear of failure, low risk-taking, a need for security, rigidity, and dogmatism, a reduction of ambiguity, a sense of urgency, a dependence on experts and authority figures. A low Uncertainty Avoidance Index (UAI) reflects a low anxiety level, more acceptance of dissent, and few rules. A high Individualism Index is recorded in cultures where personal life outside work is attributed great importance, while a low Individualism Index reflects significance attached to duty, expertness and prestige at work. A high Masculinity Index indicates aggressive, ambitious, and competitive behaviour as opposed to compassionate, modest, and friendly behaviour and the resolution of conflict by compromise and negotiation, which is characteristic of a low Masculinity Index. Cultures with clearly distinct gender roles are, according to Hofstede (1991), ones in which not only men, but also the few women in positions of authority, are 'tough'.

Hofstede finds a higher UAI among people from most Catholic nations than among those from Protestant ones. This he puts down to the Catholic emphasis on the uniqueness and infallibility of the Catholic Church. Similarly, Israel and Muslim countries have a high UAI. Protestant (especially Calvinist) cultures encourage worldly and not ritual ways of coping with uncertainty. Among other cultures with low UAI are India, the Philippines, and Ireland (which tends to be puritanical in its Catholicism).

While the English-speaking and Northern European cultures share a low PDI and UAI, German-speaking cultures have a low PDI and high UAI, and 'Latin' and Japanese cultures show both a high PDI and a high UAI. South-east Asians have a low PDI and a low UAI. A high level of individualism is shown in the English-speaking cultures and, to a lesser extent, in Northern Europe, where identity is based on the individual ('Protestant ethic'), and a low level in the Latin American cultures and among South-east Asians and Pakistanis, where identity is based on the social system. Whereas the Latin Americans require strict authority while stressing personal independence from collectivity, Austrians and Israelis resist strict authority but are relatively dependent on collectivity. On the Masculinity Index the German-speaking and Caribbean Latin American cultures rate highly, the Northern European and non-Caribbean 'Latin' cultures low, and the Asian and English-speaking ones in the middle. The rather disparate results (Austrians high, 'Yugoslavs' low, Italians and Latin Americans high, Spaniards low) make it difficult to reconcile Hofstede's Masculinity Index with our data.

Hofstede's range of cultures is limited by his data, which do not include Eastern European groups apart from 'Yugoslavs' as the multinational company under consideration did not, at the time, operate in their countries. The notion of the national culture is very useful, but also open to question. This has been exacerbated by recent events. The difficulties arising from German unification demonstrate the much higher collectivity and uncertainty avoidance in the east than in the west through the strong reactions to the changes that had occurred in the east. It is unclear what is meant by 'Yugoslavs' and whether there are some differences between the ethnic/national groups. The recent playing down of 'nation-states' in Western Europe and general political changes in Europe show that 'national boundaries' are not an altogether suitable basis for describing cultural variation. Also, class, group, gender, age, and other factors interrelate with such parameters as 'individuality/ collectivity', which suffer from the weaknesses of polarities generally (see e.g. Wierzbicka's criticism of 'direct'/'indirect', 1.3.4). I shall, however, utilize Hofstede's framework for want of a better one while complementing it with broader cultural units.

These points do not detract from the usefulness and significance of Hofstede's model and categories. His findings will be referred to again in 6.2 when I attempt to relate cultural variation in our data to cultural values systems.

1.4   Closing remarks

This chapter is an attempt to put the present study into the general context of linguistic theory and research. The field of inter-cultural communication within linguistics is a relatively new and rapidly developing field which has been supplied with its theoretical and methodological insights by pragmatics, discourse analysis, and areas of sociolinguistics. The studies under review bring out the diversity of discourse patterns, including sequencing, and the expectations of discourse, which are related to general cultural parameters to be discussed in Chapter 6. As in cross-cultural pragmatics studies in general, particular cultural discourse patterns in interactive studies will be described and perceived differently, depending on which other culture they are contrasted with. This is a strong argument for multilateral studies, involving different groups.

2 Setting up the project

2.0 Australia's multilingual and industrial situation

In this chapter, I will discuss the setting up of the project which is providing us with our data on verbal communication in English between immigrants of different non-English-speaking language and cultural backgrounds. Australia's ethnolinguistic diversity offers challenges and opportunities to sociolinguistic research. It is estimated that over one hundred languages are spoken on a regular basis in Melbourne, the city in which the data were gathered. According to the 1986 Census, 22.7 % of the population then used a language other than English at home. This does not include the many people who employ a language other than English regularly but not in their own homes (cf. Clyne 1991).

The wide cultural diversity of the Australian population provides rich contexts for research into inter-cultural communication. In Melbourne, for instance, Croats, Sinhalese and Vietnamese, Maltese, Poles, and Chinese have co-settled and worked together. These groups – in contrast to, say, Greeks and Turks, Germans and Croats, Italians and Maltese, Chinese and Vietnamese – have had no history of interaction as groups and are unlikely to share communication patterns that they do not share with the 'mainstream' Australians (i.e. those of British descent and those who have assimilated into that dominant group). With people of non-English-speaking backgrounds constituting 40 % of the work-force in manufacturing industries, with 28.6 % of the total manufacturing work-force born in non-English-speaking countries, and 90 % of the males in this group in production work (Matheson 1991), there is a considerable chance that people interacting in the work domain will be native speakers of different languages other than English with varying cultural expectations of communication.

At the end of the Second World War, Australia had a population of barely seven million and a predominantly agrarian economy. Australia's post-war industrial expansion was due almost entirely to its mass immigration scheme. The required supply of unskilled workers was imported in the late 1940s from the Central and Eastern European human resources available in refugee camps. Further supplies were sought first in Britain and then in the North-Western European countries which were culturally similar, and gradually the sources were diversified with the most recent groups becoming increasingly distant, ethnically and culturally – first Italians, then Greeks, followed by a new wave of Yugoslavs, then Latin Americans and Turks, then Lebanese, and most recently, Vietnamese refugees and their families and ethnic Chinese from South-east Asia. These brief comments mention only the main waves of immigration during this period. Because of rapid socioeconomic mobility, the factory floor was seen by most as a temporary means for peasants and *déclassé* professionals to establish themselves in Australia before setting up small businesses or regaining their professional status respectively. An ethnic group soon gained greater acceptance in the community and at least higher-status jobs within the workplace as newer, more disadvantaged and culturally more distant groups arrived on the scene. This has changed with economic recession and the decline of the industrial sector. The above remarks will indicate that the socialization of people into workplace culture from an early age, described for England by Willis (1983), is not commonplace in Australia.

Before the fairly recent arrival of large numbers of Asians in Australia, non-English-speaking immigrants perceived that they shared a common set of communication patterns, even though they might not have a common language other than English. These patterns gave them a common identity to mark them off from English native speakers. The assumptions of 'mainstream' Australians of British (or assimilated non-British) background have also been that the non-Aboriginal Australian population can be lumped together in two major groups – 'Anglos' and 'Ethnics'.

Previous interactional cross-cultural research has been generally oriented towards communication between native and non-native speakers (see e.g. House and Kasper 1981, Kasper 1981, Færch and Kasper 1983, Olesky 1989). Similarly, models and frameworks have been based on an absolute contrast (e.g. between English and German, English and Japanese) rather than a culture continuum (core-peripheral) which multilateral research would call for. Models have catered for a 'majority group' and one or more 'minority groups' interacting with, and usually converging towards, it. The Australian situation that we are working in calls for a multicultural framework where there are various ethnic minorities interacting with Anglo-Celtic Australians and with one another, with some converging more than others.

2.1
Criteria for selecting workplaces

Due to the availability of appropriately priced housing in particular parts of Melbourne at the time of arrival of particular groups, chain migration, and the allocation of particular immigrants to one or the other migrant hostel, some ethnic concentration has occurred (Jupp 1988). Some groups (Italians, Germans) have dispersed more; others (Maltese, Macedonians, Vietnamese) have concentrated more, even in areas of dispersion. This influences the ethnolinguistic composition of particular workplaces. Although many travel long distances to work, there is a tendency for home and workplace to be in the same region of the sprawling metropolis. Thus, the selection of the workplaces for data collection has been influenced by their *location* within the Melbourne metropolitan area (northern, western, south-eastern, eastern suburbs). It was also felt that four major *industries* employing large numbers of non-English speakers should be represented, *viz.* heavy (automotive), textiles, electronic, catering. Finally, the *national origin* of the parent company (US, Japan, Germany), if appropriate, was taken into account in the selection of the workplaces.

The workplaces selected were:

Amcar.	A car factory of American origin in the northern suburbs.
Nipponcar.	A car factory of Japanese origin in the south-eastern suburbs.
Weavers.	A textile factory of Australian origin in the western suburbs.
Elektro.	An electronics factory of German origin in the eastern suburbs.
Catering.	The catering section of a migrant hostel in the south-eastern suburbs.
Education Office.	An office of a government operation.
Employment Office.	An office of a government department.
Parent Group.	Meetings of a multicultural parents' group at a high school in the south-eastern suburbs.

The data collection at Catering, Education Office, and Employment Office was kindly undertaken by teacher-researchers from Adult Migrant Education Services in Melbourne (see Acknowledgements).

At Amcar, the entire plant has 22 % of its work-force born in Australia or the United Kingdom. Turks (13 %), Vietnamese (12 %), people from

Table 2.1 *Data by workplace : audio and video*

	Audio	Video	Total (hours)
Amcar	18	0	18
Nipponcar	16.5	0	16.5
Weavers	28.5	6	34.5
Elektro	48	0	48
Catering	36	0	36
Education Office	12	0	12
Employment Office	11	0	11
Parent Group	6	0	6
Total	176	6	182

Yugoslavia (10%), and Italians (9.5%) constitute the largest groups of non-native speakers of English, followed by Lebanese and Greeks (each 7%). Unfortunately statistics on the ethnolinguistic composition of the entire work-force are not available for the other workplaces under consideration.

The 182 hours of recordings are derived from the workplaces and shown in Table 2.1.

2.2   Identifying research sites

Prior to the identification of research sites for data selection, meetings were held with management, unions, and workers to acquaint them with the aims and methods of the research and to gain their permission for it to take place. During this process, much useful advice and information was obtained. Subsequently, visits to the plant took place and the field workers were able to spend considerable periods of time observing communication and gaining the rapport of potential participants.

Both the industry and the company determined differences in communication situations. Thompson (1967) and Yuill (1970) distinguish between three types of interdependence in organizations:

Pooled interdependence –   where there are simultaneous operations but there is no immediate work flow between roles;

Sequential interdependence –   where work flows clearly from one person to another; and

Reciprocal interdependence –   where work flows back and
                                  forth, e.g. tools are passed
                                  back and forth.

In car factories, interdependence in work patterns tends to be sequential
(receiving a part from someone else and doing something to it) rather
than reciprocal. Each person works independently on the assembly line
and most communication takes place either with the person next to them
(geographically horizontal) or with one who is the superordinate or the
subordinate (socially vertical), especially in a crisis situation. Job function
and status give some people unusual opportunities for an extension of
their communication radius. High noise level in the factory is not
conducive to verbal communication and there is much shouting.
However, Nipponcar believes in multiskilling, so workers are moved
around to help others out. This means that, while workers spend most of
the day in solitary jobs, they also undertake co-operative, interactive jobs
on the line. Isolation and high noise level are also characteristics of the
work situation at Weavers. In contrast, the Elektro factory is much
quieter and there is far more reciprocal work. While the catering industry
also involves much sequential work, there is also routine planning
involving the co-operation of the workers. The noise level is not as high
as in the car and textile factories. Office communication entails habitual
dyadic communication between the same people rather than workers
explaining things to a subordinate. Thus, it is not hierarchical. (We have
not included communication between bosses and their secretaries.)
    The   research   sites   were   selected   on   the   basis   of
ethnolinguistic composition (to achieve maximum diversity in our
corpus, including different levels of hierarchy and both genders), a
relatively low noise level, and (concomitantly) communication richness
of the work situation. As will be gathered from the above section, these
conditions are met more in some work-places than in others. To balance
this, data was also collected at meetings of employee participation groups
at Weavers. In addition, meetings chaired by people of different
ethnolinguistic backgrounds at Employment Office are included for
comparison, as are meetings of Parent Group.
    At Amcar, most work in the door trim and trim lines is dyadic and
sequential. There are five trim lines, each with a top and a bottom end
and little or no communication between the two ends. The door line also
comprises two sections. The largest ethnic component in the trim lines
(see Figure 1) are Vietnamese and Italian speakers (each 9 %), followed
by Greek speakers (8 %) and speakers of the Yugoslav languages (5 %),
Arabic (4 %), and Turkish (4 %).

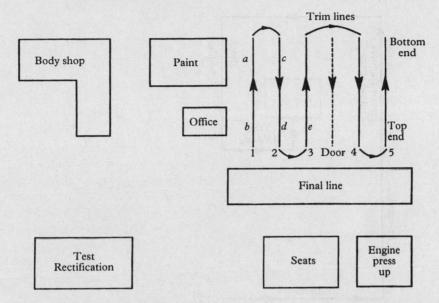

Figure 1. Amcar (Plant 1)

The door trim assembly at Nipponcar comprises 6 activity areas, 3 of which are predominantly manual work and relatively communication rich activities, 2 of which are machine-driven work and therefore noisy, with single operators, and the remaining 1 combines the 2. The communication rich activities are:

Cutting tables – Stimulating dyadic communication between those at each bench and frequent communication with the leading hand or supervisor about quantities.

Trim – Co-operative work.

Quality check – This area is in the middle and workers tend to congregate there and talk when they have finished their work.

Assembling – There are large tables with operators standing around which also give opportunity for interaction despite the fast manual work that has to be carried out. The machines involve only one operator.

The areas not conducive to verbal communication are:

Welding and Stapling – Here there is a high noise level and either solitary work or shouting (see Figure 2).

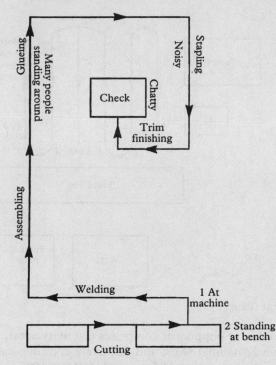

Figure 2. Nipponcar (Assembly line)

Of the thirty-two employees in the door trim assembly, 44% are Chinese speakers, the other non-English speakers being Maltese, Sinhalese, Finnish, French, and Turkish. The gender ratio is 60:40 female.

At Weavers, most communication takes place at the office (The thick lines indicate the glass windows.) Workers report the progress of their work to the office. Some communication occurs out of the office (where the machines are situated). However, the noise level is quite high and people are required to wear ear muffs.

At Elektro, the research site is the section assembling circuit boards. Most of the work is soldering. Here (see Figure 4) the 'noisy' areas are in the middle, the communication rich ones on the sides. In the middle, the manual insertion section, the operators (predominantly South-east Asian) are seated in rows, something that is also not conducive to conversation. The more communication rich sections are:

Preparation –   Here operators are seated around tables.
Assembly –   Here they are seated in groups, suitable for interaction.

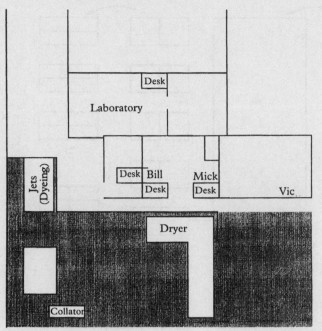

Figure 3. Weavers (Research site)

Final assembly –   Operators are sitting at a table: tend to talk in dyads.

Quality control –   Mainly technicians sitting at partitioned benches. This area was not used for research as most of the participants are Australians.

Like the other research sites, this one yields a useful ethnolinguistic mix, with 36% of the 40 workers of Chinese-speaking background, and the remainder with backgrounds in Vietnamese, Polish, German, Croatian, Indonesian, and Malay.

At Catering (see Figure 5), the activities and noise level vary according to the time of the day. Most taping has taken place between 4.30 and 6.30 p.m. This includes a cleaning period from 4.30 to 5.15 and a serving time from 5.15 to 6.30. The noise of extractor fans intrudes on the whole kitchen area while cooking is taking place (i.e. 4.00 to 6.30). Some taping has been undertaken outside this period to gauge the effects of the extractor fan noise on communication.

The interactants here are two speakers of Sri Lankan English, one Hindi speaker from Fiji, two Hakka speakers from Cambodia, one

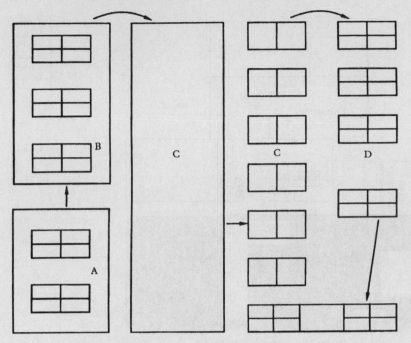

Figure 4. Elektro (Research site)
A, B, D, E – four-way desks, communication is possible because of proximity.
C – lines, operators seated in rows. More difficult to talk.

Croatian, one Vietnamese, and one Spanish speaker from El Salvador (as well as one English person). Females outnumber men 2:1.

2.3   Role of, and criteria for, selecting informants

Most of our corpus comprises spontaneous communication of workplace interactions audio-taped at the research sites. Following observation (see above, 2.2), key informants from non-English-speaking backgrounds were selected to wear a lapel microphone for 90 minutes at a time. This enabled us to audio-record their communication with other people from different non-English-speaking backgrounds. Criteria for their selection as key informants were:

(i)   their willingness to participate in this way;
(ii)   their ethnolinguistic background, gender, and workplace status;
(iii) their frequent need to communicate at work with people from different non-English-speaking backgrounds; and

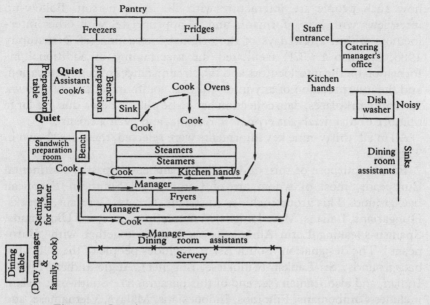

Figure 5. Catering

(iv) their range of communicative acts in the work situation, such as receiving and making requests, instructions, and complaints, and giving advice.

The communicative acts should not be merely formulaic routines. *Where feasible*, cultural background, gender, and workplace status were balanced and alternated in the choice of key informants at different research sites. This enabled us to assess the possible effects of such variables on communication patterns. So if at one research site, one of the key informants was a male Croatian 'superordinate' who communicated frequently with female Vietnamese 'subordinates', we endeavoured to engage in other research sites, say, a Croatian female and a Vietnamese male of equal status working together, as key informants. It should be remembered that through the key informants, the microphone wearers, we obtained data from a much wider range of people of different ethnolinguistic backgrounds (thirty-seven in all), both genders, and with differing status and functions in the workplace. (Incidentally, all those taped indirectly were also willing for this to happen. These people were identified on the tape by the key informant following *each* interaction.) In this way we have also obtained data on how the same person is interacting with people of different cultural and ethnolinguistic backgrounds and how such people are interacting with the same person. Follow-up interviews with key informants and, if appropriate, with other inter-locutors within a few days of the original interaction (cf. Neustupný 1985, see also 1.3.3.1) facilitated the ascertaining of additional in-formation on the interlocutors and the circumstances of communication, and the interpretation of any inter-cultural communication breakdown. In some workplaces, data collection had to be phased down due to a large number of dismissals for economic reasons, and even a closure.

All in all, thirty-nine key informants were selected, these are shown in Table 2.3.

For the purpose of this study: 'European' encompasses continental Europeans, most of whom are of Central and Southern European background. This group includes Austrians, Croats, Germans, Greeks, Hungarians, Italians, Macedonians, Maltese, Spaniards, and Ukrainians. Spanish-speaking Latin Americans are treated together with 'Euro-peans'. The designation 'South Asian' includes people of the following backgrounds: Sri Lankan (Sinhalese, Burgher), Anglo-Indian, Fijian-Indian, and also Iranian (see end of this paragraph). 'South-east Asian' includes Cambodians, Filipinos, Indonesians, Malays, Vietnamese, and ethnic Chinese from various South-east Asian countries. A small number of informants of Lebanese, Syrian, and Turkish backgrounds are treated as a separate group. This classification was drawn up after a considerable amount of data had been collected, and allocations and differentiations were influenced by progress results. The inclusion of the one Iranian under 'South Asian' is supported by the observation of other Iranians (outside our sample) in inter-cultural communication in Australia, but this classification would need to be verified by further research.

2.4   Nature and purpose of the corpus

This project is concerned with human verbal interaction. As in other human behaviour, it can be expected that variation in verbal interaction is determined by individual and sub-cultural (gender, social class, occupational) as well as cultural variables. Communication occurs not only in a social setting, but also in a cultural context in which people conform to, or contravene, behavioural norms. While the emphasis in this study is on cultural differences, these interact with sub-cultural and individual ones, and it is neither possible nor desirable to separate them, particularly since the interrelation between cultural, gender, age and status variables is in itself culture-bound. Our corpus of 182 hours of recordings of inter-cultural communication is derived principally (150 hours) from audio-tapes of spontaneous communication. The method of

Table 2.3 *Key informants by gender, language, and workplace status*

(H = high, M = Medium, L = Low)

Workplace	Gender	Language (Cultural group)	Status
Amcar	m	Serbo-Croatian	H
	m	Vietnamese	H
	m	Greek	H
	m	Greek	L
	m	Macedonian	H
	m	Turkish	M
	f	Greek	L
	m	Bahamian[1]	L
	f	Spanish	L
Nipponcar	m	Maltese	H
	m	Sri Lankan English (Burgher)	M
	m	Vietnamese	L
	f	Filipino	L
	f	Finnish	L
	m	Turkish	L
Weavers	m	Italian	H
	m	Sinhalese	H
	m	Maltese	M
	m	Ukrainian	M
	m	Vietnamese	L
Elektro	m	Croatian	H
	m	Indonesian	H
	f	Hokkien (Malaysian-Chinese)	M
	f	German (Austrian)	M
	f	Filipino	L
	m	Hungarian, Czech	H
	f	Hungarian	L
	m	Turkish	L
Catering	m	Hindi (Fijian-Indian)	H
	m	Croatian	H
	m	Sinhalese	L
	m	Hakka (Cambodian-Chinese)	L
	f	Spanish (Salvadorian)	L
	f	Vietnamese	L
	f	Hakka (Cambodian-Chinese)	L
	m	Iranian (Farsi)	H
Education Office	f	Croatian	M
	m	Vietnamese	M
Parent Group (Meeting only)	f	Croatian	M
	f	Italian	M

[1] *But this informant did not himself yield any useful discourse.*

recording this is described in 2.2 above and, as will be gathered from that section, the data represents communication between people of quite diverse language and cultural backgrounds, notably Central and Southern European, South-east and South Asian.

Much of the data covers speech acts such as directives (requests and instructions), commissives (promises and assurances), complaints, and apologies. Some of the communication has taken place in crisis situations. On the other hand, there are also instances of small-talk at work. Not by any means all of the data can be regarded as examples of communication breakdown (miscommunication or non-communication). In fact, our data enables us to throw some light on what constitutes and promotes successful and unsuccessful inter-cultural communication.

A second, smaller source of data consists of tapes of meetings from Weavers (9 hours audio, 6 hours video), Employment Office (11 hours, audio), and from Parent Group (6 hours, audio). The meetings of employee participation (quality circle) groups at Weavers involve people from different cultural groups. Presentations are prepared and made and the other participants respond. This data complements the tapes of spontaneous communication in four ways. It compensates for the communication paucity in the research sites at Weavers, due to solitary or sequential patterns and high noise levels. It adds more formal, as opposed to more spontaneous, data. Like the audio-taped data from meetings at Employment Office, where the meetings are a routine part of work, it enables us to assess how the various non-English-speaking groups interact in such groups and respond to training in formal meetings, something that is vital for the development of industrial democracy in a multicultural/multilingual workplace (see 7.4). Finally, the videos give us a non-verbal record of what is going on.

In Section 1.3.3.1, arguments in favour of, and against, various data gathering practices are discussed. The emphasis on spontaneous communication in our study departs from the established tradition in this field to use elicited role-play to gain data. We have found that 90 minutes of taping is a sufficient length of time to ensure that people are not just 'playing roles'. This is especially significant as a good deal of our data was collected in crises, or at least in non-routine situations when interlocutors had to concentrate on the content of their communications.

The only use that is made of role-play in this study is a test of informants' ability to decode both information and attitude in inter-cultural communication situations through reactions to a film of role-play based on data we have collected (Sections 2.6, 4.8). We had intended this to be a useful attitudinal addendum to the project rather than a substitute for naturalistic data. As it was, the actual response data turned

Table 2.4 *Spontaneous data and meetings data by workplace : audio and video*

Workplace	Hours of audio recording			Hours of video recording	
	Spontaneous	Meetings	Total	Meetings	Total
Amcar	18	0	18	0	0
Nipponcar	16.5	0	16.5	0	0
Weavers	19.5	9	28.5	6	6
Elektro	48	0	48	0	0
Catering	36	0	36	0	0
Migrant Education	12	0	12	0	0
Employment Office*	0	11	11	0	0
Parent Group	0	6	6	0	0
Total	150	26	176	6	6

Grand total: 182 hours.

* *Note that 10 hours of this total has been recorded as a sub-total not included in the speech act distribution (Chapter 3) or the turn-taking comparison as the interaction includes some native speakers of English as well as one of Irish.*

out to offer additional information on argumentation styles, something for which the videoed role-plays acted as a stimulus.

2.5   Method of transcription

The method of transcription adopted for this project takes over many of the principles of Ehlich and Rehbein's (1976) Halbinterpretative Arbeitstranskription (HIAT). These are that the system should be simple to use, easy to learn, authentic in that any unexpected issues can be incorporated and taken up at a later stage, and avoiding phonetic and grammatical detail. We have followed Ehlich and Rehbein in that simultaneous (overlapping) speech is indicated, and therefore turn changes, including interruptions, can be easily identified. We have also followed Ehlich and Rehbein in indicating volume: ⟨ (louder) and ⟩ (softer), and speed: → (faster) and ← (slower). Intonation is shown by: ↑ (raised) and ↓ (lowered). Individual words that are emphasized are underlined. = indicates a false start or a stutter, and the anacoluthon / indicates a repair due to change of sentence planning.

xxxx represents passages that are not identifiable; { } indicates speech that has not been identified with certainty. A full stop . indicates that the previous symbol no longer applies, e.g., intonation, volume and/or speed has returned to what it was previously. The full stop is used only where another speaker has not interrupted or taken over the turns. Pauses are shown, with each + representing a pause of 0.5 second. For longer pauses, the number of seconds is marked in, e.g. +2.0+. Pauses shorter than 0.5 second are represented by a double space between words. In the interests of consistency, we have not attempted to show deviations from the standard language in the spelling. This would be particularly problematic since we are dealing with non-native speakers of English. Standard English spelling is therefore adopted. Punctuation (e.g. full stops, commas, question marks or exclamation marks) is not employed to indicate the structure of the text since this will sometimes 'beg the question'. Minusculization is used for all words except for I and personal names. Where they are necessary, editorial comments are included italicized in brackets: (*italics*).

Full notation is not included in single-utterance quotations integrated into the text of this monograph. In such instances, a dash - denotes a change in speaker, while a full stop . marks the end of an utterance, indicating that any following utterance does not follow immediately from the previous quotation. Pauses are indicated by a double space, but in these short examples, pause *length* is not recorded.
(See examples of data, Chapter 3)

2.6   Video experiment

Three role-plays based on our data were acted out by pairs of people who were easily identifiably from different cultural groups. Each of the scenes, which were recorded on video, represented an instance of inter-cultural communication breakdown. The intention was to ascertain if there are inter-cultural differences in reactions to inter-cultural communication breakdown, and if the expectations expressed or implied match our data on the communicative behaviour of the person's culture (cf. Chapter 4). The findings are reported in 4.8.

The three situations were (Clyne, Giannicos and Neil 1994):

1. A German female supervisor prefixing an instruction for her Vietnamese subordinate with some small-talk about what he will be doing on the forthcoming public holiday. There are long silences before the Vietnamese responds. (Based on the text *FIVE DAYS OFF*.)
2. An older Central European male supervisor reprimands a younger Singaporean-Chinese female worker for returning late from lunch. She is not given a chance to give an explanation because of the supervisor's interruptions. (Based on *WORK ETHICS*.)
3. A younger South-east Asian-Chinese woman supervisor is confronted by an older Central European man, who apologizes profusely for a

mistake. Impatiently the supervisor trivializes the mistake. He keeps apologizing until she finally says "I'll fix it up for you!" (Based on *SELF-REPROACH*.)

Fifty-two informants were selected from workplaces and video-recorded watching the video. They represented some of the same cultural groups that form part of the main study. They were then asked to comment on the scenes and to answer a number of questions relating to the communication breakdown. This was also video-recorded. Non-verbal as well as verbal information was therefore available. The responses provided valuable data on argumentation styles of different areal groups (and sub-groups).

2.7   Closing remarks

In this chapter, I have described the study from which the corpus of inter-cultural communication discourse has been derived. The selection criteria, workplace contexts, and data gathering conditions have been discussed. In the following chapters, the data will be analyzed cross-culturally, first in relation to speech acts, then in relation to turn taking. Apart from cultural and gender variation, there are also workplace (institution)-specific differences which will be highlighted. Finally, some practical implications will be drawn for workplace communication.

3 Speech acts in inter-cultural discourse

3.0 The interactions[1]

In this chapter, I shall discuss some of the interactions that form part of our corpus from the point of view of their predominant communicative function or intent. The purpose of this is twofold. There are few corpuses of workplace communication that have been described in detail. Such a description may contribute to an appreciation of the diversity of the categories. Moreover, because of the inter-cultural nature of the communication, it is possible to focus on cultural variation (as well as gender variation and variation between workplaces) in the incidence of particular speech acts and the way in which they are performed. A more 'holistic' treatment of the corpus may be found in Chapter 4.

Because of the manner in which our data was collected, the tapes include periods of silence, speech that is inaudible because of industrial noise, and brief question–answer interactions of the kind:

- do you know where Jack is.
- yes he went over there.

Such interactions are generally successful and, if so, will not be discussed in this account. Also, responses to such questions are often non-verbal (i.e. by gesture).

Some of the interaction sequences in the corpus are *simple* in that they involve a single speech act and perhaps a response to it (i.e. adjacency pair) and a lead-up. There may be a repetition or paraphrase, e.g.

> don't do that don't do that.
> tell him to stand in the queue make him stand in the queue.

Most of the interaction sequences, however, comprise realizations of several connected and interdependent speech acts (e.g. complaint and directive) by some or all of the participants. The relation between these

[1] For transcription mode of examples, see Section 2.5. Please note that not all transcriptions are included in this monograph.

48

is generally less automatic and routinized than is usually described in terms of adjacency pairs, e.g. invitation and acceptance. Such sequences will be designated as *complex* and labelled according to their focal speech act. This task is a well-nigh impossible one because most speech acts are ambiguous and 'multi-functional' (e.g. commissive and self-directive). However, it is hoped that a classification according to more traditional categories will help describe variation in the kind of inter-cultural discourse that is contained in our corpus. Single speech acts or simple sequences within complex ones are also recorded separately in our corpus inventory and therefore included in statistical counts. A new sequence will often be determined by a change in the communicative setting, e.g. in the interlocutors, with at least one person entering the conversation or leaving the scene or becoming a passive participant.

Neither the cultural variation nor the workplace variation for any of the speech acts is statistically significant (x-squared) due to the small size of the sample. However, I believe that the figures given at the end of the sections do give contrastive insights.

We have 88 complaints, including 54 whinges (for the distinction, see 3.1, 3.1.1), 133 directives, 73 commissives, 25 apologies, and 29 that could be characterized as 'small-talk'.[2]
In many cases, cultural variation and inter-cultural communication breakdown may be identified through the way in which the message is embedded in the organization of the discourse, e.g. through turn-taking behaviour. This will be discussed in Chapter 4.
(For transcription mode, see 2.5.)

3.1   Complaints/whinges

3.1.0   *Definitions*

Complaints are speech acts in which disappointment or a grievance is expressed. Austin (1961: 13) categorizes complaints as behabitives – 'statements of reaction'. But some complaints would fit better into the group of exercitives – where someone is exercising a power. I would prefer to organize complaints into two categories – whinges (behabitive complaints) and exercitive complaints. Whinge is an Australian-English word for a long or repeated expression of discontent not necessarily intended to change or improve the unsatisfactory situation. Whinges are a regular feature of general and workplace conversation in Australia.

---

[2] This count does not include those meetings tapes from the Employment Office which include Anglo-Australians, a New Zealander, and/or an (Irish-speaking) Irishman in the interactions.

However, Australians (especially Anglo-Australians) frequently attribute them to English immigrants, who are often stereotypically described as 'whingeing poms' because it is claimed that they find many things in Australia disagreeable.

It is conceivable that a complaint and a whinge may use the same words in an utterance. The distinction rests with the interlocutors and the speech situation. An exercitive complaint can be made only:

(a) by someone who is in a position to do so, and/or
(b) to someone who is in a position to receive such a complaint.

There are also occasions where a whinge can lead to an exercitive complaint, as I shall show.

3.1.1   *Complaints as behabitives (Whinges)*

Whinges are very common in work situations, especially between equals and near-equals. They provide an outlet for emotions and can be regarded as a type of phatic communication which establishes and maintains solidarity between colleagues.[3] Fifty-four whinges have been recorded, mainly in the Education Office context and in Catering. Unlike the exercitive complaints, the whinges are not directed towards achieving any particular goal. No justification is required in this type of complaint.

An example of this kind of discourse is EVERYTHING WENT WRONG, where Boba, a Croatian woman, and Quoc, a Vietnamese man working with her at the Education Office, whinge co-operatively about the boss, the computer, and the evening staff stealing pens. Here, as in many whinges, there is fairly symmetrical communication between the participants. Quoc sometimes offers some advice.

EVERYTHING WENT WRONG - [Employment Office]

---

1 Boba] I don't know if she needs me to + type it + + or not + 18.0 +
2 Quoc]   ↑ aah I still

---

3 Quoc] now have the waitlist you know half an hour already came in eight thirty

---

[3] I do not quite agree with Wierzbicka's (1991: 181–2) representation of the difference between *complain* and *whinge*. To her, complain has a component of [I want someone to know about this] and whinge [I want someone to do something because of this] as a component as well as an element of helplessness. While I agree about the helplessness, I believe the other components mentioned are each attached to the wrong item.

| 4 | Boba |] | it's that slow ↑huh |
| 5 | Quoc |] | and tried to get into the computer and still now I have   yeh and |

| 6 | Boba |] | [laughs: *she is* |
| 7 | Quoc |] | still now I have the waitlist wait over half an <u>hour</u> xxxxx |

| 8 | Boba |] | *looking for a pen*] you see + + it's <u>never</u> <u>there</u> + all my pens + and |

| 9 | Boba |] | there's markers and everything everything is gone |
| 10 | Quoc |] | uh   you uh + try to get a |

| 11 | Quoc |] | few more this one black one + <I don't know where + <maybe in the |

| 12 | Boba |] | <what for they just take you know [laughs faintly] |
| 13 | Quoc |] | box in ↑there   just get |

| 14 | Quoc |] | a few + two or three you know or maybe you put your ex and my ex |

| 15 | Boba |] | there I'll = I'll go through the + cabinet and then <I'll = I'll look |
| 16 | Quoc |] | er + |

| 17 | Quoc |] | →↑actually. <you know + + <even the er people from the evening they |

| 18 | Quoc |] | just took my black pen all the time + not you know too many but you |

| 19 | Quoc |] | know usually you know + lost one or two every week + not ↑like you |

| 20 | Boba |] | <and because of that I'm not taking |
| 21 | Quoc |] | [laughs] lost every night every day |

| 22 | Boba |] | them out any more   it was full |
| 23 | Quoc |] | yeh but well you know   yeh |

Where whinges occur on the factory floor, they can take the form of parallel discourse, like the following, where Raymond, a Sri Lankan Burgher leading hand and Frank, a Maltese supervisor, are whingeing independently, with one prompting the other's complaining:

PARALLEL WHINGEING - [Nipponcar]

1	Frank	]	look I was wondering ↑why we are + + construction there there's + +

2	Ray.	]	now what happen I told her + she was keeping a bit of space + and

3	Frank	]	Lola
4	Ray.	]	putting it + about oh {what's that xxxx know who I mean} Lola and→

5	Ray.	]	I came and I said. you will do the normal that woman doesn't understand

6	Frank	]	who ↑Lola why I wonder why
7	Ray.	]	a word of english mm →she doesn't know xxxx

8	Frank	]	I said to her looks
9	Ray.	]	→here the xxxx →to ↑me nothing bloody four seconds

10	Frank	]	I say look + spray a little bit on the corner of the
11	Ray.	]	flat I finished the corner

12	Frank	]	trim ah + and send it to the heat you ↑know what she done. she send it

13	Frank	]	on + to the heat without + put any glue at all oh
14	Ray.	]	she doesn't know + +

15	Frank	]	no ↑you know why. because I don't want construction there that's why I
16	Ray.	]	yeah

17	Frank	]	want the system running + how it should be
18	Ray.	]	→↑and I said look. I have done about

19	Ray.	]	three bloody ↑door trims + + →and I go on the cutting table and another

20	Ray.	]	one is coming. + ↑fucking hell. it's not + hard for me →just four seconds

| 21 | Frank |] | even I said many |
| 22 | Ray. |] | for me to do that one + like < ↑that wack wack wack |

| 23 | Frank |] | times →even one day said so my so my daughter is coming they get upset |

| 24 | Frank |] | + but + ↑we are not behind we are actually we are ahead |
| 25 | Ray. |] | →yeah now |

| 26 | Frank |] | yeah but + I want you after tea please we |
| 27 | Ray. |] | ↑there be in there extra xxxx |

| 28 | Frank |] | start doing those door trims because I've got the truck here + |
| 29 | Ray. |] | ah okay |

| 30 | Frank |] | have a cup of coffee before the siren goes |

Raymond's opening complaint 'look I was wondering why we are + + construction there there's' is interrupted and the conversation diverted to the inadequacies of Lola and her work, especially her tendency to misunderstand directives and carry out her duties inadequately and slowly. The complaints are generally made independently, and the only co-operation is in identifying her. Both Frank and Raymond are relating incidents. Frank manages to divert the discussion back to construction tasks and Raymond to other work. Most whinges in the work situation appear to be complaints about other people.

3.1.2 *Complaints (exercitives) as complex interactions*

The complaints that are exercitives are usually part of complex interactional sequences which begin with an explicit or implicit accusation. They can be complaints about, or to, another person. Where the accused is present, there will often follow a defence or justification. The sequence will essentially include at least one directive (request for action) which will usually be explicit, but sometimes implicit, in the accusation (e.g. *PASSING ON THE COMPLAINT* below). A return accusation is an optional part of this complex sequence and an apparent disclaimer may appear as a rhetorical device (see below). Often an apology is part of the complex complaint sequence with either the accused or the accuser (making an unjustified complaint) apologizing.

Let us proceed from the more simple to the most complex complaint sequences. One simple interaction, from Catering, is characterized by co-operative repetition involving three speakers. Daniel and Lee, Cambodian-Chinese kitchen-hands complain to Tim, the Fijian-Indian cook, about a woman whom they accuse of jumping queues. The accusation is first realized by Daniel:

> she didn't line up.

then extended by him:

> she didn't line up in the queue.

echoed by Lee:

> she didn't line up in the queue.

and repeated by Daniel:

> she didn't line up in the queue.

As we will see (4.3.3), repetition and parallelism are strategies often employed by Tim himself, which have become widespread in his section, because of the work situation and/or due to his influence.

The success of the above complaint is demonstrated in the following exchange, *PASSING ON THE COMPLAINT*. Here Tim conveys to Ivan, his Croatian superior, the complaint about the lady who jumps queues and causes trouble generally:

> this lady always create too much problems.
> this lady always create too much problem.
> now she's coming between the queues.

First Ivan does not hear or does not take any notice of what Tim is saying. The complex nature of the sequence is due to the need for Tim first to capture Ivan's attention away from a communication on kitchen matters. We do not know if the desired effect is achieved, but the message is at least presented. A behabitive complaint can lead to an exercitive one. An instance of this is to be found in the exchange, *BAD SERVING*. Here Tim whinges to a passive Lee about dining-room patrons using the wrong plates for the soup or the sauce. In each case the whinge to his subordinate is followed by a directive in the negative, addressed to the accused. The first such realization:

> hey don't use that bowl for the sauce eh that's for the soup.

is repeated:

>don't use the bowl for the sauce.

The same message is conveyed to another person accused:

>hey don't use the bowl for the sauce.

and the directive to a third person is similar in structure:

>hey don't use the bowl for the soup.

The change of addressee is marked, e.g. by clearing of the throat and/or by the words:

>see another one.

addressed to Lee. A further comment is added after the directive:

>why don't you take in a plate.
>what do you people do.
>bloody shit.

His directives in the complaint cycle tend to be short, direct, and repetitive.

In *INTERROGATING THE GREEDY MAN*, Cam, a Vietnamese woman dining-room assistant, complains to Tim about people taking plates of food for people who are not accompanying them. When one such man is sighted, Tim and Cam descend on him together. They use quite different strategies. Tim produces five directives, three negative and two positive, all employing modal verbs:

>from tomorrow you have to be here with your wife.
>you cannot take the meals out.
>you cannot take the food out from the hostels.
>your wife and you all of you have to eat here in the dining-room.
>you cannot take the food out from tomorrow.

Tim's utterances are again short and repetitive. He introduces a highly bureaucratic note:

>they put the big notice there.

Cam first asks:

>are you married are you married where's your wife I didn't see
>   her.

She follows this with an explanation and a directive:

>I take two plate one for you and one for your wife but why not

come deposit of two plate huh and after pick another plate
okay.

and justifies both her own and Tim's directives with an explanation,
indicating positive politeness (cf. Brown and Levinson 1987, see 1.3.2):

that's not fair for the other people they don't have enough plate.

Cam completes the complaint cycle with a polite closing routine:

oh alright thanks a lot anyhow bye thank you

incorporating a number of Australian solidarity markers as well as
performing a female 'caring role'. We will return to the cross-cultural
variation in this interaction in 4.3.

An instance of a simple complaint occurs in a meeting discussion at
Employment Office highlighting part-time employment. Anglo-Indian
Elvira complains:

if I could get gazetted into the position it's not going to be
considered that's what the problem is.

The complex sequence *BAD SOLDERING*, recorded at Elektro, comprises two shorter complaint sequences and one apology. The apology
will be discussed under 3.4 below. (The full transcription is to be found
in Appendix 3.) The intent of this interaction between Slobodan, the 45-
year-old Croatian supervisor, Blanche, a Malaysian-Chinese leading
hand, and Ricarda, a Filipina process worker, is marked by Slobodan's
opening 'Blanche good morning a ha complain again'. Bremer et al.
(1988) consider this kind of topicalization a good way of preventing non-
understanding. Slobodan's complaint is expressed as three propositions:

(a) you put Ricarda on the soldering hand soldering.
    (Accusation expressed as a fact)
(b) I can't sit there and check every.
    (Implicit accusation about Blanche's judgment and reliability)
(c) once she soldered {a bit} she'd be alright.
    (Implicit accusation about Blanche's judgment)

This is followed by an apology in the form of a vindication from Blanche:

I can't take someone beside me I've got to check + haven't got
anyone.

Blanche avoids any blame for Ricarda's incompetence at soldering.
Slobodan interrupts her, employing an apparent disclaimer (Van Dijk
1991: 128):

> I am agreed you cannot sit beside but sometimes if we check it
> and we find it wrong we have to + show care.

as well as a downtoner (sometimes).

He also uses the first person plural pronoun as a downtoner, implying an element of solidarity (and face saving) which is not present in the rest of the discourse. Slobodan, who seems to see himself as an upholder of work ethics, reacts negatively to Blanche's suggestion that Ricarda perhaps does not like the job, having missed the suggestion the first time it was made:

> if somebody doesn't like a job then try to escape from a job
> because doing it wrong no hope about that if people want a
> better job or position or something like that they should prove
> themself on any other work.

Turning to Ricarda, he again marks the complaint sequence with an opening:

> Ricarda let's have a talk about the quality of soldering joints.
> (lines 38,40)

However, the apparent disclaimer:

> Ricarda I understand that you don't have any experience with
> soldering you've been on that area for a week week and a half
> to be trained on it and I know another things that whoever is
> trained for a couple of weeks on soldering cannot become
> expert and we don't expect that you are expert in these two
> three weeks.

precedes the directive, expressed with downtoners:

> I think is what we would like happening to concentrate yourself
> a little bit more. (lines 48–9)

which, in turn, is followed by the face threatening accusation:

> you didn't heat it properly or you did it without any flux.

Ricarda defends herself effectively to another worker Franca, an Italian woman, in the presence of Slobodan. Because it is intended for him to hear, this is a complaint rather than a whinge:

> I didn't do this one.
> look what you have shown to Blanche all the worst jobs.

and a directive to Slobodan:

> well you better make sure who did it.
> I can solder much better than that.

The interface of complaints, apologies, directives and commissives in this complex complaint interaction is apparent in lines 112–25 where Slobodan directs another woman not to do soldering:

> please don't do soldering.

vindicates (i.e. apologizes for) the directive:

> the soldering is the job was supposed to be done with the training.

complains:

> well we see that some job is done in here which is really really unskilful and ugly er that's not acceptable at all.

gives another two directives:

> and please don't do a soldering.
> if you on waiting time and have nothing to do you see me or Blanche.

performs a commissive:

> if you interested in soldering no problem at all we will put you on that area on that training and you will be trained.

returning to the negative directive again as a summary at the end:

> please don't do a soldering.

The complexity of such discourse makes it difficult to sum it up in a cultural script (cf. Wierzbicka 1991, 1993) such as:

> I think: You have done something bad.
> I say: You have done this badly.
> You must do this well.

Another female worker, Inge, a German, successfully disputes Slobodan's accusations in another of his complex complaint sequences in *CHALLENGING SLOBODAN*. This sequence commences with an implicit accusation:

> there is supposed to be the five seven ones what you already did I think yesterday or then.

responded to by a question of clarification:

> the which ones the eight seven ones

Inge tries to resolve the problem by declaring:

> no I didn't order because it's just filled with the xxxxxxx.

Further doubts cast by Slobodan are refuted by the statement:

> because no I haven't anything.

Following a first (formulaic) apology from Slobodan, Inge anticipates any further accusations:

> because I haven't got anything.
> you know that's right.
> so you don't need them at all today.

All further interrogation is answered or anticipated:

> but so from where are those ones please.
> look that's from before maybe.
> because whatever Liesl got I haven't got yet.
> that's eight-seven-three isn't it.

This is followed by an apology from Slobodan (see 3.4).

Like other exchanges, WORK ETHICS is an instance of Slobodan's efforts to teach his Chinese-speaking female subordinates work ethics. Like other interactions (see below), it begins with a vocative:

> Jennifer listen you now and all you people here.

An explanation follows:

> you know how much we need the soldering we desperately need
> soldering people to do Petersons or to do any er job on
> soldering in the area.

leads to a directive:

> from now on I don't want to see anybody who is competent with
> solder to do the cleaning.

It is only then that the focal point of a complaint sequence, the accusation, is introduced – indirectly:

> I don't understand why every ten or twenty minutes people who
> are nominated to clean those boards alright are off from the job
> I don't understand the one things how peoples are not ashamed
> to sit here doing nothing.

After another directive:

> keep it under control look nominate the people.

as in *BAD SOLDERING* above, he produces an apparent disclaimer:

> I know it's er not ah it's not easy job but.

summarizing his main point in the form of an implicit directive:

> we need output.

Then there begins another accusation, this time a direct one:

> I see people who are soldering then cleaning boards.

interrupted by another directive in the negative:

> we can't do that.

followed by a repeated accusation:

> and people are here sitting doing nothing.

Slobodan then appears to be asking for an explanation (justification):

> what's the reason.

which is repeated three times in slightly different forms:

> I would like to see what's the reason is there any reason for that
> tell me.
> yeah I would like to have a reason.

the last time being in response to Jennifer, who has been trying to give an answer and then asks:

> you want a reason.

but is not given a chance (see 4.6.1). It may be that he is eliciting an apology (cf. Rehbein 1972). The sparse use of downtoners and strong formulations would make such a speech by a native speaker of Australian English unlikely in the circumstances. All these interactions are marked by a substantial power hierarchy and social distance, and reflect a cultural obligation to protect one's own face in the first instance and the interlocutors' in the second place (cf. Brown and Levinson 1978, 1987).

3.1.3   Cultural and gender variation in complaints and whinges
(*see comment on significance*, 3.1.0.)

The above description of data indicates the context of the speech acts and the complexity of the inter-cultural implications in which they are performed. An analysis of our data in Table 3.1.3 below shows that complaints are performed predominantly by men, especially Europeans, but that people from all groups whinge. (It is impossible to assess if the opportunities for whingeing are equal!) South-east Asian women are least likely to complain or to whinge. It would appear from the figures in the table below that whingeing was the particular pastime of Central European women. However, most of the examples in this category (ten out of fifteen instances from European women) were derived from one informant, Boba at Education Office. Similarly, most of the South-east Asian instances of whinges (seven out of twelve) were recorded from Boba's colleague, Quoc. In fact, there is not much cultural variation in the whinges. The speakers simply state what they do not approve of. Whinges tend to be concentrated in particular kinds of workplaces (cf. 3.1.4). Exercitive complaints have tended to be rather explicit and come from people with a higher status. However, even those South-east Asian women with superordinate status tend not to complain to, or about their subordinates. The two complaints from South-east Asian men are from Daniel complaining about diners, something that is part of the discourse of his workplace (see below, 4.5.1).

Table 3.1.3 (*Exercitive*) *complaints and whinges: cultural and gender variation*

| | Complaints | | | Whinges | | |
	M	F	Total	M	F	Total
European/Latin American	15	2	17	0	19	19
South-East Asian	5	3	8	12	2	14
South Asian	5	4	9	16	0	16
Turkish/Lebanese	0	0	0	5	0	5
Total	25	9	34	33	21	54

Complaints were performed by people from the following cultural groups: Croatian, Greek, Maltese, Spanish, Lebanese, Turkish, Anglo-Indian, Fijian-Indian, Sinhalese, Cambodian-Chinese, Filipino, Vietnamese, and whinges by Croatians, a Finn, Poles, a Spaniard, Lebanese,

Turks, a Fijian-Indian, a Sinhalese, Cambodian-Chinese, and Vietnamese.

3.1.4   *Workplace variation in complaints and whinges*

The distribution of differences between complaints and whinges is due to the functions of communication in specific types of workplaces. Whinges were recorded mainly in the workplaces (Catering and Education Office) where a small number of people work together habitually, social distance is minimal, and there is plenty of time and scope for comments. The more goal-directed institutional nature of communication in the factory, as well as the hierarchial and sequential work patterns, make whinges a less common type of interaction there. Exercitive complaints, while not so prevalent in our corpus, are somewhat more evenly distributed between workplaces, though again most common in research sites outside heavy industry. Their prevalence in the Employment Office is due to our data from that workplace being derived from meetings intended partly to air complaints and difficulties:

Table 3.1.4. (*Exercitive*) *complaints and whinges : comparison between workplaces*

	Complaint	Whinge
Amcar	0	5
Weavers	0	0
Nipponcar	0	6
Elektro	11	6
Catering	12	18
Migrant Education	1	18
Employment Office	10	1
Total	34	54

3.1.5   *Complaints and whinges : summary*

'Complaints' are divided into whinges, (long or repeated) non-goal-driven statements of discontent, and complaints, goal-driven exercises of power. Both categories are common in Australian society as a whole. Whinges are part of the social discourse of the workplace, and are often about other people. They are least common on the factory floor, where communication is goal-directed. They occur particularly in workplaces where there is time and scope for them, social distance between a small number of colleagues is minimal. Whingeing tends to be a solidarity

promoting speech activity, through repetition, echo, or parallel discourse.

Complaints, which usually form part of a complex sequence, occur
across workplaces. The central part of the complaint, the accusation, is
toned down through apparent disclaimer, modal, explanation or justification, or implicit directive. Complaint sequences typically include other
speech acts, such as directives, apologies, and commissives.

Although cultural and workplace variation are not statistically significant in our rather limited corpus, complaints are most common among
men, especially Europeans, people with higher status, while South-east
Asian women are relatively less likely to whinge or to complain. Among
Europeans, whingeing is gender-independent.

3.2   Directives

3.2.0   *Definition and sub-categorization*

For the purpose of this monograph, directives will include both requests
and instructions, the distinction being hard to justify in the corpus.
Directives are the most frequently employed speech act in our data from
work situations and, as we have seen, also form part of the complaint
sequence. I will differentiate between positive and negative directives
and between explicit and implicit ones. Examples of explicit ones are:

- tomorrow bring the picture. (Filipina)
- hey don't use the bowl for the sauce. (Fijian-Indian man)
- you must ask then. (Croatian woman)

Examples of implicit ones where the message of the directive is expressed
'indirectly' are:

- we need output. (Croatian man) (Meaning: Stop loafing)
- your fax is here. (Croatian woman) (Meaning: Go and collect
  your fax)
- are you going to repair them (Fijian Indian man) (Meaning:
  Repair them)

In some cases, grammatical conventions are employed for implicitly
expressing a directive:

- I was wondering if I can have... (Maltese man) (Meaning:
  Give me...)
- Maybe you could put her on there insertion. (Croatian man)
  (Meaning: Put her on the insertion work over there)

Where there was any doubt, the intended meanings were verified in follow-up interviews. The problem with such instances is that they bear the literal meaning.

Negative directives direct someone not to do something. One of the directives discussed in the text *WORK ETHICS* under complaints (3.1.2, full text 4.1.1) from Slobodan is a negative one:

> from now on I don't want to see anybody who is competent with solder to do the cleaning.

The reader is reminded that, in addition to autonomous directive sequences, there are directives which are part of complex complaint (and other) sequences. However, there are also complex directive sequences which include other sub-sequences (e.g. complaint, promise) and speech acts (e.g. justification, accusation, promise).

An instance of a directive combined with a justification or explanation (indicating 'positive politeness', cf. Brown and Levinson 1987) is:

> tell Ken to bring the certificate on Tuesday you know why because it's p.d.o.[4] on Monday if he doesn't bring the certificate he doesn't get paid for today. (Maltese man)

A directive is combined with a whinge in *BAD SERVING* (see also 3.1.2) where Tim is whingeing to Lee about dining-room guests and unsuccessfully directing him to reproach them at the same time. He ends up instructing them while maintaining the conversation with Lee:

BAD SERVING - [Catering]

1	Tim	]	see what they're doing they're washing the bloody spoons + + in the

| 2 | Tim |] | coffee machine   eh Lee Lee tell tell this one here + + |
| 3 | Lee |] | yes mate + 1.5 + |

| 4 | Tim |] | come + 2.5 + come + + I'm very sick an' tired oh she's coming there |
| 5 | Lee |] | oh |

| 6 | Tim |] | why don't you take it in a plate (*clears throat*) + 3.0 + hey don' use that |

| 7 | Tim |] | bowl for the sauce eh that's for the soup + don't use the bowl for the |

---

[4] p.d.o. – Programmed day off.

8	Tim	]	sauce		see another one is there hey don't use the bowl
9	Lee	]		yeah she always	

All these uses are common in Australian English.

3.2.1   *On the nature of directives at work*

Directive sequences differ from complex complaint sequences in that the former are largely sets of instructions, e.g.:

> you put it on.
> > see if we can load it up on winch.
> > have a roll of fleecy or something from the old exacto stock.
> > just see how it runs.
> > and we try to dye it on that winch.
> > take the young chap what's his name Mike.
> > and see if you can put it on winch two before it starts to ...
> > (Maltese foreman, Weavers)
> > push this one in press the button lock up wait two second.
> > (Turkish operator, Amcar).

Often directives require no response other than backchannelling, e.g.:

> yeah yeah.
> Okay

This is because persons giving directives have both the authority and the information. However, sometimes factual information has to be sought through questions, e.g.:

> how much does it turn to. (Sinhalese kitchen-hand, Catering)

Sometimes complex directive sequences include background information which the person being directed requires, or a justification for the directive ('positive politeness'), e.g.:

> please we start doing those door trims because I've got the truck here. (Maltese foreman, Nipponcar)

Justification (vindication) or explanation (giving details or reasons), like other forms of politeness, is a way in which the interactant who has the power to make directives can allow the other some face.

Some of our subjects display much variability in their use of directives, perhaps according to who they are talking to, e.g. at Catering, Tim gives an explicit directive to Daniel:

> you can start with the cauliflower.

and to Cam:

> just give them.

but an implicit one to Marisa, a Salvadorian female kitchen hand:

> if you keep a spoon I think it will be better for you to take the potatoes when you press it it breaks.

Tim gives directives to the same group of offsiders 'more explicitly', e.g.:

> give them ...
> take out ...

and less explicitly, e.g.:

> they can have ...
> it should be ...

Directives can contain different degrees of forcefulness, ranging from Slobodan's:

> Like or not like we have to do it alright.

(but NB the first person plural indirect formulation of directive), to Boba's equally determined but milder:

> and so if you don't mind to go up again don't send me there again please.

Perhaps the simplest directive in our corpus is:

> Cam chicken chow mein.

shouted by Tim to Cam.
One effective way to get people to do things for you is through the skilful use of *want* and <u>can</u>, e.g.:

> You want some more potatoes. (Meaning: Add some more potatoes)
> You can do it at home. (Meaning: Do it at home)

Let us examine some examples of directives in some complex sequences. The complaint sequence *WAITING TIME* above is preceded by a directive sequence from Slobodan beginning with an vocative, then please followed by a modal:

>   Jennifer please I would like to clear something with you.

then appellation, please, and an imperative:

>   Rosie please come here.

with the please sometimes being reinforced by be kind and:

>   Jennifer you are also on waiting time please be kind and come
>   here.

Within the complex complaint sequence, directives are employed to gain and keep control. There is an implicit directive:

>   I would like to see what's Ling's doing where she is.

and then explicit ones:

>   Jennifer organize this shop there alright.
>   if it's not enough working place look do it on the other.
>   if you find a difficulty look just see me and inform me.

Both the simple imperatives and the ones with please (be kind and) would be considered 'non-native' directives in Australian English.

CHECK IT is a complex directive sequence which contains not only numerous directives, but also a shorter complaint sequence, justification, and promises.

CHECK IT - Elektro

1 Slobo.] + 2 + I was informed from storemens that two items they didn't deliver

---

2 Slobo.] this morning   some kind of capacitors and connectors
3 Jennifer]   I will check   I will

---

4 Slobo.]   and er miss summers said the capacitors are okay + +   {you
5 Jennifer]   I will check that

---

6 Slobo.] get 'em}   check it and er see if you are in short supply we
7 Jennifer] afterwards + 2.0 + I after

---

8 Slobo.] can an action otherwise er
9 Jennifer]   yeah

Slobodan, having asked questions about production matters, produces a very implicit complaint addressed to Jennifer:

> I was informed from storemans that two items they didn't deliver this morning.

Slobodan then gives details and each time Jennifer gives an assurance that she will check:

> I will check.
> I will check that.
> I will check that afterwards. (See also under 3.3.1.)

In spite of this, Slobodan follows this with a directive in a direct mode to confirm that the message is understood, thereby exercising his authority:

> better check it and see if you are in short supply.

with an alternative directive:

> we can an action otherwise. (Meaning: Go ahead otherwise)

to which Jennifer replies:

> yeah yeah.

Within the same sequence, there is another directive:

> look if you find the problem bring them in here and they can do a job they can share a job.

In *DYEING AND LOADING* at Weavers, the Maltese foreman Bill is giving instructions to the Macedonian, Bob, in the presence of the Sinhalese supervisor Dulip and the Ukrainian foreman Mick. He employs a technique frequently used in instructions on the factory floor of first focussing on the object to be featured in the instructions:

> listen see that truck with the with the cuffs.

followed by the actual directive:

> you put it on see if we can load it up on winch.

and then:

> take the young chap what's his name Mike and see if you can put it on winch two before it starts to.

While Slobodan tends to use a politeness marker please or please be kind and or the interjection look! in his directives (as does Frank the Maltese foreman at Nipponcar, for example, at the start of 3.2.1), Slobodan's fellow-Croatian Ivan at Catering does not. Ivan's English communication patterns appear to have converged far more to Australian usage. This is why we have to be cautious with generalizing about particular ethnic cultures from a small sample. It is why I will be referring to tendencies. Like that of his Fijian-Indian colleague Tim, Ivan's discourse is marked by repetition and positive and/or negative imperatives. Unlike Tim, he gives justifications or explanations as part of directive interactions, e.g.:

> the chicken don't leave it out.

(NB Left dislocation for emphasis, according to Bremer et al. (1988) a good technique for preventing non-communication.)

> don't leave it out of the fridge because it's.
> don't leave it in the water any more because it'll start smelling.

Raymond, the Burgher at Nipponcar, similarly elaborates justifications, e.g.:

> so I cannot give you at least a couple of days because you have to go and check it out from the sister again.
> it's for everybody not for one person because I don't want to take a risk on my job.
> so that's why I'm not giving you but you have to go on Monday or Friday.

Like his fellow-Maltese Bill, Frank also justifies directives, e.g.:

> I want you after please we start doing those door trims because I've got the truck here.

Like Slobodan (see 3.1.2), Irma, the Croatian Parent Group co-ordinator, employs the first person plural pronoun as a second person, e.g. (directed at Maria, her Italian colleague):

> so we have to buy what about pizza you're expert how many we need for.

3.2.2   *Cultural and gender variation in directives*

Directives were imparted overwhelmingly by men, especially European men. Of the nineteen directives performed by women in our corpus, thirteen came from Croatians.

Table 3.2.2. *Directives : cultural and gender variation*

	M	F	Total
European/Latin American	65	15	80
South-East Asian	18	4	22
South Asian	19	0	19
Turkish/Lebanese/Syrian	12	0	12
Total	114	19	133

Directives were performed by people from the following cultural groups: Croatian, Finnish, Macedonian, Maltese, Lebanese, Syrian, Turkish, Cambodian, Filipino, Indonesian, Malaysian-Chinese, Vietnamese, Fijian-Indian, Iranian, Sinhalese.

3.2.3   *Workplace variation in directives*

The distribution of directives across the workplaces is indicative of where most of our data has been gathered, but also shows the importance of this speech act in most work communication:

Table 3.2.3. *Directives : comparison between workplaces*

Amcar	15	Catering	27
Nipponcar	12	Education Office	23
Weavers	9	Employment Office	7
Elektro	38	Parent Group	2
		Total 133	

3.2.4   *Directives : summary*

The directives in our corpus vary in their explicitness. Some are positive, often negative. Some are expressed by simple imperatives, which may be quite forceful or just give basic information, others by simple imperatives and a politeness marker or other downtoner. The directives are typically performed by men, especially Europeans, often to women. They are not always performed in the same way to different types of interlocutors. Note, for instance, Tim's lengthier, more polite and implicit directive to the Salvadorian woman Marisa than to Daniel, the Cambodian-Chinese man of the same workplace status or to Vietnamese and Cambodian-Chinese women (3.2).

Directive sequences tend to be more complex than complaint sequences (other than whinges). This is because of the variability of the
structure of complaint sequences, and because directive sequences tend
to be simply a clustering of directives and (usually positive, sometimes
delaying) responses to them. Directives are sometimes accompanied by
an explanation or justification, and sometimes form part of a complaint
sequence. Something that complaints and directives have in common is
their importance in gaining and maintaining control and power. Getting
people to co-operate through language by routines and markers that are
perceived by members of particular other cultures as more or less urgent
or more or less polite (and face saving).

3.3 Commissives

3.3.0 *Definition*

In his classification of illocutionary acts, Searle (1969) categorizes as
commissives those in which, by promising and offering, Speaker S 'is
committed to a future act A'. They are thus a sub-class of predictives. In
this case, they are predicting one's own future behaviour. This includes
committing yourself to do something or not to do it (i.e. positive or
negative commissive), whether such a commitment is imposed or
voluntary. It includes both conditional and unconditional promises. In
our corpus, commissives include both simple spontaneous responses and
the process and result of involved negotiation. A commissive is one
possible response to a directive. The difficulties with commissive-type
utterances in our data are:

(i)   that they do not employ a performative verb and it is therefore not
      certain that they are really promises in Searle's (1969: 60) sense, i.e.
      that S intends to do A; and
(ii) that Searle's (1969: 62) distinction between sincere and insincere
      promises may not be culturally relevant to both (all) the interlocutors
      (see 6.5, 6.6).

3.3.1 *Categorization of commissives*

There are few complex commissive interactions in our corpus because
they are usually simply responses to another speech act, e.g. directive or
complaint. Unlike complaints and directives, commissives can normally
be analyzed in terms of adjacency pairs – A requests B to do something
and B gives an assurance that (s)he will – e.g., in an exchange between
Bill and Bob at Weavers (*DYEING AND LOADING*):

BILL: get Joe to give you a bit have a roll of fleecy or something
BILL: from the old Exacto stock right
BOB: alright

Offers are an exception in that they are self-initiated commissives:

Quoc to Boba: I will give you a lift home tonight.

The commissive-like assurances in our data fall into four categories:
(i) Active first person utterances/complete or nearly complete sentences,
e.g. in CHECK IT, Jennifer is responding to a directive from Slobodan,
see 3.2.1:

I will check.
I will check that.
I will check that afterwards.

Another utterance in this category also produced by Jennifer is in
response to a complex apology sequence (SELF-REPROACH).

Jennifer: I'll fix up for you.

Commissives are sometimes at the same time self-directives where the
speaker is reciting to him/herself what they are going to do (in this case,
in the presence of another person), e.g.:

got to check with Kim okay. (Turkish process worker, Elektro)
I'm going to call them myself by 'phone and then I'll send them
letters. (Secretary, Education Office)

While Slobodan uses the first person plural pronoun as a false solidarity
marker in complaints (3.1.2), Irma, the Croatian co-ordinator at Parent
Group, employs it as a collective self-directive commissive (i.e. for the
entire group), e.g.:

and then we will follow up with lunch.
we'll have to make sure whether in C 40 or upstairs in centre.
(i.e. we will have to make sure where the function is being
held.)

(ii) Single-word routines, e.g.:

DULIP: you are going to do this next are you
VLAD: yeah
(See also e.g. the quotation from Bill and Bob above.)
A variant of this is the non-lexical mm, e.g.:

IVAN: you can do your ham right
TIM: mm

  IVAN: and then change the menu like last time
  TIM: mm

(iii)   Assurances through formulaic expressions, e.g.:

  No worries. (Jennifer, several instances)
  No problems. (Jennifer to Krysztina)
  That's no problem. (Jennifer to Slobodan)

('No problems' is common to Australian and South-east Asian and other Englishes, while 'no worries' is typical of Australian English – Mark Newbrook, personal communication.)

(iv) Implicit assurances in the form of complete or incomplete sentences, e.g. in the context of negotiation about a fax which Quoc wants Boba to send for him, which she wants to avoid doing, Boba says (*THE FAX*, see 4.3.1):

  this time never again.

This is accompanied by a reciprocal commissive from Quoc:

  I never will ask again.

Both these utterances express negative commissives (i.e. assurances concerning S's future actions), but Boba's is also an implicit positive one in relation to the present. A variant of these assurances covering only part of the ground of the directive is, e.g. in a dialogue between Tim and Lee:

  TIM: you can start with the meat
  LEE: okay but now we have to clean

While Lee is formally giving an assurance, i.e. promising to do the meat, she is implicitly assuring Tim that she will not do it now as she is being asked while at the same time offering an implicit directive.

  Similarly, in a complex interaction (*TAKING ON CELIA*), Jennifer, on being asked by Slobodan to take Celia into her team, gives a commitment in the affirmative:

  Slobodan that's no problem in my area.

a refusal for the present:

  but at the moment we don't have many jobs right.

and a conditional promise at the same time:

  but if we have jobs in future coming in Celia can when I get my new cassette next month when my new cassette come in next month Celia is handy on my area you see there's no worry about that.

In both cases, the South-east Asian Chinese-speaking woman is culturally bound to give an assurance while feeling unable to do so. So, she performs an affirmative commissive, restricted by a negative commissive (see also 4.6.3). Similar responses to directives are:

> after lunch yeah.
> right after lunch yeah.

The cultural values underpinning this are discussed under 6.4. Another instance from the same text:

> we can work something out.

is of quite ambiguous commitment.

Single-word and non-lexicalized commissives (twenty-one instances) are exceeded in our corpus by those in category (i) (twenty-eight instances). Since the 'assurances' are realized by very common lexical (and even non-lexical) items, there may not be a tacit consensus as to how binding the assurance is. The same applies to the multi-purpose idiomatic expressions in category (ii) and (iii), the former, among other things, being frequently employed in back-channelling.

3.3.2   *Commissives in complex sequences*

Most complex sequences involving commissives are actually part of complex exchanges where the focus is on another speech act, such as a directive or apology. In *CAN I LEAVE IT*, a clarification precedes the actual commissive due to the interlocutor's clarification question:

CAN I LEAVE IT   -   [Elektro]

1 Tom]	Farouk + + ↑can I leave this with you		it's for the wire that
2 Farouk]		{what's this} +	

---

3 Tom]	Leon xxxx + 1.6 +		< ↑huh +
4 Farouk]		↑don't we got ↓any stock in +	haven't we in

---

5 Tom]	yeah bu' it's passed + 1.8 +		from inspection + 2.7 +
6 Farouk]	stock	yeah but xxxxxx	

7	Tom]	↑can I leave it with you + ↑can I leave
8	Farouk]	well if you + 1.4 + come back +

9	Tom]	it with you on your = on your desk +
10	Farouk]	yeah but/ yeah you can leave it

11	Tom]	↑yeah so when you come
12	Farouk]	yeah but er + + when you = when you gonna when

13	Tom]	↑it's already <u>passed</u>
14	Farouk]	the pass you gonna get it + 1.5 + yeah but I haven't

15	Tom]	yeah I know + 4.0 + yes
16	Farouk]	got it alright when you leave here and you get it

17	Tom]	Farouk + ↑so I leave it with you yeah
18	Farouk]	mm

This clarification occurs because 'can I leave it with you' is an instruction (You do what you normally do with this), an adjunct to an informative, and a question.

I have already referred to *TAKING ON CELIA*, which involves several commissives. In *SELF-REPROACH*, which I would consider to be a complex apology sequence (see 3.4), Krysztina is trying to extract from Jennifer a commitment that she is not going to be penalized for something that she has done wrong. She apologizes profusely and Jennifer attempts to calm her down with the following utterances:

> look Krysztina for me is nothing worrying me.
> these things happen. (twice)
> don't worry. (twice)
> I can understand.
> I understand.
> don't worry just take it just take it as it comes.
> oh no worries yes.
> oh Krysztina don't worry
> oh don't worry.

It is only the final commissive:

> oh don't worry I'll fix up for you.

which is interpreted as the binding promise that was being sought because of the first person singular and the active verb. This is the culmination point of the complex interaction.

Sometimes a commissive is simply a repetition of a directive, e.g. (in response to Ivan's directive: Give it (i.e. the salad) to him.):

> Tim: yeah give it to him.

The above discussion has given a small indication of the complex and variable nature of commissive use. This makes this category potentially very susceptible to inter-cultural communication breakdown.

3.3.3   Cultural and gender variation in commissives

The predominance of male directives and complaints contrasts with the relatively large incidence of commissives performed by women. The striking result is that most of these speakers are ethnic Chinese.[5] Relatively few of the commissives came from Central European men. In fact, in most cases the commissive performed by a South-east Asian was a response to a directive from a Central European man. As the number of commissives is limited, individual personality factors may play a significant role.

Table 3.3.3 *Commissives: cultural and gender variation*

	M	F	Total
European/Latin American	15	15	30
South-East Asian	9	22	31
South Asian	10	0	10
Turkish	2	0	2
Total	36	37	73

Those who performed commissives were from the following cultural groups: Croatian, Greek-Cypriot, Macedonian, Maltese, Salvadorian, Turkish, Cambodian-Chinese, Malaysian-Chinese, Indonesian, Vietnamese, Fijian-Indian, Sinhalese.

---

[5] In a separate sub-corpus, commissives were also well represented in the discourse of Anglos and an (Irish-speaking) Irishman.

3.3.4   *Workplace variation in commissives*

The distribution of commissives in the workplaces seems to relate to the number of South-east Asians represented in our research site(s) or in our corpus.

Table 3.3.4. *Commissives : comparison between workplaces*

Amcar	0	Catering	14
Nipponcar	7	Education Office	17
Weavers	2	Employment Office	3
Elektro	30	Parent Group	0
		Total 73	

3.3.5   *Commissives: summary*

As is the case with directives and complaints (other than whinges), the distribution of commissives indicates the power relationships in the workplaces as well as cultural differences. The commissives in our corpus tend to be performed by women rather than men and by South-east Asians (often in dialogue with European men). One difference has emerged between European and South-east Asian styles of performing commissives – i.e. clarifying the issue about which an assurance is required (European) as against giving some kind of assurance, even about something (slightly) different (South-east Asian).

3.4   **Apologies**

3.4.0   *Definition*

Apologies fall into Searle's (1969) category of expressives in which S makes known feelings to H. Under the term 'apology' are subsumed the three acts defined in the *Concise Oxford Dictionary* (1976: 43–4) as:

> regretful acknowledgement of failure or fault
> assurance of no offence intended
> explanation or vindication.

Apologies are very much concerned with face saving. Therefore it is important to consider, for each apology, how they were initiated, by a complaint or a situation in which S feels that it is in his/her interests to apologize, and how this apology is performed.

3.4.1 *Simple apologies and apologies in a complex sequence*

In none of the twenty-five instances of apologies in our corpus is the apology a simple, clear-cut case of the second pair of an adjacency pair. In most of them, the superordinate is 'apologizing' to the subordinate. As many of the 'complaints' in the corpus are whinges, and one other is a complaint to a third person, adjacency pairs – where the apology is a response to a complaint, are not appropriate.

Sometimes, apologies are performed simply through a formulaic routine, e.g.:

> sorry. (Slobodan to Inge, in *CHALLENGING SLOBODAN*)
> okay Slobodan. (Jennifer to Slobodan, in response to a complaint and directive, i.e. acknowledgement of a fault, *WORK ETHICS*, line 25, see 4.1.1)

In the exchange *SELF-REPROACH*, referred to under commissives (3.3.2), Krysztina, the Polish operator, is 'apologizing' to Jennifer, her superior, in a self-intiated stretch of discourse. Ostensibly she wants to be 'freed from her guilt' for she fears the consequences of an error she committed at work. Actually she is 'fishing' for an assurance that nothing will happen to her, or rather, that Jennifer will support her if necessary. The apology follows the following schema:

(i) admission of guilt:

> I was probably it was my fault alright.

(ii) doubts about her guilt:

> I don't know whose fault but I take my (*prompted by Gabi*: '*you blame yourself for it*') I blame myself for it.

(iii) explanation of 'what went wrong':

> because I find that in the middle of the job was accidentally I find oh I said what's going wrong and after all I check every part I put in but I didn't know how many had done it and on the end I just check that and was nine wrong.

(iv) anxiety about the reactions of another worker:

> she was so angry so upset when she said you are worst person. probably she thinks I'm bad xxxxxx because she wants that job.

(v) appeal for compassion:

> you know I'm very sensitive.
> and I said to my husband you know that's life and everything
> and and he said oh you should leave that job.
> he says you should leave that job you should stay at home.

Statements under (iv) and (v) give a clue that Krysztina's fear is that her job may be in jeopardy, something that is not a reality.

(vi) an assurance that the delay in reporting the matter to Jennifer is not the result of antipathy (or prejudice?):

> the reason was because was mixed up the components alright
> and I want to fix it myself because that was my fault alright
> xxxx I got nothing against you or I I didn't want to {give} you
> or I didn't want to give you because I don't like your company
> so it's the only reason I can't give you the boards alright.

(vii) seeking a reassurance:

> but not many xxxxxx mistake anybody can do.

In Wierzbicka's (1991, 1993) terms, the cultural script is something like:

> I have done something bad
> I feel something bad because of this
> I say: I have done something bad
> I want you to say to me: You do not need to feel something bad
>   about this
> I want you to say to me: Nothing bad will happen to you because
>   of this.

For most of the interaction, Jennifer does not understand the nature of Krysztina's concerns and responds by:

(a) multiple use of 'don't worry';
(b) expressing her sympathy, e.g.:
> I understand these things,
> these things happen;
(c) advising her to forget it;
(d) diverting her:
> is your husband back back from Atlantic; and
(e) advising her to 'take it as it comes'.

The interaction does not terminate until Jennifer's commissive, which was the goal of the apology. I shall later (6.2.1, 6.2.4) relate this to Eastern

European 'patronage' and to the Catholic sacrament of Reconciliation (Confession).

The next two texts demonstrate the close relation between complaint and apology. In *BAD SOLDERING*, after Slobodan had complained to Blanche, the Singapore-Chinese, about untrained workers doing soldering, and to Ricarda, a Filipina, about her shoddy work, it is revealed that Ricarda did not do the faulty work. He 'apologizes' to all concerned in ways which would not cost him face.

(To Blanche:)

> not much sorry about it you have to talk to people otherwise people doesn't know why they're they're doing a good (job).
> (lines 84–7)

Here he is, in fact, transferring the blame for his error back to her.

(To Ricarda:)

> now I am sure then that some kind of mistake is done. (line 101)
> whatever is happened if we blame you for things what you didn't done we apologize on it but anyway it would happen. (lines 107–8)

By the use of the passive and the first person plural and the shift from the indicative (real) to the conditional (hypothetical), he first rejects personal responsibility for it and then conjures it away altogether. His final dismissal of the incident is a summarizing pontification which contains the nearest thing to a personal apology for which he then gives an acquittal:

> I'm sorry we apologize for this mistake and that's okay everybody can make mistakes.

The entire interaction is indicative of great social distance and a strong power hierarchy in the workplace as well as of Slobodan's hierarchial orientation.

In the exchange *CHALLENGING SLOBODAN*, the same Croatian supervisor is interacting with a German woman worker (Inge) of the same rank as Blanche. It is a complex complaint sequence in which the request for an explanation is inherent in a number of statements concerning some parts that should have been finished (see above, 3.1.2). When Inge makes clear that she did not have the parts, he apologizes, first formulaically:

> ah sorry.

and, after further evidence has been provided by Inge, giving an explanation:

> I'm sorry I'm sorry oh.
> sorry I thought xxxxxxx I didn't er look for in the on the paper.

The next two exchanges involve Raymond, the Ceylonese Burgher leading hand at Nipponcar. Both are vindications. In SICK LEAVE, he is explaining to a Vietnamese operator that she cannot be given overtime when she is on sick leave. Two justification schemata are employed:

> don't get angry but that's that's how the company is doing if you're being sick and you're going home early and you come the next day to work you won't be given overtime it happen it's for everybody not for one person because I don't want to take a risk on my job.

It will be clear that the vindication is based on company policy, the generality of the policy, and his personal risk if he does not follow it. A similar example is MEDICAL CERTIFICATE, where Frank vindicates his directive for a certificate to be brought by referring to the danger that Ken would otherwise not be paid for the day. In MULTISKILLING, Raymond is responding to a reminder from Rose, a Filipina operator, for him to reply to Mary's complaint concerning overtime. He answers with a very lengthy, highly rhetorical and repetitive explanation of multi-skilling. This vindicates him of any responsibility to give Mary overtime. Rose simply replies: 'fair'.

Another example is in an exchange between Quoc and Boba (GENDER ERROR). In a letter concerning superannuation, Quoc has been marked as female. Boba teases him:

> you should think about it (laughingly) why did they cally you female (laughingly).

and then 'apologizes':

> I'm sorry Quoc I'm a bit naughty.

which is less of an apology than a marker of a joke.

Several of the apologies have more than one function in terms of the dictionary definition given at the start of 3.4.1. The apologies in SICK LEAVE and MULTISKILLING (explanation/vindication) and Self-reproach (regretful acknowledgement of failure/fault) also indicate assurance of no offence, something that is central to BRIEFING ON CHANGES (see 4.1.8). CHALLENGING SLOBODAN also represents acknowledgement of fault, as does to some extent BAD SOLDERING, which can be regarded as a 'non-apology'. Like commissives, apologies are direct reflections of culture-specific face saving devices.

3.4.2   *Cultural variation in apologies*

In the relatively small amount of data on apologies, there is a concentration among Central Europeans of both genders and some representation from other groups. However, this conceals the enormous effort that goes into the appropriate choice of apology schema by Central Europeans to save face, and the variation in type of apology, as has been discussed above.

Table 3.4.2. *Apologies : cultural and gender variation*

	M	F	Total
European/Latin American	11	9	20
South-East Asian	0	2	2
South Asian	3	0	3
Total	14	11	25

Apologies were performed by people from the following cultural groups: Croatian, Italian, Polish, Ukrainian, Burgher, Iranian, Singapore-Chinese. Four of the apologies from 'European males' were statements by Slobodan representing an acknowledgement of fault. The three apologies to South-east Asian women all avoided any loss of face on his part – by playing down the need to apologize or at least by depersonalizing responsibility for the mistake or wrong accusation. The apology to Inge, the German woman, was far less verbose, but without any downtoning of the act of apology. It should be noted that Slobodan and Inge work for a German firm and that Slobodan had been a guest worker in Germany prior to his migration to Australia, so that he might perceive Inge to have a higher status than the South-east Asian women of the same rank in the workplace. But, more importantly, Inge's challenge to Slobodan's complaint indicates a competence to deal with his communication style and consequently a refusal to be intimidated. Among the other Europeans to apologize are Boba with her 'ritual apology' on teasing Quoc, and Krysztina the Polish woman who has been discussed at length. The latter apology is both an acknowledgement of fault and an assurance of no offence. Both apologies from Raymond, one to a Vietnamese man, the other to a Filipina are explanations and vindications. Another South Asian example, from Khalil the Iranian, to Alfonso (*BRIEFING ON CHANGES*), is an assurance of no offence despite changes that he explains have taken place during Alfonso's absence on leave. The only two apologies from female South-east Asians are single-word routines, from a Malaysian-Chinese and a Singapore-Chinese.

From the above, it would appear that, to the South-east Asians, something that you do wrong does not require a great deal of fuss. This is discussed in 6.3.3. To South Asians, it is more a question of maintaining good relations so that there is no ill-feeling – i.e. the apologizer explains why something has to happen or he or she is not responsible for it. The face significance of apologizing gains large-scale dimensions among Central Europeans as is indicated by the length of complex apology sequences and the constituent turns. Not apologizing is not an option. But an apology to a person of 'subordinate' status can be degrading unless worded in such a way as to avoid losing face. Hence, Slobodan's 'non-apologies' and his unusual hesitancy when he has to apologize to Inge. Moreover, apologizing can have another primary goal, such as to extract an assurance of support, as in the case of Krysztina (see also 6.2.1). To at least some Central Europeans, apologies like requests may require a (verbal) response, in this case to indicate acceptance.

3.4.3   *Workplace variation in apologies*

Almost all the apologies come from Elektro. Since the apologies in our corpus are nearly all from Central Europeans, the main source is due to the clustering of Central Europeans at this German firm.

Table 3.4.3 *Apologies: comparison between workplaces*

Amcar	0	Catering	0
Nipponcar	2	Education Office	1
Weavers	1	Employment Office	0
Elektro	21	Parent Group	0
		Total 25	

3.4.4   *Apologies: summary*

Most of the apologies in the corpus are performed by the superordinate to the subordinate. They are intended mainly to vindicate the speaker and/or to offer an explanation (cf. Zimmermann 1984 on '*subsidiäre Handlungen*' ('subsidiary actions'), where the interlocutor's possible actions or communicative reactions are anticipated). The hearer has no option but to accept the apology which, in some cases, is no real concession to the aggrieved.

The apologies in the corpus are largely from Europeans, both male and female. Some of them are quite lengthy because the apologizer employs several schemata to apologize and requires or presupposes some kind of reassurance. South-east Asians, especially women, who rarely apologize themselves will sometimes try to terminate an apology. In *BAD SOLDERING*, the miscommunication between Slobodan and the South-east Asian women may be attributable to an expectation of an apology that does not eventuate. Europeans will apologize in such a way as to avoid losing face. This puts both Europeans and South-east Asians at variance with Anglo-Australians, who occupy the middle ground in that they tend to apologize as a formality according to conventions of politeness but do not make a 'big deal' out of it.

3.5   Small-talk

3.5.0   *Definition*

Small talk, though thematically considered unimportant, is an essential aspect of conversation in that it provides a means of 'easing things along' (Schneider 1988). Some of our informants use small talk to initiate a conversation on a work topic. There is also institutionally oriented small-talk about people's activities in the workplace, the people they work with, their networks, likes, and dislikes. So some of the exchanges in our corpus are entirely composed of small-talk. This type of communication plays an important function in the social cohesion and solidarity that characterize the multilingual workplaces in which this study has been conducted. However, small-talk requires common expectations among participants about its appropriateness and a common willingness to take part. The tolerance for small-talk generally and in particular work contexts is subject to some cultural variation.

3.5.1   *Small-talk in the corpus*

In most of the twenty-nine instances of small-talk, people who are habitually working together develop phatic communication unrelated to the actual communication required by their jobs. Sometimes it concerns their weekend plans and activities, sometimes their families or their appearance, or the weather. Sometimes it is close to whingeing.

In the first of the following excerpts, the small-talk exchange is more symmetrical than in the second. *ROY'S WEEKEND PLANS* is a conversation between Tim and Roy, a Sri Lankan burgher kitchen-hand at Catering. There is a consensus that they should talk about Roy's plans for the weekend.

ROY'S WEEKEND PLANS - [Catering]

1	Tim	] so Ray have a nice weekend +2.3+ and I hope to see you with a cheer-
2	Tim	] ful face on Monday +10.0+ oh my god +1.8+ you know why we get
3	Tim	] late today we got late because of the stop all the steams an' everything
4	Roy	] eh

5	Tim	] no they off er off the power today +4.5+
6	Roy	] oh the steamer broken no

7	Tim	] so when you picking the ↑chair +1.4+ when you gonna
8	Roy	] worries +4.5+ xxxxx xxxxx

9	Tim	] pick the chair do ↑you know what time is the function then
10	Roy	] yes + seven

11	Tim	] ↑oh +10.0+ ↑what are you getting ↑what are you getting for
12	Roy	] o'clock ↑eh

13	Tim	] the party ↑what are you gonna have for the party
14	Roy	] ↑huh ah I'm having my

15	Tim	] but ↑what she's making
16	Roy	] girlfriend's mummy's cooking all the food rice

17	Tim	] ↑what curry
18	Roy	] curry er chicken beef er what er/ um chicken tandoori style

19	Tim	] oh ↑tandoori chicken tandoori yeah
20	Roy	] tandoori chicken

On the other hand, in the conversation between two operators, Faith, a Filipina, and Minh, a Vietnamese man at Elektro (*PERSONAL QUESTIONS*), Faith is bearing responsibility for generating the interaction (see 4.1.4).

PERSONAL QUESTIONS - [Elektro]

1	Faith	]	how are ↑you ↑I'm good + how's the baby
2	Minh	]	oh fine thanks how are you

3	Faith	]	↑yeah she'll be a one year old soon you
4	Minh	]	mm good + baby is bigger now

5	Faith	]	said you're gonna bring me picture ↑where is it. ↑you promise me
6	Minh	]	mm alright (*laughs*) ah

7	Faith	]	↑again ↑where
8	Minh	]	→I did not find one very busy I move yeah I've moved there

9	Faith	]	yeah this is the one that close where Hung live mmm how is it
10	Minh	]	now xxxxx xxxxx

11	Faith	]	how many + how many bedrooms mm ↑that's good. how
12	Minh	]	three bedrooms and

13	Faith	]	much ↓that's alright mm + + ↑well
14	Minh	]	then ah next week I one hundred eighty yeah

15	Faith	]	good on you ↑to work why
16	Minh	]	and next week I return back to Richmond yeah

17	Faith	]	↑ah they need you in Richmond is it well what about your little
18	Minh	]	no job yeah

19	Faith	]	↑boy
20	Minh	]	yeah

Where power relations permit it, a hearer will terminate the speaker's small talk if it is unacceptable, unnecessary or incompetently handled, e.g. in *WEATHER*, where Bob is not interested in listening to Dulip's mumbles about the weather:

THE WEATHER   -   Weavers

```
1   Bill      ]   morning everbody                                              yeah nice
2   chorus ]                            morning
3   Dulip    ]                              good morning  ↑is it a good morning +
```

```
4   Bill      ]   ↑yeah  well that's good + 2.0 +                                    yeah
5   Dulip    ]                              if it's a good ↓day. when it's ↓cold.
```

```
6   Bill      ]                         yeah
7   Dulip    ]   normally it's a good day      yeah it's warm  you know  sun +
8   Bob      ]                                                              ↑what's
```

```
9   Bill      ]                  I'm wired for sound   they= they checking my heart beat
10  Dulip    ]        sunny day
11  Bob      ]   that
```

Another form of small talk which is quite prevalent in factories is ritual joking (including ritual inter-ethnic insults). An example is *REASONABLE REQUEST*.

REASONABLE REQUEST - [Elektro]

```
1   Peter    ]   ah + say if you've got a problem if it's reasonable request + ←can be
```

```
2   Peter    ]   ↓done. but if it's just one of those requests with no purpose + +
3   Jennifer ]                                                              I beg
```

```
4   Peter    ]                          I say if you've got a reasonable request      it
5   Jennifer ]   your pardon +1.6 +                                        ah ha
```

```
6   Peter    ]   will be done    if it's just one of those easy ones
7   Jennifer ]                    oh                                  we always very
8   Celia    ]   reasonable request              er we always reasonable
```

9   Jennifer]   reasonable ←we asian always reasonable xxxx (*laughter*)
10 Celia   ]   (*laughter*)

Ritual inter-ethnic insult is exemplified in the following interchange between Seyit the Turkish relief operator and Michael, the Lebanese operator at Amcar:

RITUAL INSULT - [Amcar]

1   Seyit   ]   alright Michael + 8.0 + what's happen your mama
2   Michael]   okay stupid bloody

---

3   Seyit   ]   ↑how
4   Michael]   stupid →take the gun and put the leave in the h= hand   ↑how I don't

---

5   Seyit   ]   no brain   (*same foreign*
6   Michael]   know how you ask ↑how   ↑no brain (*foreign word*) brain

---

7   Seyit   ]   *word*) (*slight laugh*)
8   Michael]   you know + 1.0 + →we put the xxxxx in here leave

---

9   Seyit   ]   eh Michael Greek what can you ↑do
10 Michael]   it and press + 4.0 +   no never Nick

---

11 Seyit   ]   I said Greek + no Nick (*laughs*)
12 Michael]   because never see   all the Greek silly + +

---

13 Seyit   ]   silly sausage

As can be seen from the above discussion of a selection of examples, small-talk is found in the discourse of people from most of the cultures represented in our corpus. It is particularly prevalent in communication between people of the same gender or those from a similar cultural background. However, non- or miscommunication will arise where small-talk occurs in a context in which some other kind of discourse is expected by the other party because it is conventionalized in the workplace or that person's culture. For examples and discussion, see 4.6, 6.1.

3.6   Foreigner talk

There are hardly any instances of syntactically or phonologically marked foreigner talk (cf. 1.3.5). Generally little or no modification is made to the speaker's normal grammar according to the hearer, apart from the pragmatic variation mentioned above. One exception is Aija, the Finnish operator at Nipponcar, when she speaks to a Vietnamese and a Timorese work colleague (in the exchange *FOREIGNER TALK*), e.g.:

> it's bad weather yuk no good yeah long one week extra yeah but yeah and then next year no roster days and this year plenty next year nothing.

3.7   Closing remarks

This chapter has described the actual corpus, the diversity of speech acts and how they are realized, in inter-cultural work situations, focussing on apologies, commissives, complaints and whinges, and directives. It has been demonstrated that speech acts tend not to be autonomous, but to cluster interdependently as part of complex patterns. It been found that culture interacts with gender and, to a lesser extent, other power-related variables in the cultural variation of speech acts in inter-cultural communication. Differing cultural expectations of people in particular status contexts cause people to react differently to the power structures and work interdependence of the various workplaces. This is evident, for instance, from the large number of directives from male Europeans and the high incidence of commissives from South-East Asian women in response to directives and apologies from Europeans. In the following chapter, some of these will be taken up again in the interface between speech acts and turn-taking.

4 Variation in communication patterns and inter-cultural communication breakdown in oral discourse

4.0 Opening remarks

This chapter discusses cultural variation in communicative behaviour in a broader context than does Chapter 3. The focus is now on turn-taking, relating to the interactions as a whole. The notion of communication breakdown will be considered with examples of different inter-cultural dyads, all of whom are responding, in their own way, to the power structures of a multicultural Australian workplace. Cultural differences in coping with communication breakdown will also be explored. The notion of broad areal communication styles will be canvassed, with some ethnolinguistic groups at the centre and others on the periphery.

It will be apparent from Chapter 3 that emerging patterns of cultural variation are represented not only in individual ethnolinguistic groups, but across groups from the same parts of the world. In this chapter I will endeavour here to describe the overall tendencies that cluster together. The tendencies in communicative behaviour will be considered in relation to the notion of a 'centre' and a 'periphery'. There may be other styles represented in our corpus which cannot be examined because of their scant representation in the data. On the basis of a rather limited and very diverse sample, it will not be possible to say much about individual cultures. (This is something that remains a priority for subsequent research.) Any cultural tendencies need to be seen as applying to this corpus and situation. If our data were concentrated on people from a more limited area, we would be in a better position to contrast styles and groups within the region, but not those in different regions. However, we will, in Chapter 6, be able to refer to values of particular cultures to explain the specific motives for broader areal communicative behaviour.

4.1 Turn taking

In Chapter 3, I have alluded to a close relation between discourse rhythm (turn taking) and the illocutionary force of the speaker's utterance. This applies particularly when we consider variation in cultural styles and its role in the success and failure of communication. The terminology adopted widely in the literature is expanded here (as it was in Clyne, Ball and Neil 1991) in order to cater explicitly for all the possibilities in the data.

Turn giving –	A yields the turn to B.
Turn receiving –	A yields the turn to B, B accepts the turn from A (B wants the turn, A does not).
Turn maintaining –	A keeps the turn, whether B wants it or not.
Turn appropriating –	A wants to maintain the turn but B takes it.
Turn terminating –	A's turn comes to a close. This may end the whole exchange or give the others the option (or the responsibility) to take it up.
Turn direction –	A allocates turn to B by asking a question.
Turn deflection –	A appropriates B's turn in order to assign it to C (usually to prevent B from maintaining it).

Any instance of turn receiving or appropriating will be termed a turn change.

4.1.1 *Turn maintenance*

From the above framework, it will be obvious that turn maintenance will occur either where there is no attempt at turn appropriation or where such an attempt has failed. Let us examine a number of examples of these from our corpus.

CHECK IT has been discussed under 3.2.1 (Directives) and 3.3.1 (Commissives). The exchange begins with an interrogation, to which Jennifer gives an explanation, maintaining her turn (with two instances of back-channelling from Slobodan) – until Slobodan gives his implicit complaint:

> I was informed from storemans that two items they didn't deliver this morning.

Slobodan maintains his turn even after he receives three assurances, one after the other, from Jennifer that she will check. Perhaps he feels he must be the one who gives an explicit directive as the last word. Perhaps he just needs confirmation that it will be done in response to an explicit directive.

Another instance of Slobodan's turn maintenance is WORK ETHICS, referred to under 3.1.2 (Complaints).

WORK ETHICS - [Elektro]

1   Slobo.   ]   <u>Jennifer</u> Jennifer please +3.5+ I would like to clear something with you

---

2   Slobo.   ]   +6.0+ who else is on waiting time   you on waiting no <u>Rosie</u> please
3   chorus   ]   Rosie

---

4   Slobo.   ]   come here   ah Rosie who else is on waiting time <u>Jennifer</u>
5   chorus   ]   xxxxxx xxxxxx

---

6   Slobo.   ]   +4.5+ Jennifer you are also on waiting time +   please be
7   Jennifer]   yes I am

---

8   Slobo.   ]   kind and come here +3.0+ who else is waiting time + from that area

9   Slobo.   ]   +5.0+ those three people is anybody on waiting on that area there

10 Slobo.   ]   +4.0+ what about those people who assemble these there
11 Jennifer]   well that's

---

12 Slobo.   ]   yeah what about Van +
13 Jennifer]   what they are doing now   ↑Van xxxxx xxxxx

---

14 Slobo.   ]   Jennifer listen you now and all you people ↓here
15 Jennifer]   queue one six one four

---

16 Slobo.   ]   + + you know how much we need the ↓soldering + + we desperately

17 Slobo.   ]   need soldering people to do Petersens or to do any er job on soldering in

18 Slobo.   ]   the area + look from now on I don't want to see anybody who is
19 Jennifer]   yeah yeah

---

20   Slobo.   ] competent with solder + to do the cleaning + + alright and ↑only one

21   Slobo.   ] things I don't understand + <u>why</u> + every ten or twenty minutes people

22   Slobo.   ] who are nominated to clean those boards + alright are off from this job

23   Slobo.   ] + + < ↑I don't understand the one things how peoples are not <u>ashamed</u>

24   Slobo.   ] to sit here doing nothing + alright +2.2+ doing nothing and er er

25   Slobo.   ] in = instead er to = to give us something to + to produce something +

26   Slobo.   ] and its really + + look it = its embarrassing +2.7+ keep it under control

27   Slobo.   ] + look nominate the people + who are waiting time to clean these

28   Slobo.   ] boards there + ←the job has to be done. + I know it's er not ah it's not

29   Slobo.   ] +2.0+ easy job but I don't know is it right word to say easy or hard

30   Slobo.   ] job + we don't select in job here in our area ah that's hard that's easy

31   Slobo.   ] you know the all job are practically the same though sometimes people

32   Slobo.   ] prefer one job than the other but +1.5+   we may not do it
33   Jennifer]   okay Slobodan
_____

34   Slobo.   ] like that ↑alright   look we need output from that area and I see
35   Jennifer]   yeah   xxxxxx xxxxx xxxxxx xxxxx
_____

36   Slobo.   ] people who are ←soldering then cleaning boards + →we can't do that
_____

37   Slobo.   ]   a = and people are here sitting doing nothing +1.5+ what's the
38   Jennifer] okay + +
_____

39   Slobo.   ] reason + + if they go there and they sit there ten minutes and after that

40   Slobo.   ] they just ↑disappear +2.7+ I would like to see what's the reason + is

41   Slobo.   ] there any ↑reason ↓ for that ↑<u>tell me</u> +2.3+   yeah
42   Jennifer]   the rea =   ↑you want a
_____

43   Slobo.   ]   yeah I would like to have a reason alright then I = I'll take people
44   Jennifer] reason   oh
_____

45 Slobo.] and I talk to them alright   here is one two three four
46 Jennifer]   okay +2.2+ yeah

_____

47 Slobo.] people who are availiable   alright I would like to see what's Ling doing
48 Jennifer]   okay

_____

49 Slobo.] + where she is   you
50 Jennifer]   ↑Ling. I'm putting her on connector at the moment

_____

51 Slobo.] did   oh
52 Jennifer]   yeah   xxxxx xxxxx the pee cee bee's ready +2.0+ from Petersens

_____

53 Slobo.] oh   Jennifer organize this job there
54 Jennifer]   so I'm putting her on connectors

_____

55 Slobo.] alright   if it's ↑not enough one working place + look do it on the
56 Jennifer]   okay

_____

57 Slobo.] ↓other   ←I am agree and I understand. if one person is there for a
58 Jennifer]   okay

_____

59 Slobo.] week or two + days you know +2.0+ probably get tired of something

60 Slobo.] like that look but we have a three people or or four people that share a

61 Slobo.] job +1.5+ alright +2.1+   if you find a ↑difficulty + look +
62 Jennifer]   alright   I will

_____

63 Slobo.] just see me and ↓inform me   it's not fair it's just <u>unfair</u> + + we have the

64 Slobo.] work + we have the work that's supposed to be done and people say

65 Slobo.] I'm on waiting time + + you know but +1.5+
66 Jennifer]   after lunch + I

_____

67 Slobo.]   fine   yeah   xxx   sorry girls
68 Jennifer] organize them xxxxxxxxx right after lunch ↑yeah Marie xxxx xxxxxx

_____

69 Slobo.] but that's how it works
70 Jennifer] xxxxx xxxxxx xxxxx xxxxx after lunch ↑yeah

Here Slobodan gives the South-east Asian women a pep talk about work ethics and urges them to keep soldering, This is the exchange where he appears to be 'asking for a reason'. Slobodan does not permit any response other than back-channelling (e.g. yeah, okay, you want a reason).

In *SELF-REPROACH*, referred to under 3.3.2 (Commissives) and 3.4.1 (Apologies), Jennifer manages to break in only a few times for back-channelling and clarification (e.g. briefly: yes, yeah, the transistors, who which girl; longer interruption: so you just brought it in mistake). However, Krysztina does maintain her turn except for the advice and diversions from Jennifer, e.g.:

> don't worry.
> is your husband back from Atlantic.

As has been mentioned under 3.5 in *JENNIFER ANSWERS BACK*, Jennifer is making a determined effort to interrupt Slobodan, mid-utterance if necessary, in order to take the floor and present the case. However, he does not yield turns, but still controls 70 % of the conversation. In *BAD SOLDERING* (see also 3.1.1), Slobodan maintains his turn throughout. Others get turns only when he wants their explanations or information. The first part of the exchange with Ricarda (lines 40–52) is one long turn, a monologue. Ricarda herself maintains her turn (lines 89–95) despite two attempts on Slobodan's part to appropriate the turn (Slobodan's only failure in this regard in our corpus). He also maintains a turn (lines 112–25) without any interruption when he directs the Asian women under his charge to refrain from doing jobs for which they are not trained.

Raymond is the main participant in both *MULTISKILLING* and *SICK LEAVE*. In the latter, where Raymond is explaining company policy about not giving overtime to people on sick leave (3.2.1), there is only back-channelling (e.g. oh, mm, no, okay) from the interlocutor, a Vietnemese woman (who requires the information). In *MULTISKILLING*, the interlocutor (Rose, the Filipina), whose complaint conveyed on someone else's behalf had triggered off Raymond's monologue on the need for people with multiskills, makes no attempt to break in. (There is only one contribution by Rose: 'fair'.)

4.1.2   *Turn appropriation*

Turn appropriation is the classic case of competition for control of the 'floor'. An example of this is the following excerpt, *FEELING BETTER*, where Vin and John (Vin's Pakistani subordinate who is on light duties), are conducting small-talk about John's health and work:

FEELING BETTER - [Weavers]

1 Vin   ] yeah when you feel better xxxxx xxxxx xxxx xxxxx and ←plus
2 John   ]   →<now when I'm better I tell you   yeah

3 Vin   ] ←plus when is a = all the time available xxxxx   is always the xxxx xxxx
4 John   ]   ↑yeah   yeah yeah no you

5 John   ] haven't →no I told Dulip yesterday

Both parties appropriate one another's turns. The competition may be seen as a type of co-operation to keep the conversation going.

Some examples of unsuccessful turn appropriation ('butting in' in the sense of Nordenstam 1992: 88) may be found in Jennifer's encounters with Slobodan in WORK ETHICS (e.g. line 35), and CHECK IT, under 3.2.1. The only instance of Slobodan being prevented from appropriating a turn is in BAD SOLDERING, where he tries three times to enter a conversation between Blanche and Ricarda in which both are trying to defend themselves against allegations (see 4.1.1). The first two times he is unsuccessful and succeeds in regaining the floor only at the third attempt (lines 89, 92, 94). Under 4.1.6 we will discuss the strategies. Slobodan's failure here may be related to more acute face threatening (see 6.2.6).

In a meeting (TRAINING) at Employment Office, superordinate Irishman Mark and Vietnamese-Chinese woman colleague Tran are unable to take the floor from the Spanish public servant Manuela. They are able to interrupt, and sometimes their ideas are taken up, but she always regains her turns:

TRAINING - [Employment Office]

1 Manuela] I say as long as the cell works tonight + and help each other
2 chorus]   yeah mm

3 Manuela] it works it really works because in the moment George did confront er the

```
4   Manuela]  person + it was as smooth as a glove + isn't it    so is not em + 1.96 +
5   George  ]                                                              yip
```

```
6   Manuela]  I think er I think that that's the main thing to for this question of character
```

```
7   Manuela]  or the                     < angry        clients   and that
8   Patrick ]          as long as the training is = is is realistic
9   Tuk     ]                                                        training is also very
```

```
10  Manuela]                                         you mean training for < us
11  Patrick ]              don't you reckon                                  for us yeh
12  Tuk     ]  important training
```

```
13  Manuela]                              mm
14  Patrick ]      is realistic so that we can get our message of what we're trying to do
15  Charlie ]  mm
```

```
16  Manuela]          I find that I have been in two two places again er twice they have
17  Patrick ]  across  xxxxx xxxxxx xxxxx xxxxxx xxxxxxx xxxxxx
```

```
18  Manuela]  offered me training you know when they in the xxxxxx and in the other
19  Manuela]  thing we went to xxxx and I don't see I got all that much er out of the
20  Manuela]  training + it just + show the same things we doing + 1.2 + couple of
21  Manuela]  hints there only
```

Where turn appropriation does not work, the speaker has to wait until an opportunity is afforded by the interlocutor. So, in *SELF-REPROACH*, Krysztina (line 22) tries twice to break in to Jennifer's consolatory remarks, but only gets a turn following Jennifer's turn termination marker 'that's all':

JENNIFER: just have to discuss and sort it out that's all
KRYSZTINA: it's just it's just   Hung told me…

Sandor, a Hungarian foreman at Elektro, and an Austrian leading hand, Liesl, about ten years his senior, engage in simultaneous speech and reciprocal turn appropriation, e.g. in the exchange *INVENTORY*:

INVENTORY - [Elektro]

1	Sandor]	see we got <seven now. + seven xxxxx seven seven you already
2	Liesl]	seven xxxxx xxxxx xxxxx

3	Sandor]	change + change change from five to s = to to six
4	Liesl]	xxxxx you just have to wait for oh ah I must probably write a new one

5	Sandor]	seven seven seven
6	Liesl]	anyway by the time you get some more in you might be more

7	Sandor]	company
8	Liesl]	xxxxx and Kim's got a <u>new</u> lot and er

It is particularly the response of the first interlocutor to talk on regardless of an interruption that promotes simultaneous speech.

Raymond appropriates turns by a combination of increased speed and rising intonation in his interaction with Frank, e.g.:

> FRANK: you know why because I don't want construction here that's
> RAY.:   yeah
> FRANK: why I want the system running how it should be
> RAY.:   ↑→and I said look I
> RAY.: have done about <u>three bloody</u> →door trims
>   (From *PARALLEL WHINGEING*, lines 15–19)

Dulip and Bob, his Macedonian subordinate, increase the volume to appropriate turns, e.g.:

> DULIP: give it a wash first   yeah just you know
> BOB: yeah   ⟨how many metres is
> DULIP: ⟨one forty metres in er each
> BOB: that part
> BILL: oh we don't   ea = each string
>   (From *DYEING AND LOADING*, lines 22–5)

4.1.3   Turn deflection

An instance of this is *THE WEATHER* where, in a small-talk situation, Bob, tired of Dulip mumbling about the weather, asks Bill 'what's that' (indicating the lapel microphone), thereby directing the floor to him. Bill replies:

I'm wired for sound they they checking my heart beat.

Later in the exchange, Bob again tries to deflect the turn away from Dulip to Bill, but the former reappropriates it (see the above excerpt from *DYEING AND LOADING*, 4.1.2). Turn deflection is frequently employed by chairpersons in meetings to achieve a more 'democratic' communication flow.

4.1.4   *Turn direction*

Turn direction has a number of basic functions. One is to ensure the development and continuation of a conversation. Another is to ensure that a particular person gets the turn (i.e. You give the person the turn). This can be to encourage democratic participation, to reinforce a particular position or to prevent someone else from gaining the floor.

In *ROY'S ACTIVITIES*, Khalil is interrogating Roy, his subordinate, about his personal activities. The exchange becomes a sort of question and answer session. A short excerpt will illustrate this.

ROY'S ACTIVITIES - [Catering]

| 1 | Khalil |] | how's it going Roy ↑good   you started at ↑school or ↓not yet |
| 2 | Roy |] | good good |

| 3 | Khalil |] | you're starting on ↓Monday   ↑is what time |
| 4 | Roy |] | aah starting on Monday   yeah |

| 5 | Khalil |] | to/ what time is it eight to twelve ←or   ↑eight to <u>one</u> |
| 6 | Roy |] | ah eight to one   that's |

| 7 | Khalil |] | ↓oh right + +   ah + no Saturday no |
| 8 | Roy |] | right +   start at eight in the morning or |

| 9 | Khalil |] | Sunday |
| 10 | Roy |] | okay + →but sunday we have er = we have to be involved in |

| 11 | Khalil |] | | always or/ just happen once a month |
| 12 | Roy |] | church ↓time. church ↓ministry + + |

| 13 | Khalil |] | probably isn't it |
| 14 | Roy |] | no + + better if they say if we can get involved every |

| 15 | Khalil |] | yeah |
| 16 | Roy |] | week |

PERSONAL QUESTIONS is a similar kind of text, this one between Faith and her male work-mate, Minh. The latter's responses are very limited. They are merely intended to promote the conversation flow.

4.1.5   *Turn termination*

Turn termination often overlaps with the act of closing. In many cases in our corpus, the way in which turn termination takes place is indicative of the power structures in the workplace, e.g. On the one hand, Jennifer terminates her exchange with Krysytina about her guilt (*SELF-RE-PROACH*), and thereby deprives Krysztina of further turns, by starting a conversation with another interlocutor:

> (To Krysztina) no it's nothing some people is a bit sensitive you know.
> (To another person) good morning Lisa.

On the other hand, Jennifer vainly attempts to terminate some of her superordinate Slobodan's long complaint turns, e.g.:

> okay Slobodan. (*WORK ETHICS*, line 33)

Thanks (plus name), like alright and okay, are indicators of turn termination employed by Slobodan, Tom, Mustafa, and Lee, for example. Sometimes such indicators relate to what had preceded it in the discourse, e.g.:

> now you understand good. (Aija, *FOREIGNER TALK*)

Turn termination is frequently a means of exercising authority, i.e. giving yourself the final say. For instance, Slobodan puts a stop to discussion by declaring:

> sorry girls but that's how it works. (*WORK ETHICS*, lines 67, 69)

where the deictic anaphora implies that the workplace power structure
has been predestined.

As I indicated in 3.4.1, an apology can act as a closing of the entire
exchange as well as a turn termination by the interlocutor in the power
position.

4.1.6 *Strategies for turn maintenance and appropriation*

The strategies for turn maintenance and for turn appropriation are
similar. In *MULTISKILLING*, Raymond employs repetition, partly to
prolong his turn after he has already said all that he needs to:

MULTISKILLING - [Nipponcar]

1	Rose	]	did you ask Mary about the overtime she's mad again she's always

---

2	Rose	]	bloody hell + you know
3	Ray.	]	I have to get people who can operate right

4	Ray.	]	round the clock ↑right if I put you on the cleaning you can clean if I put
5	Ray.	]	you on the glueing you can glue if I put you on the stapling you can if I
6	Ray.	]	put you on the clipping you can if I put you on corners you can + that is
7	Ray.	]	how + that's + it's not gonna have anything against anybody edith I
8	Ray.	]	know but she said it's not my concern anymore but then in overtime it's
9	Ray.	]	not like those days we now take + we now take + ten + we take ten
10	Ray.	]	people + those ten people have to know everything + this is a training
11	Ray.	]	for 1993 when they have the award restructuring + that is when every
12	Ray.	]	operator can operate on every type of job a full day's production that's
13	Ray.	]	how you'd be you'll be granted the awards ↑right if there's fifty dollars
14	Ray.	]	come in on one job for stapling that you are have to do all day and you
15	Ray.	]	can ↑do it then you are be like there for example you'd be paid fifty
16	Ray.	]	dollars + but if it's if you can not you're not you're not classed as one of
17	Ray.	]	those operators it's going to be right around the country and then in 1993
18	Ray.	]	that's going to be enforced so that's what I'm trying people don't
19	Ray.	]	understand me here I'm trying to do it but I don't want you to be a stapler

20	Ray.	]	and I'm an all-rounder and you get a lesser wage and I get a more wage
21	Ray.	]	how will it suit you + ↑right but she can not do that at the moment
22	Rose	]	fair

23	Ray.	]	if I put jan on corners she does corners if I put her on trimming she does
24	Ray.	]	the trimming if I put her on the cutting she does the cutting if I put her on
25	Ray.	]	stapling she does stapling if I put her on clipping she does clipping she
26	Ray.	]	even does can do the other girls' job but she well she can do clipping she
27	Ray.	]	can do the glue that's about it + excuse me man I'm just talking to you
28	Ray.	]	+ ↑okay

(See, for instance, lines 3 ff. and lines 16 ff.)
Jennifer repeats herself to prevent Krysztina from regaining the floor in her long apology (*SELF-REPROACH*) when the latter starts interrupting:

> sometimes people just overlook yes it's just overlook like they did it's just overlook.

Slobodan (*BAD SOLDERING*) maintains the floor even when he is searching for words by repetition:

> if someone doesn't like a job they said oh I'm going to/ to make it fair I'm going to/ to make a scrap.

In *BAD SOLDERING*, too, Slobodan tries to appropriate turns by calling the interlocutor by name or simply by shouting 'excuse me' (another example of 'positive politeness'). This strategy succeeds twice in this text and fails to succeed twice. Incidentally, Slobodan is a person who frequently uses appellations, e.g. at the start of an exchange.

A third strategy is to increase the volume. Both increasing and decreasing the speed can contribute to turn maintenance and, under certain conditions, to turn appropriation. Increasing the speed prevents someone else from interrupting and gaining the floor[1]:

> if people want a better job or = or job position or

---

[1] To refresh the reader's memory, in the transcription system described in 2.5:
→ indicates an increase in speed
← indicates a decrease in speed
↑ indicates an increase in volume
↓ indicates a decrease in volume.

→something like that they should prove themself on any other work. (Slobodan, *BAD SOLDERING*, lines 27, 29)

After Jennifer has tried to terminate Slobodan's turn in the complex complaint sequence *WORK ETHICS*, 4.1.1 by responding:

alright I will.

he increases the speed:

→if you find a ↑difficulty look just see me and inform me.
if →someone doesn't like a job they said ⟨ oh I'm going to = to make it fair I'm going to = to make a scrap and something like that. (Increased speed coinciding with increased volume for stress; *BAD SOLDERING*, lines 31, 33.)

In this exchange, Slobodan slows down whenever there is no attempt by anyone else to appropriate his turn. However, the effect of turn maintenance (and avoidance of appropriation) can also be attained by slowing down and elongating words (similar to repetition, above). When Jennifer tries to appropriate Krysztina's long turn in *SELF-REPROACH*, she frequently employs elongation in her interjections:

←for ↑me [mi:::]. is nothing worrying me. (line 20)

Elongations are also employed to maintain turns:

I can under↑stand [ʌndəstɛ:::nd]. (line 52)

when the interlocutor is starting to regain her turn.
   Several strategies are often employed in combination:

←why [wa:i:] ↑Krysztina just forget it. (lines 6,9)
←for ↑me [mi::] if there's ↑problems [prɔ:::bləmz] just have to discuss it. (line 23)
oh don't worry ⟨ I'll fix up for you. (line 78)

In *BAD SOLDERING*, Slobodan both slows down and repeats himself in order to maintain his turn:

SLOBO.: even   even u/ no no even u = university
BLANCHE: maybe she doesn't like the job

Raymond takes over a turn from Frank (*PARALLEL WHINGEING*) by increasing speed and rising intonation (see 4.1.2).
   Competition for the floor between one person who wants to appropriate a turn and another who insists on maintaining the turn can lead to simultaneous speech ('co-speech') in the sense of Nordenstam 1992:82), which may continue for a shorter or longer time. For example, in *PRIZE*

GIVING, Irma, the Croatian chairperson of the Parent Group and Maria, the Italian member, keep on interrupting each other and simultaneous speech ensues:

PRIZE GIVING - [Parent group]

1	Irma	]	you know what we're planning <u>next</u> Wednesday is a award time eleven
2	Irma	]	thirty period four and we will give award to multicultural students who
3	Irma	]	↑participated + we'll take teachers and teachers' aide who did er for
4	Irma	]	multicultural a lot of activities this year was really + and then we will
5	Irma	]	follow up with er lunch not lunch yes something like lunch we'll have um
6	Irma	]	I have to make sure where by maybe in ↑C-forty or ↑upstairs in xxxxxx
7	Irma	]	centre + because whole assembly for whole school will be period ↓four

---

| 8 | Irma |] | assembly for students   for ↓students |
| 9 | Maria |] | all the students lunch then   lunch   no no lunch |

| 10 | Irma |] | who performed nearly hundred students multicultural who everybody |

| 11 | Irma |] | performed then we have lunch er erica next week we have er lunch for |
| 12 | Maria |] | oh I see |

| 13 | Irma |] | students who performed and teachers aide and teachers   we have |
| 14 | Maria |] | oh right |

| 15 | Irma |] | period ↓four assembly and we will give award and then go up when it's |

| 16 | Irma |] | lunchtime and eat lunch not I mean we won't I think maybe order pizza |

| 17 | Irma |] | everybody like pizza ↑hmmm |
| 18 | Maria |] | I don't know we did once ah like this last |

| 19 | Irma |] | no we ordered chinese food   you order I order chinese food |
| 20 | Maria |] | year we did   yeah   we did chinese   what about the sandwich we had |

| 21 | Irma |] | oh no |
| 22 | Maria |] | one day one day one day we had a last year sandwich and a sausage |

23	Irma]	ah that was five years ago that Mary O'Donnell's husband
24	Maria]	rolls this was for what [laughs] not

25 Irma]   had restaurant and they brought food ah that was five years ago my love

26	Irma]	not for us canteen makes last time
27	Maria]	the canteen make the sandwiches ah it's not

28	Irma]	canteen makes last time the canteen make sandwiches when
29	Maria]	for the multicultural but the students

30	Irma]	aboriginal group came that's what we're trying to make next ah next
31	Irma]	monday if aboriginal group can come then I could organise something ...

They are recounting the catering arrangements on a previous occasion. In order to appropriate the turn and change the topic from Chinese food to sandwiches, Maria has to interrupt and talk over Irma until she is silent. Later in the same interaction (lines 26–31), Maria interrupts Irma's recollection that the canteen made sandwiches last time to stress that the food was for the students. In the ensuing simultaneous speech, Irma's utterance could not be fully heard and she interrupts, regaining the floor through the production of simultaneous speech.

Another instance of simultaneous speech occurs at Weavers in an exchange between Vin and his Pakistani subordinate John. Vin is trying to maintain his turn and John increases his tempo to appropriate it (*FEELING BETTER*).

4.1.7   Turn taking : Summary

Turn change and the procedures for it are largely determined by power relations. Central Europeans and South Asians are the speakers in our sample who are most successful in turn maintenance. Often members of these groups attempt to appropriate one another's turns, resulting in simultaneous speech. Turn direction and deflection are the results of more goal-oriented behaviour – turn direction to keep a conversation going or to involve particular people at a meeting, and turn deflection to promote a more 'democratic' control of the floor. Among the methods of turn maintenance and appropriation are: increase in volume, increase in speed, decrease in speed with or without elongation, rising intonation, repetition, addressing a person by name, and the use of 'excuse me'.

4.1.8   *The notion of turn length*

Length of turn was measured objectively. In SELF-REPROACH, Krysztina's longest turn is 1 minute 20 sec. before a single interruption and then another 17 seconds after an interruption from Jennifer. Slobodan's turn in WORK ETHICS, where he is lecturing Ricarda about the quality of soldering joints, is 1 minute 25 seconds, extending to 1 minute 54 seconds following a single interruption. Slobodan's monologue in BAD SOL-DERING, where he is complaining about people not working hard enough, comes to 2 minutes 35 seconds, with only four attempts at turn appropriation on Jennifer's part. Krysztina's turns are generally 8 to 10 seconds, but can be as long as 22 seconds and 25 seconds. In meetings at Employment Office, the turns of Manuela, a Spanish employment officer, are the longest. In TRAINING, for example, she manages to maintain her turn of 1 minute 33 seconds amid attempts at appropriation by her Maltese male superior, from whom she had appropriated back her turn, and an (Irish-speaking) Irish male superior. Her longest uninterrupted turn in that exchange is 51 seconds.

The longest single uninterrupted turns are those of Khalil, the 35-year-old Iranian catering manager at Catering, explaining to Alfonso, a Uruguayan kitchen hand about five years his junior, what procedural changes had occurred since the latter had gone on holidays and why (BRIEFING ON CHANGES). A 40-second turn on the reasons for procedures is maintained because of Khalil's breathless delivery. A brief period of interaction with responses and back-channelling is then followed by a section where Khalil holds the floor for a minute. The few turn appropriation attempts made by his interlocutor are unsuccessful. All in all, Khalil keeps these turns for a total of 4 minutes 46 seconds.

BRIEFING ON CHANGES - [Catering]

1 Khalil] outside businesses alright so when you get into outside businesses it

2 Khalil] means + uh + you get + uh + outside the xxx that's the reason we do

3 Khalil] the little bit changes an' we try a little bit here than we have because it

4 Khalil] wasn't good enough with the + ah + this one not good enough till now

5 Khalil] at that point you you collaborate absolutely with each other as you xxxx

6	Khalil	]	be having now as you notice you organise here to be helped our chef +
7	Khalil	]	on top I taught this one everybody before we have the chef here on the
8	Khalil	]	top and we got our cooks + they don't have anybody from the kitch =
9	Khalil	]	kitch/ about the kitchen kitchen hand is the right alright an' there's xxxxx
10	Alfonso]		xxxxxx

| 11 | Khalil |] | xxxx I'm telling you xxxx xxxx a thoroughly good worker and he did a |
| 12 | Alfonso] | | xxxxx xxxxx was a good worker you know |

| 13 | Khalil |] | good job   that's only the people when they short |
| 14 | Alfonso] | | that it's only the people |

| 15 | Khalil |] | ah productivity   not much you understand what's happening I mean if |
| 16 | Alfonso] | | yeah I I know |

| 17 | Khalil |] | I am able to give eight not just ah three or four hours support xxx on top |
| 18 | Alfonso] | | yeah |

| 19 | Khalil |] | of the job xxxx   in that is charge Tim   Tim is off one |
| 20 | Alfonso] | | each hour is payment   yeah |

| 21 | Khalil |] | month's off he go and er xxx he go he will let you cut enough to cut for |

| 22 | Khalil |] | tomorrow for the day after as well I mean such vegetables |
| 23 | Alfonso] | | we didn't |

| 24 | Khalil |] | that's no no no no   I tell you no no xxxxx |
| 25 | Alfonso] | | touch the cooking xxxx   because |

| 26 | Khalil |] | beer you know what happened   I know what happened okay I |
| 27 | Alfonso] | | that's right |

| 28 | Khalil |] | want to say something every week we change the week or to a point it's |

| 29 | Khalil |] | up to us   xxxxx maximum xxxxx is possible Tim so he can run the |
| 30 | Alfonso] | | oh yeah |

---

31 Khalil   ]   good thing about the Tim because he's the chef he have to look after for

32 Khalil   ]   the deep sea fish xxx have to make sure the fish cook if something at first

33 Khalil   ]   I can't find I call him actually perhaps that's the reason he has to go he

34 Khalil   ]   will check the other two now what I expect only from you I know you are

35 Khalil   ]   doing sometime possible if you don't have much until such time you work

36 Khalil   ]   as all together what can happen that they can call your assistance I

37 Khalil   ]   prepare for you you prepare for do it that way   try to keep
38 Alfonso]   no worries

---

39 Khalil   ]   working if xxxx doesn't do it I angry I tell you once then very nice I get

40 Khalil   ]   maximum work I can well but + if somebody's not nice and is try for me

41 Khalil   ]   they go straight away I know what I mean   er straight away if
42 Alfonso]   yeah yeah

---

43 Khalil   ]   somebody   that's right if I have good people work together if I have
44 Alfonso]   xxxx xxxx

---

45 Khalil   ]   good people I don't have   make   mistake   if the people they
46 Alfonso]   xxxx than the other people

---

47 Khalil   ]   don't collaborate with me I have to xxxxx if they don't collaborate help us

---

48 Khalil   ]   that's correct okay   if we all do our
49 Alfonso]   we have to help in production   xxxxx

---

50 Khalil   ]   task that's the point   but anybody can do that wash the
51 Alfonso]   you have people

---

52 Khalil   ]   vegetables cut...

(tape switched off briefly)

53 Khalil   ]   ...be changed everybody with three thousand eight hundred eight hundred

54 Khalil   ]   something wages okay I got now what I can do I get that three thousand

55 Khalil   ]   eight hundred and I put everything xxxxx and I put 'em xxxxx is good an'

56 Khalil   ]   I'm sure what quality I'll get with one per cent in the xxxxx I put three

| 57 | Khalil] | thousand eight hundred on top of to what I want   about ten dollars |
| 58 | Alfonso] | maybe |

| 59 | Khalil] | now for all the nine dollar xxxx   I can save thousands of dollars for the |
| 60 | Alfonso] | xxxxxx |

| 61 | Khalil] | time go up   it won't work I just want to ask you to help me |
| 62 | Alfonso] | but now   yeah |

| 63 | Khalil] | alright we help each other   work with Tim as much as you xxxxxx ask |
| 64 | Alfonso] | yeah   mm |

| 65 | Khalil] | hiw what he has to need to be done and ah ask us all about nothing else |

| 66 | Khalil] | okay I didn't see you yesterday and er all the best I am sure |
| 67 | Alfonso] | xxxxx |

Another exchange characterized by one speaker's lengthy turns comes from *PRIZE GIVING*. Despite a number of unsuccessful interruptions from Maria, an Italian committee member, Irma continues her turn for 1 minute 43 seconds.

Long turns were recorded for the speech acts of apology, directive, and (exercitive) complaint. Cultural style is a more important factor in turn length than speech act (see below, 4.4). However, there are a number of concomitant factors that generally coincide with long turns:

1. the speaker is interrupted only by back-channelling
2. a large number of words in the utterance
3. the complexity of argument and interaction sequence (involving several speech acts often including justification)
4. success in turn maintenance and/or in preventing turn appropriation
5. competence in employing one or more of the strategies mentioned under 4.1.6.

Often, long turns are related to negative politeness and face saving strategies on behalf of the hearer as well as oneself (see 6.2.3, cf. Brown and Levinson 1987).

Short turns, on the other hand, are usually related to adjacency pairs, e.g.:

TOM: can I leave this with you   it's for the wire
FAROUK: what's this
                                        (*CAN I LEAVE IT*)

Our corpus indicates that whinge and commissive turns tend to be relatively short. While directive turns tend to be long in complex sequences and short in simple sequences (i.e. those with only one directive).

It is not necessarily the case that long turns are taken by speakers with a high competence in English and short ones by those with a low competence in the language. Seventeen intercultural dyadic exchanges involving a total of 27 speakers were selected from the corpus to test this. Eleven high-competence speakers took predominantly long turns as against 4 low-competence speakers. The turns of 7 high-competence speakers and of 5 low-competence speakers were predominantly short. (Some of the speakers appeared in several dyadic exchanges.) However, the correlation with cultural groups was much stronger. All those in the sub-sample with short turns were South-east Asians, and only three South-east Asians (including one Filipina) mainly took long turns. On the other hand, all the Europeans, Latin Americans, and South Asians in the sub-sample took predominantly long turns.

All those whose turns were lengthened by repetition were highly competent speakers of English, all from European or South-east Asian backgrounds.

Table 4.1.8 *Relation between English competence and length of turns* (Sample of 17 exchanges)

	Long Turns	Short Turns
High Competence	11	7
Low Competence	4	5

4.2   Back-channelling

4.2.0   *Definition*

Back-channelling (see also 1.3) gives the speaker an indication that the hearer(s) is (are) still listening. It is intended to keep up the communication flow by confirming or reacting to a preceding statement (cf. Bublitz 1988: 189–90) and can be regarded as a 'positive interruption', in fact as an encouragement for turn maintenance (see below, 4.1.1).

4.2.1   *Back-channelling in our corpus*

The most frequent instances of back-channelling in our data are (in order): yes/yeah (99 instances), mm (50), and oh (25) (cf. Heritage 1984). Other examples include right, no, okay, and I know (cf. Heritage 1984). Sometimes keywords used by the conversation partner are repeated as back-channelling, e.g. by George, a Greek employment officer, and Elvira, his Anglo-Indian colleague at the Employment Office:

> ELVIRA : you know three or four you know xxxx exercise
> GEORGE :   exercise yeh

Sometimes really is used for back-channelling, e.g. by Tuk, a Vietnamese-Chinese employment officer reacting to something Muntha, his Cambodian female colleague, had said:

> MUNTHA : she will get a hundred and twenty dollars a week
> TUK :   really

Because of the use of some of the items as commissives (see above, 3.3), it is popularly believed (e.g. in factories and other places where inter-cultural communication occurs) that back-channelling is ambiguous and leads to communication breakdown, especially with groups who back-channel a great deal. There is little data in our corpus to support this, virtually all the instances of commissives being in the context of a directive or complaint and those of back-channelling outside this context. It should be noted, however, that there is a tendency for the same people to prefer a particular item or items for both commissives and back-channelling. (A good case in point is Boba at Migrant Education.)

Some examples of back-channelling:

In *ABOUT BRAINSTORMING*, where six men of different ethnolinguistic backgrounds are conducting a quality circle meeting at Weavers, while one or another is giving a presentation, the others are back-channelling:

> MICK : it's one of our problems we had in the work area
> DULIP :   yeah

and later:

> DULIP : because we had listed thirty problems
> MICK :   yeah

In *EVERYTHING WENT WRONG*, Boba is narrating to Quoc what their boss had said:

> BOBA : yesterday afternoon when I spoke to her   she told me
> QUOC :   yeh

No as well as yes (yeah) can act as a back-channelling device, where it harmonizes with the interlocutor's discourse, as in Inge's argument with Slobodan (*CHALLENGING SLOBODAN*):

> SLOBO.: are they in frame ah no ah he didn't put them all
> INGE: no no   no

In *FINGERNAILS*, Quoc is commenting on Boba's long fingernails. When he runs out of words, Boba back-channels to assure him that he is being understood:

> QUOC: somebody just scratch the em
> BOBA: mm

Jennifer and Hung are both back-channelling during Slobodan's negotiations in *TAKING ON CELIA*:

> SLOBO: automatic insertion machines yeh since Petersons stop we
> SLOBO.: don't have much work on that area   and I have one
> JENNIFER: yeh
> HUNG: oh
> SLOBO.: operator too many   one operator is Celia
> JENNIFER: eh   oh

4.2.2   Cultural variation in back-channelling

All categories of subjects engage in back-channelling, Europeans, South-east Asians and South Asians. men and women (in that order). Table 4.2.2 indicates the large incidence of back-channelling in the speech of South-east Asian women:

Table 4.2.2 *Back-channelling: cultural and gender variation*

	M	F	Total
European/Latin American	57	41	98
Turkish/Lebanese	14	–	14
South-east Asian	19	61	80
South Asian	40	4	44
Total	130	106	236

The people who provide instances of back-channelling in our corpus are from the following cultural groups: German, Greek, Italian, Macedonian, Maltese, Polish, Salvadorian, Spanish, Ukrainian, Uruguayan, Lebanese, Syrian, Turkish, Cambodian, Cambodian-Chinese, Filipino, Malaysian-Chinese, Singapore-Chinese, Anglo-Indian, Burgher, Fijian-Indian, Iranian, Sinhalese.

The different back-channelling phenomena are subject to some cultural and gender variation, with mm used mainly by European and Latin American women (28 instances out of a total of 52) and oh/ah principally by South-east Asian women (12 instances out of a total of 25). mm as opposed to yes can probably be attributed to expectations of female behaviour in European cultures being restrained (Negative politeness). Oh/ah expresses a different kind of negative politeness. As the above instances from Jennifer and Hung demonstrate, it represents an acknowledgement of their status in relation to Slobodan. Jennifer is inviting him to proceed with a proposal with which she does not agree, and Hung is indicating that she has not been familarized with the information and wants to hear more. The men, who are less constrained by 'good manners' constraints, provide the bulk of the instances of yes and its variants (yeah, yeh). Yes/yeah, mm, right, and Okay are all very common in 'mainstream' Australian discourse.

Table 4.2.2.1 *Some actual back-channelling phenomena : gender and cultural variation*

	European		S. E. Asian		South Asian		Turk/Leb.		Total	
	M	F	M	F	M	F	M	F	M	F
Yes	25	6	15	23	28	1	11	–	79	30
mm	11	28	–	9	3	1	–	–	14	38
oh/ah	3	2	2	12	5	–	1	–	11	14

Note: *Yes* includes *Yeah*.

4.2.3   *Workplace variation in back-channelling*

This phenomenon is especially prevalent in workplaces where the informants are co-operating in a team situation, as in Weavers, Elektro, Catering, and Education Office. The sequential interdependence and the relative absence of South-east Asian women, who back-channel a good deal, keeps the scores for this phenomenon low at Amcar.

Table 4.2.3 *Back-channelling : comparison between workplaces*

Amcar	15	Catering	60
Nipponcar	22	Education Office	27
Weavers	40	Employment Office	37
Elektro	60	Parent Group	2

4.3   Negotiation

4.3.0   *Definition*

Negotiation involves 'conferring with a view to agreement' (*Concise Oxford Dictionary* 1976: 730). Thus, the dynamics of the group are of great importance in understanding how the negotiation takes place and is or is not successful and how turns are taken. There are two main types of negotiation – symmetrical and asymmetrical. In asymmetrical negotiation, one person dominates, i.e. in Bayrataroglu's (1991) terms, there is an interactional imbalance (see 1.3.2). In symmetrical negotiation, there is more text-sharing between the interlocutors (Watts 1991). Long turns make for asymmetrical negotiation while short turns contribute to symmetrical negotiation.

4.3.1   *Negotiation in the corpus*

In *BAD SOLDERING* and *WORK ETHICS*, Slobodan's pep talks are examples of the asymmetrical type of negotiation, where the others can do little but respond with commissives. Being both 'boss' and hierarchially oriented, he does not allow Blanche or Celia any input into the decision making. Another context of asymmetrical negotiation is where one person is explaining a procedure – i.e. 'discussing' with them why something is to be done, e.g. in *SICK LEAVE*.

In *TAKING ON CELIA*, Slobodan negotiates with Jennifer (and an almost silent but occasionally back-channelling Hung, a female Vietnamese leading hand), employing the following schema:

1. Appellation and announcement:

> Hung I have to talk to you now and ah Jennifer as well let's go and talk together.

2. Appeal for help:

> I need a help from you now in the moment.

3. Statement of general problem and explanation:

> since Petersons stop we don't have much work on that area and I have one operator too many.

4. Statement of specific problem with implicit directive:

> one operator is Celia.

5. More explicit directive (couched in first person plural):

> we have to utilize her somewhere on this area.

6. Procedure starting with least unacceptable aspect, with the kind of antithesis inherent in apparent disclaimers:

> she will work one of those two areas and be back-up in automatic insertion machines if somebody is missing or sick or whatever she will pop there or if we are hm overloaded or things like that but.

6a. General justification:

> ah I'm forced to take ah one operator out from that area.

6b. Specific justification:

> I cannot take Eleanor because she's longer time there and trained and ah et cetera and there's the only Celia.

7. Implicit directive:

> now yes what do you think where we can utilize her.

Up to this point, there is nothing for Jennifer to do but to offer back-channelling, e.g. yeh, mm, right. She is being presented with a *fait accompli* and initially has no opportunity to take a turn. I have referred elsewhere (3.3.1) to her conditional commissive at one of the points where she is successful in turn appropriation in this exchange. In this exchange of 8 minutes 30 seconds, Hung speaks for only 43 seconds.

It is not the case that it is impossible for a woman of south-east Asian background to negotiate with Slobodan. In *JENNIFER ANSWERS BACK*, where Jennifer is on her own with him, he expresses his disapproval and exercises his authority through interrogatives, imperatives, and modals (cf. Kress and Hodge 1979: 122):

> what do you stop changing these things.
> tell me how many connectors you changed hundreds of it.
> you may not you may not destroy these connectors.
> you may not push them in the rubbish.
> you can keep them separate and count them you know that.

Jennifer responds to each accusation and reproach immediately:

> these are all from last week monday all good ones.
> but monday we have already started with the new carrier.
> I did told them.

I did show them.
I knew xxxxx to clean them and they're very good.

An example of fairly symmetrical negotiation is *DYEING AND LOADING* (Comments on the earlier part of this text may be found in 3.2.1). Here Dulip, Vin, Mick, Bill, and Bob, all skilled and frequently working together, are discussing how they should carry out a particular job. Bill (he foreman) starts off with some directives (in the form of advice):

> you put it on see if we can load it up on winch three even if you have to get a leader if you have to get a leader get Vin to give you a bit ah have a roll of fleecy or something from the old exacto stock right xxxxxx you got fleecy exac= exacto we might need a bit just see how it runs and we try to er dye it on that winch.

Up to now, Bob has been back-channelling (e.g. alright, yes yeah). From this point on, each of the participants contributes:

BOB: maybe we have to Al said to re = to replaid you know

BOB: because
BILL: replaid it
MICK: but you can replaid it from here Bill...

DULIP: put it on the winch as it is give it a wash first.

Instances of negotiation occur in the data from quality control circle meetings at Weavers which are, after all, intended for discussion. In *ABOUT BRAINSTORMING*, they are talking about a forthcoming presentation to management. Here there is a balance between symmetrical and asymmetrical communication, with Dulip dominating and Vin needing to state everything himself to be sure of what is happening, the others, Mick, Bill, and Luke (a Greek-background operator), in more or fewer words, indicating their positions to what has been stated or confirming that a particular procedure has been followed. The excerpt reproduced will illustrate this.

ABOUT BRAINSTORMING - [Weavers]

1   Vin   ]   so + after we have had the ↑solution. we will have the er ↑recommend-

---

2	Vin	] ation +
3	Mick	] well we + it's already
4	Gary	] no it's already been done
5	chorus	] no xxxxx xxxxx xxxxx

6	Vin	] xxxxx xxxxx
7	Mick	] been done we're getting the wheels replaced again xxxxx it's

8	Vin	] xxxxx
9	Mick	] all xxxx
10	Dulip	] wha = what we you know the attack probably is that + +

11	Dulip	] when we were collecting + data + + er you know another + problem

12	Dulip	] + did come to light + + and this action was taken and this this solution

13	Mick	] well that it's one of our + 1.8 + problems that we had in the
14	Dulip	] was arrived

15	Mick	] work area we decided to do a mini + + another problem while we
16	Dulip	] yeah

17	Mick	] worked xxxxx this is what it was + 2.1 + xxxx xxxx
18	Dulip	] that's that's all the

19	Dulip	] bit of data collection + that's xxxx and er + that's when we we shall

20	Mick	] yep
21	Dulip	] take the other project up
22	chorus	] yep

(one minute later)

23	Vin	] the problem is the slitting and the ballooning + +
24	Mick	] no xxxx talk about
25	chorus	] xxxx xxxxx

26 Mick] this + 3.2 + problems in the work area how we come about getting +

27 Mick] picking tangles + of what ←oh. proper choice how many problems we've

28 Mick] come up with + ↑right + 1.3 + (*shuffles paper*) we come up with about

---

29 Vin   ]   yeah but after
30 Mick] thirty + different + + problems right xxxx xxxx + 1.8 +

---

31 Vin   ] you have picked one
32 Mick]   →we did brainstorming. + we're talking about brain-

---

33 Vin   ]   mm
34 Mick] storming + problems in the work area +   you did problems in the work

---

35 Vin   ]   right
36 Mick] area   next person xxxxx xxxx
37 Dulip]   Vin at the presentation we go through
38 chorus]   that's right

---

39 Vin   ]   ←all the xxxx
40 Mick]   xxxxx xxxx we go
41 Dulip] all the steps we went through in the + y'know + in the circle

---

42 Vin   ]   no I know + + I
43 Mick] through it + week by week + what we were doing

---

44 Vin   ] thought + + I that   the main problem but we/ for the presentation
45 Mick]   no that's

---

46 Vin   ] chose only one the tangle the ballooning and that xxxxx xxxxx
47 Mick]   no no no   the

---

48 Vin   ]   < everything
49 Mick] presentation you're talking about   everything that   first
50 Dulip]   number f =

---

51 Mick] first presentation right
52 Dulip]   yeah + number four
53 Bill]   how to come about it   how did you

| 54 | Dulip |] | number four + in that list is problems... |
| 55 | Bill |] | you pick that problem + + |

The question of face in directives is crucial in inter-cultural negotiation such as *THE FAX*, where the office colleagues at Education Office, Boba and Quoc are interacting. Quoc, who is well educated and overqualified for the job he is doing, would like Boba to collect a fax for him and send the reply. He is evidently not confident that he can send faxes. Boba does not want to send it, perhaps because doing the two messages for Quoc, her equal, would threaten the face of someone from a hierarchially related culture. On the other hand, a direct refusal would entail contravening her rules of politeness which includes doing favours for a colleague. She therefore indirectly declines by making him feel that it is very simple and in his interests to send the fax himself. (This is what Watts (1992) terms 'linguistic politeness as a mask'.) She also justifies her reluctance to send the fax by the rainy weather. All this is achieved through explicit or implicit directives:

> yeh I mean you know you don't mind going. (Quoc – implicit)
> you know how to send a fax. (Quoc – implicit)
> you know how to send it. (Quoc – implicit)
> did you try to send it before. (Quoc – implicit)
> if you need to send it send it this way. (Boba – implicit)
> please Boba. (Quoc – implicit)
> I can send go to collect it just don't send me back today. (Boba – explicit)
> I'll go there to collect it but   then go   er back again. (Boba – explicit)

In a follow-up interview, Boba indicated that it was impossible for her to say to Quoc 'I can't (won't) do it'.

4.3.2   *Cultural variation in negotiation*

In negotiation, most of the cultural groups represented in our sample avoided giving a negative response to a directive (including a request). How this manifestation of negative politeness works in practice, varies across cultures. In Central European cultures – especially Croatian – as we have shown, an appealing option is to persuade the interlocutor that the request is not really in his or her interests. In South-east Asian cultures, most particularly among our Vietnamese speakers, the response is to say as little as possible and to co-operate by saying what they think they are expected to say and, where appropriate, by focussing on the positive rather than the negative. It is in accordance with the values systems of the South-east Asians (cf. 6.2.7) that they are generally not prepared to engage in 'verbal duelling'.

Although Quoc emerges as a confident and articulate communicator, he is rather exceptional in that he is a highly qualified professional working in a clerical job for which he is overqualified. The fact that he is communicating habitually with one Central European female colleague perhaps contributes to his confidence. The communication style of the other Vietnamese in our sample, both men and women, is quiet or silent, and reticent. So in exchanges between Slobodan, Jennifer, and Hung, the latter, who is of the same status as Jennifer, restricts her responses to back-channelling. In PERSONAL QUESTIONS, Faith demonstrates her 'superiority' over Minh at small-talk.

I have referred elsewhere (e.g. 3.1.2) to the bureaucratic tone employed by South Asians. The difference between the style of a South Asian (Burgher) male and a South-east Asian (Vietnamese-Chinese) female is seen in INTERROGATING THE GREEDY MAN, where Tim and Cam are both interrogating a dining room patron as to his eligibility to eat there. Tim uses a string of directives and adopts a bureaucratic tone, making a number of assumptions about the practices of the man and his wife. Cam first asks the questions which give the information and, when she gives directives, he explains the reasons for the rules and concludes with a polite closing.

On the question of silence, the one Finnish informant does not provide us with any evidence of the 'silent Finn' (1.3.5, see also below). If the Finnish tolerance for silence is, in fact, high, her deviation from this norm may be due to her personality. Another explanation would be that Finns are initially silent and pensive in formal communication with 'outsiders', but do have the competence to be talkative and outgoing for communication with their primary networks. On migrating, Finns can, if they choose, adopt this pattern of communication for all contexts. In 1.3.5, I refer to Lenz's (1990) study of Finno-German business encounters, which suggests that the problem of inter-cultural communication between Finns and some other Europeans is not one of silence, but of cultural variation in turn-taking rules – which Aija has either overcome or not experienced.

4.3.3 *Negotiation or clarification of meaning*

One specific form of negotiation is clarification of meaning. Among the numerous strategies employed for clarifying meaning are: defining, adjusting, repeating, reducing, and expanding, with several strategies sometimes employed in the same exchange. An example is *WE HAVE A COMPANY*. Here four of the kitchen staff at Catering – Tim (Fijian Indian, male), Betty (Burgher, female), Daniel (Cambodian, male), and Cam (Vietnamese, female) – are involved in negotiating what Daniel means by the utterance rendered incomprehensible by the indefinite article:

> we have a company here.

Tim, not understanding, due to the (probably hypercorrect) unusual use of the indefinite article, asks:

> who.

Daniel simply repeats:

> we have a company here.

Tim tries another means of asking for clarification, by deleting the inappropriate indefinite article:

> company.

and receives two explanations, one from Daniel himself:

> someone is not living here come here and eat.

the other from Betty:

> you know if he eats here he doesn't live here but he has (Interrupted by Daniel: 'this one').

She does not complete the utterance because it overlaps with Daniel's and by then, Tim has sought exemplification:

> who this one.

This exemplification he receives from Betty:

> no the one behind.

There is some more negotiation over the identity of the 'culprit':

TIM: this one   yeah in the
BETTY: ah the one over there with the glasses yeah

There is then some disagreement about whether this person is really intruding:

> TIM: he's staying here
> BETTY: I heard that he's not

with further negotiation of meaning:

> TIM: the fat one the one last or this one   which one
> BETTY: this one
> DANIEL: yeah

This negotiation is essentially 'meaning-focussed' in the sense of Long (1991) – meaning cannot be understood. However, it began as 'form-focussed – one in which the form cannot be assessed. An example of form-focussed negotiation is SPOILER, in which two relief operators at Amcar, Seyit, a Turk, and Joe, a Syrian, are negotiating procedures – a part called a 'spoiler' (a device used to maintain ground friction by arresting air flow) has to be added to a new car with a powerful V8 engine. This is difficult at first because Seyit does not know the word 'spoiler' used by Joe. Negotiation of the task proceeds co-operatively so many utterances are expended in the process, and non-verbal means are employed.

SPOILER - [Amcar]

1 Seyit]	↑Joe + red sport car is red one ↑spoiler ↑what's that		
2 Joe]	spoiler yeah should be		

---

3 Seyit]	xxxx I don't know just I/ I see yeah you
4 Joe]	two door yeah + + why xxxxx xxxxx

---

5 Seyit]	got I.D.T.C. uh hu yeah spoiler that's
6 Joe]	yeah and it's a spoiler spoiler you put you

---

7 Seyit]	like er + doesn't matter
8 Joe]	put the spoiler you know the spoiler like I told you

---

9 Seyit]	no tell me later (laughs) yeah no worry
10 chorus]	what's everybody doin' ↑here

| 11 | Seyit |] | yeah   big spoiler |
| 12 | Joe |] | + 7.0 + ↑here   ah it's a big spoiler you see that on the boot on the |

| 13 | Seyit |] | ah you got one rubber   like ah like sports car sports car |
| 14 | Joe |] | back lid   yeah xxxx xxxx xxxx xxxx xxxx xxxx xxxx |

| 15 | Seyit |] | ↑yeah   vee eight |
| 16 | Joe |] | xxxx if it says ↑ee you do put that alright   vee eight   vee |

| 17 | Seyit |] | eight yeah put the vee eight on the spoiler and all that stuff al↑right |
| 18 | Mario |] | you |

| 19 | Seyit |] | must understand mate   yeah must |
| 20 | Mario |] | alright ↑now   we we work by by paper |

21	Seyit	]	understand yeah yeah they put all out + + already
22	Joe	]	xxxxxx
23	Mario	]	it's vee eight

| 24 | Seyit |] | they send it ↑everyone   yeah they say to me le = le = |
| 25 | Joe |] | what even xxxxxx |

| 26 | Seyit |] | leave to xxxxxx   vee eight + vee eight spoiler |
| 27 | Joe |] | xx13.0xx vee eight car huh |

| 28 | Seyit |] | is wha/ they put something specials + 2.5 + |
| 29 | Mario |] | today you see five four five |

| 30 | Mario |] | years ago we have all mixed up the car here Laser Telestar vee eight |

Two instances are from the sub-corpus of Employment Office meetings. One is due to George's misinterpretation of a response from Rachel.

The other results from Tuk's use of migrant instead of migrants and his lack of explicitness (from SINGULAR FOR PLURAL):

TUK: what happen to other migrant   what
RACHEL: I'm sorry Tuk

TUK: what happen to Cambodian

Sometimes it is only content that needs to be clarified, e.g.:

what's this. (*CAN I LEAVE IT*),

or:

the which ones the eight seven ones. (*CHALLENGING SLOBODAN*)

In preparation for a meeting the following day (*NEW LEAVE ARRANGE-MENTS*), Aija and a number of other women have been discussing new leave arrangements for the following year. Anh, a Vietnamese woman, later comments 'I don't understand', and Aija explains:

NEW LEAVE ARRANGEMENTS - [Nipponcar]

1	Aija]	and then next year no roster days
2	Anh]	no more no more no more holidays

3	Aija]	no not every month maybe on Christmas time we don't have no holidays
4	Anh]	(*laughter*)

5	Aija]	next year at all this year plenty next year nothing
6	Anh]	next year yeah yeah this yeahr alright

7	Aija]	nothing (*laughs*) only public holiday
8	Anh]	but next year no nothing holiday (*laughs*)

9	Aija]	days no good never mind + can't do much
10	Anh]	yeah no no good yeah

11	Aija]	otherwise some of us have to go if we don't agree with that
12	Anh]	yeah

As I mentioned under 3.6, Aija is unique in our corpus in her use of syntactically marked foreigner talk. Generally, little or no modification is

made to the speakers' speech according to interlocutor, apart from the
pragmatic variation mentioned above, under 3.2.1.

The simplest type of interaction negotiating meaning is where one
interlocutor does not know how to express a particular concept. For
instance, Seyit and Mario, a Turk and an Italian at Amcar (*INJURY*), are
talking about Mario's injury:

> SEYIT: yeah how is your finger now
> MARIO: what a finger I go for my shoulder
>
> SEYIT: your back   ah back here
> MARIO: here   no here er through here

A more complicated process is the negotiation of communicative intent
from a pragmatic point of view. In *WORK ETHICS*, Jennifer attempts to
clarify Slobodan's intentions:

> you want a reason.

but the answer she receives:

> yeah I would like a reason.

only confuses the communication because of the 'metaphorical' nature of
the utterance.

4.3.4   *Negotiation: summary*

The above discussion of negotiation in the workplace shows both
symmetrical and asymmetrical patterns. It strengthens the link between
discourse patterns on the one hand and power factors and cultural values
on the other, but the cultural factors predominate. The Europeans show
a tendency towards well-developed schemata intended to persuade others
of their viewpoint. With a few exceptions, the South-east Asians (most
especially the Vietnamese) say what they think is expected and negotiate
as little as possible.

4.4   Meetings

We have derived our data on meetings from three sources – a 'quality
circle' group at Weavers, partly on videotape, the Employment Office,
and Parent Group. The reader is reminded that a substantial part of the
Employment Office data forms a 'sub-corpus' in which the participants
include English native speakers. In fact, some meetings are chaired by an
English native speaker.

'Quality circle' groups are formed to give employees the opportunity to discuss issues relating to productivity and to practise presentations on such topics subsequently delivered to the management. The group under consideration – comprising six men, a Ukrainian, a Sinhalese, an Italian, a Maltese, and a Macedonian, and, in later sessions, a Vietnamese – are engaged in mutual discussions. (In a few cases, an Anglo-Australian member of the management was present as an observer.) These people work together habitually, and the discourse can be characterized as collaborative, in a light-hearted atmosphere. The presentations, though formal, are given in a solidarity marked situation. Even some of the interjections are 'in fun'.

Suggestions are made for both content and lexical choice, e.g.:

TEN SOLUTIONS - [Weavers]

| 1 | Bill |] | o = out of the nine + + out of the er nine problems we + as I said before |

| 2 | Bill |] | we picked up the one that is the most concurrent which is + er balloon- |

| 3 | Bill |] | ing + which ended up at about forty-five or fifty per cent + xxxx |
| 4 | Mick |] | that was one |

5	Bill	]	yeah + and now I hand you over to er Mr Vin Boemo
6	Mick	]	xxxx
7	Dulip]		here comes the

8	Bill	]	yeah here comes the solutions xxxx <easy +4+
9	Dulip	]	solutions
10	Vin	]	the solutions

| 11 | Vin |] | to ballooning + yes + after we evaluate the + the problems and collect |

| 12 | Mick |] | xxxx solutions |
| 13 | Vin |] | the facts xxxx we come up with some solutions + + there are about ten |

| 14 | Vin |] | solutions but we decide to take out the most practical and economical + |

| 15 | Bill |] | down the bottom |
| 16 | Vin |] | which one is supposed to be + + to slit the fabric xxxx xxxx   yeah + |

| 17 | Mick |] | ↑Vin   ↑Vin + you can say we've tried these different |
| 18 | Vin |] | eh + slitting before dyeing |

| 19 | Mick |] | things xxxxxx + 3.0 + |
| 20 | Vin |] | yeah I mean this er this all + + the solution we |

| 21 | Mick |] | we have tried these out |
| 22 | Vin |] | come up but we we we practically we take only a few |

| 23 | Mick |] | on the workers xxxxxx |

(some minutes further discussion)

| 24 | Vin |] | this this is another solution we eh + I don't know if it's relevant but + |

| 25 | Dulip |] | ↑Joe   I think it's not not only because it's time consuming |
| 26 | Vin |] | er we have the filter |

| 27 | Dulip |] | |
| | | | or i= it's costing us + I think it wasn't <u>successful</u> + →it didn't solve the |

28	Dulip	]	
29	Vin	]	problem + 3.0 + xxxx xxxxx
			don't < we don't know because we scrap it

30	Bill	]	yeah yeah
31	Dulip	]	xxxxxx I
32	Vin	]	because it was + it not was economical so don't know if it was

---

| 33 | Dulip |] | I mean + if you talk about xxxxx fabric can operate by hand xxxxx |

34	Mick	]	yeah well see we haven't actually <u>solved</u> that
35	Dulip	]	reliable + 2.0 +
36	Vin	]	you got +

| 37 | Bill |] | < you can't solve it you gotta <u>suggest</u> it + + that's why you're having |
| 38 | Mick |] | you |

39	Bill	]	this presentation
40	Mick	]	no + I'm saying that this hydro business
41	Gary	]	<that's right

| 42 | Mick |] | hasn't been resolved + resolved xxxx |

There are few interruptions, with each segment becoming a series of monologues, see *ABOUT BRAINSTORMING* (e.g. lines 6–16). The echo it's already done is typical of this kind of collaborative discourse. Each person allows the other to complete their turn without interruptions (but for one small exception), even when there is some disagreement, e.g.:

VERBAL OR WRITTEN - [Weavers]

1	Mick	]	if she wants production + if you're gonna lose + if you're gonna lose a
2	Mick	]	third on some batches xxx you're not gonna meet that production xxxxx
3	Mick	]	xxxx I'm saying it
4	Bill	]	and this has been going on + since they took over + +
5	Mick	]	it should be in writing xxx
6	Bill	]	→and I'm saying it's already in writing + + ↑how
7	Mick	]	na + it's all been done verbally
8	Bill	]	else could it be done + + <hey w = when Ben
9	Bill	]	was in charge they took the number + + xxxx of each machine and they
10	Bill	]	done it in writing + + ↑where did it get us. + same story five years later

Even where there are some interruptions, the contribution of turn appropriation to collaborative outcomes is seen in the following discussion concerning grease and rust marks on fabric:

FABRIC MARKS - [Weavers]

1   Bill   ]   ah because we've got another roll there's about eighteen metres of those

---

2   Bill   ]   creases +   ↑Bill, xxxx good to have in there
3   Tuan   ]   yeah + something like that

---

4   Vin   ]   xxxx it's not xxxx this is er the machine + th= the eyes is not working

---

5   Vin   ]   properly xxxx don't work properly xxxxxxx
6   Tuan   ]   coz I= + + cos sometime when

---

7   Tuan   ]   we work on the machines + so we know what + what going on with

8   Tuan   ]   machines + so we put more attention + pay more attention for that one

9   Tuan   ]   + if its doesn't work properly + + we know we have + to do something

10 Tuan   ]   + but you know you can't do it + you must for help xxxxx xxxxx and
11 Mick   ]   xxxxxx

---

12 Tuan   ]   ask me to come for help xxxxx ↑help + +
13 Mick   ]   but in actual fact it's the

---

14 Mick   ]   + operator that's actually causing it + + he should stop + and get

15 Mick   ]   someone to give him a xxxxx he's gonna spoil that fabric   what they've

16 Mick   ]   done is they've just run it and you get eighteen metres of fabric that's no

17 Mick   ]   good xxxx see after sixteen metres it'll come good + + it straightens

---

18 Vin   ]   yeah but I mean when it's
19 Mick   ]   itself out like + you know + on its own xxxxx

---

20 Vin   ]   happening it's happening + + suddenly you are not prepared + ↑you see

21 Vin   ]   + + like the machine's good now + you pull the fabric through + +

22 Vin   ]   ↑ <oof + it's gone + xxxx the operator before it was alright + + the

23 Vin   ]   operator didn't know it was xxxx ↑you know what I mean + +
24 Mick   ]   al↑right +

---

25 Mick] what's the next one Dougal

(a minute later)

26 Bill]   no + <u>machine</u> + +
27 Mick] + + we'll put that under + 2.0 + <u>method</u> xxx + +

28 Bill] that's fitter's job + 3.0 +   < that's when they grease the housing
29 Mick]   no xxxxx

30 Bill] only + + that only happens when they grease the + + housing + +

31 Bill]   cos they don't want to xxxx grease
32 Mick] yeah but you see   yeah but they

33 Bill]   < na na na nope nope nope + i = i = it's far away from the xxxx Mick
34 Mick] shouldn't xxxxx
35 Dougal]   xxxxx xxxx

36 Bill] + it's just carelessness by the + + by the fitters + + that's what that

37 Bill] is   under the machine + when it comes
38 Mick]   what xxxx ↑under the machine

39 Bill] under the machine
40 Dougal]   well + + what you're saying here is + + Vin + you're just

41 Dougal] saying y/ w/ you load it + + <u>away</u> from the two ends + you're not really

42 Bill]   nope   when eh when
43 Mick]   xxxxx
44 Dougal] solving the problem you're just covering it up

45 Bill] they grease it + they just + overload the grease   warms up   when
46 Mick]   they put too much grease

```
47  Bill    ]  it warms up + it's er
48  Mick    ]                              xxxxxx
49  Dougal  ]                        Mick is there any way of sort of seeing it ↑ as
    _____

50  Bill    ]                        →yeah. + + they should wipe their bloody
51  Dougal  ]  soon as they've done the job
    _____

52  Bill    ]  hands instead of leaving it there
```

The person making the presentation initiates the topic, and there is hardly any change of topic, although there may be 'metatalk' about the presentation, e.g. in the discussion TEN SOLUTIONS, Mick says:

Vin you can say we've tried these different things.

There is a considerable amount of back-channelling, e.g. yeah, right, no, but not as much as in the Employment Office data (see below).

The turn taking is fairly symmetrical – probably because the group is single-sex (male), educated and experienced in their work area, and has worked together for a long time. The one South-east Asian member, Tuan, does not participate as actively as the others although he does contribute extensive turns from time to time.

The Employment Office data is also collaborative in nature. Meetings are an essential feature of the work of the employment officers. The convenor of the meeting almost invariably initiates the topic, and there is rarely any deviation from the topic. The convenor also clarifies and elucidates the issues. The other members of the group provide information, voice opinions and concerns, offer suggestions, and report on relevant experiences on the implementation of policies. There is a great deal of back-channelling (e.g. yeah, yip, mm, or echoing keyword, see 4.2), much of this coming from the English native speakers.

The turns offering suggestions or expressing concerns can be quite lengthy and, although there are more interruptions than at the Weavers 'quality circle', group members are allowed to continue their turns in a disciplined manner, e.g. Manuela's long turn in TRAINING. Her lengthy turn is followed by one from George.

The meetings discourse demonstrates the tendency for people from Latin American and Greek backgrounds to have long turns and a greater tendency for people of Anglo-Celtic backgrounds than others to appropriate turns that have become lengthy. (As this study is intended to be on English as a lingua franca, we do not have spontaneous communication data from which to verify this.) Muntha, the Cambodian woman, is given a fairly free run to make her suggestions, which she does in quite an articulate manner, e.g.:

MULTILINGUAL INFORMATION - [Employment Office]

1	Rachel]	okay
2	Muntha]	now the last time when Christina came here with the job-seeker +

3	Rachel]	right
4	Muntha]	you know clients xx Tuk and I have explained/ go through/ went through

---

5	Muntha]	with them tou know all the/ xxx in in + bilingual in Vietnemeses and in

---

6	Muntha]	Cambodian + tried to explain them but you know it
7	Penny]	easy for them to

8	Muntha]	yeh they I told them to write it ↓down ↑right
9	Penny]	forget anyway
10	Tuk]	xxx they will forget (*laughs*)

11	Rachel]	mhm
12	Muntha]	cause it's = it's not a matter of just talk and for ↑ get about it. but if

---

13	Rachel]	mm hm
14	Muntha]	you write it down you get something you know to read and + learn again

---

15	Muntha]	and + um it's gonna take + time to explain < to each of them you know

---

Muntha's and Tuk's turns are marked by long pauses (e.g. over 1.5 secs.).

The Anglo convenor Rachel and the Maltese-background convenor Charlie conduct meetings in different ways. Rachel insists on keeping some control over turn management. In her meetings, some of the members will ask for a turn. The 'next step' is subject to some cultural variation, e.g. in the following two examples both George and Patrick ask: 'can I say something'; but, whereas George waits for Rachel to respond, Patrick immediately proceeds to his point. Rachel is able to silence George by deflecting the turn to Tuk:

CHAIR'S REBUFF - [Employment Office]

1	Craig]	so you record everyone they re↑ferred
2	Tuk]	well actually I'm going to see er
3	Rachel]	well with with xxxx

| 4 | Tuk] | Vietnamese xxxxx <some people xxxx + xxx <what happen to some |

| 5 | Tuk   ] | other migrant   xxxx what what happens to some other |
| 6 | Raohel] | I'm sorry Tuk |

| 7 | Tuk   ] | migrants you know xxx they cannot communicate at all   <mm |
| 8 | George] | xxxxx |

9	Tuk]	Cambodian xxxx
10	Rachel]	well Tuk is actually talking
11	George]	can I + ↑say something

12	Tuk]	yeh
13	Rachel]	↑George yes so what you're talking about the clients whom you
14	George]	↑is he

| 15 | Tuk   ] | mm |
| 16 | Rachel] | can't communicate with |

Rachel is unable to appropriate and deflect Patrick's turn:

PATRICK'S SKILFUL TURN - [Employment Office]

| 1 | Rachel] | didn't I just go through all the things that were going to impact on what |
| 2 | Patrick] | xxxx |

---

3 Rachel] we were gonna be doing this ↑quarter   xxx <I thought we'd just
4 Patrick]   yeh + <could I/ could you/ could I

---

5 Rachel] covered this
6 Patrick] just say something here while I think. of it cause I= I keep on wanting to

---

7 Patrick] bring this subject up and I keep on forgetting it and er <u>George</u> has

---

8 Rachel]   ↑mm
9 Patrick] reminded me   mm + ↑do we + sort of consciously + uh make a list of

---

10 Patrick] ↑employers. that are ↑willing. around the area to take non-English

---

11 Rachel]   ↑do we
12 Patrick] speaking migrants   xxxxx xxxxx xxxxx
13 Manuela]   mm   well we don't xxxxx xxxxx xxxxxx
14 Tuk   ]   xxxxx xxxxx

---

15 Tuk   ] you know they uh the/ they was willing to take non-English speaking

---

16 Patrick]   yeh un=under s= under certain xxxx
17 Manuela]   <practic=   practically   every one of
18 Tuk   ] people to ↑work mm

---

19 Manuela] the employers which is in the ↑umbrella + under the umbrella is because

---

20 Manuela] they are willing to <u>take</u> + people with difficulties that includes + people

---

21 Rachel]   ↑actually that
22 Patrick]   ↑has somebody got + ↑has somebody got a list
23 Manuela] with language difficulties

===

Muntha frequently plays a secretarial role at the meetings, providing precise information and giving out material. She and Tuk appear to be more effective under Rachel's more organized meeting management than with Charlie, who allows the meeting to proceed more 'democratically' with the effect that George, Manuela, Daniela, and to a lesser extent, Elvira are allowed to hold the floor for fairly long periods. Meetings chaired by Charlie allow for a great deal of collaborative discourse, e.g. in *Who's boss*, where the group is discussing changes in the management structure and fears of 'being let down':

WHO'S BOSS - [Employment Office]

1   George] I was thinking before you know we know this centre is gonna be divided

2   George] in two units + job centre and Special Service Unit + we know about that

---

3   George]   and we know + and we know +1.3+ job centre's gonna be uh
4   Charlie] yeh xxxxx

---

5   George] supervised by Brad and + and uh Jeff all right   as er
6   Charlie]   how do you know that

---

7   George] manager er + already they're already in the positions + as the manager

---

8   George] and assistant manager er + they're already in the positions + as the

---

9   George] manager and assistant manager   now how we know who is
10 Charlie]   uh   up up until

---

11 George] gonna manage the special service unit + see we are + we are doing the

12 George] job +1.6+ and we dunno who is xxxxx you see we gonna go for a

13 George] promotion + for those positions and we dunno who is gonna give us the

---

14 George] er + the supervisor reports
15 Craig   ]   the + first point that I raised was that we

---

16 George]   you see we = we/ here we work most of the
17 Craig   ] dunno what the audience

---

18 George] days + with the service unit special service unit + and we dunno who is

---

19 George] er   I   the idea + the
20 Charlie]   your supervisors
21 Manuela]   I thought I thought I thought Charlie is the supervisor

---

22 George] idea before   with er Carolyn + she she was + supporting + the special
23 Tuk   ]   supervisor xxxx

---

24 George] service unit + she was supporting us as you see   and uh we a
25 Charlie]   mm hm

---

26 George] appreciate the help she's been doing for the unit but I can't see any

---

27 George] support from er the management you know we just + we know you

---

28 George] helping us + + I   ah well
29 Charlie]   which xxxxx what sort of support do you want
30 Manuela]   I under-

---

31 George] you can see the difference with er Carolyn she has been doing you xxxxx
32 Manuela] stand Tony is our supervisor   it's not ↑Tony
33 Patrick]   xxxxxx
34 chorus]   xxxxxx xxxxxx xxxxxx xxxxxx

---

35 George] know before   and er you know but we xxxx
36 Manuela] is our supervisor   in the cell in the migrant cell
37 Craig   ]   no he

---

38 George]   see what I mean   I thi= I think everybody if
39 Charlie]   uh
40 Craig   ] just co-ordinates the unit

---

41 George] I think everybody if you ask everybody you can see the difference I'm not

---

42 George] gonna now xxxxx xxxxx xxxxxx   mm
43 Charlie]   xxxxx xxxxx but + no well I'm having trouble um

---

44 Charlie] so what sort of support do you want Brad to give you that + that +

| 45 | George |] | | yeh I know xxxx Brad he's sitting there |
| 46 | Charlie |] | Carolyn was giving I mean there's no | |

| 47 | George |] | because he's gonna be a manager of this job centre he does | |
| 48 | Charlie |] | | we don't know which |

| 49 | George |] | | ahh (*laughs*) | |
| 50 | Charlie |] | one he'll pick | see this er the special service unit is an office |

| 51 | George |] | | yeh I know but ah I = I thought that the way they |
| 52 | Charlie |] | initiative it's not C.S.R. | |

53	George	]	set up you know is + is going to be staying	as it is
54	Charlie	]		no	not
55	Craig	]		it's a local initiative

| 56 | Charlie |] | not necessarily you may find uh + that when the + S.S.U. sets itself up |

| 57 | Charlie |] | that there might be an ASO5 in there or an ASO6 even |

As will be recalled from *PRIZE GIVING* (4.1.6), Parent Group meetings are dominated completely by Irma, who initiates the topics, changes them, and corrects the other participants.

Underlying the types of meeting behaviour, even in a context where formal procedures are not followed, are cultural styles of discourse organization which will be discussed under 6.3.3 and 6.3.4.

4.5   Turn length in relation to speech acts: communicative styles

On the whole, those initiating certain speech acts, especially complaints and whinges, have the longest turns. So, for instance, Cam, who is normally very silent, becomes a dominant vocal contributor to the whole of the exchange (*INTERROGATING THE GREEDY MAN*). The length of turns will, of course, depend partly on the goal of the communication. For instance, where one interlocutor is trying to stimulate a conversation by asking lots of questions, the turns will be short. This applies in *ROY'S*

WEEKEND PLANS, where Khalil is 'interviewing' Roy. It applies equally to *PERSONAL QUESTIONS*, where Faith is 'interviewing' Minh.

There are, however, also general tendencies which will cluster and which I will designate in terms of three styles – A, B, and C. This is not a contrastive study. What we are concerned with is inter-cultural communication. However, in order to discuss this, we need to give an indication of the 'styles' that are in contact. In terms of turn length, A and B, which I will differentiate below, are, on the whole, characterized by longer turns and C by shorter turns. In our sample, the Central and Southern Europeans, Latin Americans and South Asians *tend* to have longer turns than the South-east Asians, and all the very long turns come from the former groups. This is not only by virtue of their enjoying higher status within the workplace. Where a South-east Asian, say Jennifer, is communicating with a Central European subordinate, her turns are not appreciably longer than when she is talking to her superordinate. Nor is gender an important variable here. Irma from the multicultural Parent Group takes long turns which are very similar to that of fellow-Croatian Slobodan. However, the need to reflect authority in discourse patterns can be a factor in turn behaviour. For instance, in *CHECK IT*, after Jennifer has interrupted three times with:

I will check that afterwards.

Slobodan still insists on giving the directions for confirmation:

you get them better check and see if you are in short supply.

One of the reasons why those using Style A (continental Europeans, such as Croatians, Poles, and Spaniards, and Spanish-speaking Latin Americans), take long turns is that they enable the speaker to downtone an unpleasant speech act such as a complaint or a directive. From the point of view of the Style A user, this is a face-booster for both the hearer, who is hearing consolatory as well as bad things, and for the speaker, whose status and authority are reflected in long complaint and directive sequences. Examples of downtoners are 'apparent disclaimers' (see *BAD SOLDERING*) and apologies for having to give a directive (e.g. Raymond in *SICK LEAVE*). As exemplified by Krysztina's apology in *SELF-REPROACH*, the longer, the more elaborate and creative the apology, the more sincere it appears to be and the more effective it is believed to be (see also below). The length of Style A discourse is also partly determined by non-linearity (cf. 6.3.4). As we have seen (4.1.5), negative politeness, which contributes to extending the turns of Central Europeans, encourages those of South-east Asians to be brief. These considerations would suggest that levels of directness, on which many cross-cultural pragmatic studies such as the CCSARP (Blum-Kulka, House and Kasper 1989, see 1.3.4) rest, need to be viewed in a broader discourse context. A 'higher level of directness', for instance, can be counteracted by a longer turn in some cultures. While our corpus does not allow us to make deductions similar to those of CCSARP because the data is not comparable, we do have instances of more explicit and less explicit performance of speech acts from the same speaker in similar conditions. This appears to be attributable to the hierarchy of the workplace, reflecting Brown and Levinson's 'relative power' as well as 'social distance' (see 1.3).

Those using Style B – in our corpus, 'South Asians' such as Indians and Sri Lankans of different ethnic groups, and Iranians – tend to take long turns partly because of repetition and/or a preference for rhetorical devices, such as elaborate parallelism (cf. Kaplan (1971, 1972) and Ostler (1987) on Arabs, 5.7, 5.9) in their discourse which are characteristic of this style. Notice Tim's long turns in the following excerpt. However, Tim frequently employs short turns which are generated by the exigencies of his workplace.

BAD SERVING - [Catering]

| 1 | Tim |] | see what they're doing they're washing the bloody spoons + + in the |

| 2 | Tim |] | coffee machine   eh Lee Lee tell tell this one here + + |
| 3 | Lee |] | yes mate + 1.5 + |

| 4 | Tim |] | come + 2.5 + come + + I'm very sick an' tired oh she's coming there |
| 5 | Lee |] | oh |

| 6 | Tim |] | why don't you take it in a plate (*clears throat*) + 3.0 + hey don' use that |

| 7 | Tim |] | bowl for the sauce eh that's for the soup + don't use the bowl for the |

| 8 | Tim |] | sauce   see another one is there hey don't use the bowl |
| 9 | Lee |] | yeah she always |

An instance of rhetorical repetition is Raymond's explanation in *MULTISKILLING*. This type of pattern is a means of remembering schemata in some cultures. Kaplan (1971) has found preference for elaborate parallelism among speakers of Arabic and Hebrew, and it is also preferred by Muslims, regardless of whether they are native Arabic speakers or not (Robert Kaplan, personal communication). Examples of Tim's repetitions and parallelism in directive patterns are discussed under complex complaint interactions (3.1.2). Raymond's rhetorical parallelism (as part of long turns) has its counterpart in Tim's dichotomy concerning a couple who take it in turns to eat in the dining room and collect food for their spouse:

> when he eat the wife never eat when the wife eat, he never eat.
> (*MISSING WIFE*)

In *PRIORITY LIST*, Dulip, a very fluent speaker of English, frequently employs repetition of the same or almost the same words (despite back-channelling from other interlocutors), whether in questions:

> have you got that priority list have you got that priority list this batch one of them is this batch one of them or not is this batch one of them.

or in narratives:

> when they finish at three o'clock it wasn't ready at three o'clock it wasn't ready at three o'clock.

It should be noted that all the 'South Asians' providing us with data are very competent speakers of English – five native speakers of an Indian or Sri Lankan variety of English, a Sinhalese speaker who had conducted studies towards a university degree in Sri Lanka largely in English, and a Hindi speaker from Fiji, where English is an official language. The other two are a Farsi speaker from Iran and an Urdu speaker from Pakistan who could also speak English before arriving in Australia.

Another reason why those adopting Style A (Continental Europeans and Spanish-speaking Latin Americans) and Style B 'South Asians' tend to take long turns is that they engage in complex interactions which (to them) require justifications and explanations (see 3.2.1, 3.4.1). Such explanations can be a vindication or part of another type of apology, or attached to a directive. Khalil's long turn contains numerous explanations and justifications (*BRIEFING ON CHANGES*). While characteristic of these areal cultural groups, this practice is not restricted to them. For instance, Cam (*INTERROGATING THE GREEDY MAN*) justifies her long directive to the diner who is not accompanied by his wife. Here her cautious, caring style embracing 'negative politeness' (in Brown and Levinson's (1978, 1987) sense) contrasts with Tim's, which reflects frankness and little regard for the others' face.

Most of the complex interactions are dominated by Europeans. In the organization of his discourse, Slobodan, for instance, will often work towards a speech act through a multi-pronged strategy (e.g. a complaint comprising directive, accusation, and apology/explanation). So, in his complaint in BAD SOLDERING, he commences with an explanation. An apparent disclaimer also preceeds the accusation. In CHALLENGING SLOBODAN, too, the accusation is cushioned by its late positioning. Krysztina, in her lengthy apology, similarly tries out one strategy after the other.

As I have implied above, Style C is characteristic of the South-east Asians – the ethnic Chinese, Cambodians, Indonesians, Malays, and Vietnamese. Even members of these groups in superordinate positions, with higher levels of education and/or a high English proficiency tend to take shorter turns. Negative politeness in Style C means saying little rather than saying more and downtoning.

It should be noted that an 'Anglo-Celtic'/Northern European style, which is ever-present within the communication settings, links up with all the other ones. It is also the style towards which other groups converge, but which lies outside the scope of this investigation.

4.6   Variation in communicative styles

4.6.1   Other features of communicative styles and successful communication

From 4.1 and 4.5, similarities can be deduced between Styles A and B – as represented in our study by Europeans (especially Croatian and other Central European and Spanish) and Spanish-speaking Latin Americans, and by people of South Asian background (especially Sri Lankan, Fijian-Indian as well as Iranian) respectively. Both are characterized by long turns and a tendency seldom to listen to or tolerate interruptions. However, they are creative in different ways – Style A through lexical choice and B through rhythmical rhetorical patterns. Speakers employing these styles are successful in both turn maintenance and turn appropriation in inter-cultural communication. The main exceptions are: Dulip when he is engaged in small-talk, in which he is not nearly as competent as in work communication and meeting routines, and in which his position of power is challenged (4.1.3); Boba, who sometimes has to yield to a person with whom she is working habitually on a collegial basis;

and Slobodan on the occasion when Ricarda's face is severely threatened (3.1.2). (The reader is reminded that, while the general conclusion on Europeans applies to both women and men, we have only two 'South Asian women' in our sample.) In encounters at Weavers between Mick and Vin (e.g. TEN SOLUTIONS), both speakers appropriate turns, but Mick holds the floor for most of the time. Style C is characterized by a tendency not to interrupt, and the South-east Asians, who employ this style, are not successful in turn appropriation or even turn maintenance in competition with Europeans or South Asians (see 4.1.1, 4.1.2).

The available data indicates a preference for different strategies of turn maintenance and appropriation in each of the main groups. In a cross-section of ten exchanges, verified from other data from our corpus, turn appropriation is achieved in Style A (European) by interruptions, and both turn maintenance and turn appropriation by an increase in volume and speed. Where speakers sharing Style A (e.g. Italians and Croatians, Austrians and Hungarians) and also Style A and B communicators (e.g. Italians and Pakistanis) are engaged in communication, interruptions lead to simultaneous speech and reciprocal turn appropriation (e.g. 4.1.2). In Style B (South Asian), turns are appropriated by an increase in speed and/or volume, sometimes with also a rising intonation, but maintained through a decrease in speed. In Style C (South-east Asian), on the other hand, turns are appropriated and maintained by elongation of words, decrease in speed, and a rising intonation. All the styles employ repetition.

4.6.2   Institutional differences between workplaces

The nature of the work undertaken in the different workplaces and research sites influences the communication patterns adopted, over and above variation, according to culture and gender. As will be gleaned from the discussion of the data so far, the catering industry has yielded many short turns. In the factories, 'encounters' between the 'boss' and one or more subordinates for the purpose of directing or complaining, giving explanations, etc. have compounded cultural tendencies towards long turns there. Where people are constantly working together as in Catering, Education Office and (to a lesser extent) Employment Office, the social distance is less pronounced, and there is a tendency towards more shorter, equal turns than in a concern such as Nipponcar, where there is multiskilling and workers being moved about frequently. Conditions in the car factories, Amcar and Nipponcar, allow for relatively little verbal communication during worktime, not only because of high noise level, but also because of sequential interdependence. At Weavers, social distance is reduced because there are a number of well-qualified equals or near-equals working together, who meet to negotiate. Also, the ethos of the workplace plays an important role in determining communication. Elektro has more of a power hierarchy, which leads to longer turns and the overproportionate use of commissives (and apologies). However, it is also the company that is perhaps most aware of the need for successful inter-cultural communication. There is plenty of opportunity for verbal communication because people are sitting in fixed positions in close proximity. While there is a visible German–Central European presence at Elektro, the fact that Nipponcar is a Japanese company has no direct implication for inter-cultural communication.

Amcar seems more conscious than the others of ethnic differentiation. They are the only company in our sample which keeps statistics on the language breakdown of the workforce. They provide language-specific services to workers. However, most of the workforce are from related/ geographically contiguous cultures of Southern Europe or from the Middle East. The workers engage in quite a lot of inter-ethnic teasing and ritual insult, e.g.:

> silly Turk.
> Greek silly.
> Lebanese I love you.

While Catering has a less hierarchial structure than the factories, there is a marked us vs. them dichotomy, with the workforce ganging up against the diners. We are projected as lacking power (both within the institution and *vis-à-vis* the outsiders) and being overworked. They are destroying the order and creating more work for us. There is also some belief that 'old' immigrants feel that the 'new' arrivals are having it better than they ever did. Tim's direction is influencing the communication patterns of many of those working with him, especially in their communication with the diners. At Employment Office, successful communication is considered paramount to the work of the office but it is judged on the basis of Anglo-Australian norms. Our data from this workplace is derived from meetings at which, on the whole, turns are received from those who have terminated them and people are allowed to complete their argument. This is illustrated in *TRAINING*, a typical meeting segment from Employment Office, where Manuela, a Spanish employment officer, is holding the floor and, while she is interrupted a number of times (by an Irishman and an ethnic Chinese from Vietnam), is always given the chance to go back to where she left off.

4.6.3   *The relation between culture, gender and status in language and power*

It is somewhat difficult to deduce from Chapter 3 and the above sections of Chapter 4 contrasts in the communication patterns of men and women from the same cultures in inter-cultural communication, because the men and women from the same culture are communicating with different people in different settings. However, broader comparisons enable us to suggest the following for our corpus:

(i)   South-east Asians (especially women) tend to receive directives from European men and to return commissives to them.
(ii) Europeans (men and women, regardless of their status) tend to dominate Vietnamese (men and women) and, to a lesser extent, other South-east Asians in exchanges.
(iii) European and South Asian men in status positions use long turns, extended by explanations and justifications, to women, especially South-east Asians.
(iv) South Asians (in our corpus men, typically those in higher status positions) tend to dominate South-east Asian women in their exchanges.
(v)   South Asians (men) are the group most likely to make complaints.
(vi) Gender-specific solidarity networks transcend ethnic boundaries but are strongest among Europeans.

The interface of culture and gender indicates the importance in communication patterns of Brown and Levinson's factors, power and social distance.

4.7   Success and failure in communication: why and how?

Success in communication concerns the relation between the speaker's communicative intention, the interlocutor's expectation of the message, and communicative effects of the messages. Successful communication means that the communicative effects match the intentions. In conversations, an important issue is also to ensure that your point of view is heard and understood, and that you do not lose face or feel threatened.

Among the possible outcomes of a communicative act are:

(i)   Communication which is successful from the start.
(ii) Potentially unsuccessful communication, where a communication breakdown (including a pragmalinguistic failure in the sense of Thomas 1983) is averted through negotiation of meaning. Thus, communication is successful in the end.

(iii) Resolved unsuccessful communication. Due to the resolution of the communication breakdown is resolved. Thus, communication is successful in the end.

(iv) Unsuccessful communication which cannot be resolved.

(v) Unsuccessful communication whose resolution has not been attempted.

Of twenty-six instances of communication breakdown in our corpus,[2] eighteen are resolved through negotiation of meaning (i.e. category (iii)), e.g.:

Tom the Indonesian leading hand (*CAN I LEAVE IT*) is making a request of Farouk, the Turkish storeperson. It is phrased as a modal question:

> Farouk can I leave this with you.

and is successful the second time around after some discussion of what 'this' is and what needs to be done with it.

This is then confirmed:

> so I leave this with you.

It takes Farouk the rewording of the request to realize the function of the utterance. Six of the instances represent problems in understanding the content and/or context rather than questions of discourse or other aspects of language, e.g.:

> TIM: what about that Iranian man you know we still give him the salad
>
> TIM: or   huh   no the one I was telling you got the
> IVAN: what Iranian man   why
>
> TIM: paper from the doctor

> (from *IRANIAN MAN*)

Another example is *THE CERTIFICATE*, a conversation between Frank and Anne, a Vietnamese woman:

THE CERTIFICATE - [Nipponcar]

---

1 Frank]   ↑Lola + tell Ken to bring the {certificate} on Tuesday
2 Lola   ]   bring what

| 3 | Frank |] | medical certificate   you know why because it's a p.d.o.[#] on Monday |
| 4 | Lola |] | yeh |

5	Frank	]	+ if he doesn't bring the certificate he doesn't get paid for today tell
6	Frank	]	him make sure o↑kay otherwise he miss one day because once you take
7	Frank	]	a sickie and Monday's a p.d.o.[#] ↑right if you don't get the medical
8	Frank	]	certificate you don't get paid

[#]. p.d.o. - Programmed day off.

Six are discourse problems related to cultural background, e.g.: the following excerpt from *SACKINGS*:

> SEYIT: see Qantas gonna sack nine hundred people   Qantas
> MARIO: huh
>
> SEYIT: gonna sack nine hundred people   Qantas
> MARIO: who /kon/   we no work
>
> SEYIT: yeah
> MARIO: for Qanta

Seven are the result of lexical or grammatical decoding difficulties, e.g. the conversation between Seyit and Mario, entitled *SPOILER*, see 4.3.3.

Another example is the following discussion between Tim and Khalil from *MISSING WIFE*:

> KHALIL: I can't see the wife   the the farmer who married on
> TIM: whose wife
>
> KHALIL: Saturday
> TIM: you can't see the wife or you can't see the husband

four probably resulting from auditory perception (sometimes together with a failure to understand the context), e.g. *PRIORITY LIST*, discussed in 4.5, and one could be due to either a lexical problem or one of auditory perception. Six at least are due to expectations of communication not being fulfilled, the interlocutor reacting unexpectedly or not reacting, or to the expectations of communication being fulfilled at the wrong time. They are thus instances of Thomas' (1983) sociopragmatic failure. Five of the six instances are from communication between a Central European

(Austrian, Croatian, Pole) and a South-east Asian (ethnic Chinese or Vietnamese). The Austro-Vietnamese encounters are discussed below. Another is Slobodan's non-apology reprimand of the Singapore-Chinese woman Blanche:

> not much sorry about it you have to talk to people. (see 3.4.1)

when the feedback that Slobodan expects may not be appropriate in her culture.

The other instances of cultural expectation-induced communication breakdown (Krysztina's apology and Slobodan's complaint) have been given considerable treatment in other sections – 3.4.1 and 3.1.2 respectively. The remaining example, an interaction between a Maltese and a Turk, is discussed below. A seventh example does not lead to a communication breakdown because the interlocutor makes the necessary adjustment: (from *GREETING* – the beginning of an interaction between Marisa, the Salvadorian at Catering and Tony, her Maltese colleague):

> MARISA: good day hello good day to you   mm yeah it's
> TONY: hot today
>
> MARISA: very nice day

The resolution of almost all the instances of communication breakdown in our corpus, and the attempted resolution of all of them, speak for the inter-cultural communication expertise that has been acquired in Australian society and in the Australian workplace, and the goodwill that exists, by and large. On the other hand, it obscures the strain that accommodation of communicative behaviour and communicative expectations and interpersonal concessions may cause. (This would also arise, but to a much lesser degree, in a monocultural setting, without the advantages ensuing from inter-cultural experience.) All in all, nine of the instances of communication breakdown involve a European or Latin American communicating with a South-east Asian, seven a European and a South Asian, and two a Turk and another European, one a Turk and a South-east Asian, three a Central and a Southern European, three a Fijian-Indian and another person of South Asian background, and one a Filipina and another person of South-east Asian background.

Following Gumperz (1982), I am differentiating between:

> Noncommunication – where no message is communicated; and
> Miscommunication – where an unintended message is communicated.

Miscommunication is more serious because it can pass unnoticed by either party, something that can exacerbate ethnic and racial stereotypes and cause communication conflict in which dignity and/or trust are threatened.

Let us consider FIVE DAYS OFF, where Liesl, an Austrian female leading hand, is approached at her desk (as usual) by Hoa, a Vietnamese woman worker for some requisite parts. It is the Thursday before Easter. In addition to getting her parts as she expected, Hoa is asked by her immediate superior:

> now you get five days off what're you going to do.

This was intended as friendly small-talk, phatic communication, but Hoa's bewilderment is marked by a long period of silence. A follow-up interview suggested that she may have believed that she was being laid off for five days. This is then a miscommunication. What distinguishes this episode from a similar one, where Cam asks the diner (INTERROGATING THE GREEDY MAN) if he is married and where his wife is, is Hoa's strong expectation that she was simply going to get some parts. A clear-cut instance of non-communication also involved Liesl and a Vietnamese woman, this time Giao, who brings Liesl some damaged parts:

BROKEN PARTS - [Elektro]

1	Liesl	]	hallo Giao haven't seen you what's wrong + 2.0 +
2	Giao	]	hallo Liesl xxxxxx + xxxxx so

3	Liesl	]	oo they're breaking
4	Giao	]	xxxxxx like this yeah see + 2.0 + →I beg your pardon what

---

5	Liesl	]	I haven't seen you for a long time oh you get a little
6	Giao	]	you want ←ah yeah

7	Liesl	]	↑note. printed ↑note
8	Giao	]	yeah nice isn't it from someone ahh →↑I beg your

9	Liesl	]	I will tell Tom gee ↑always the same thing
10	Giao	]	pardon xxxxx

Again Liesl's use of small-talk to put the Vietnamese woman at ease is not understood and she gives the Austrian an unexpected response of 'I beg your pardon what do you want.' In order to relax the atmosphere, the Austrian woman then reverts into the small talk in a most unusual place in the discourse, and her Vietnamese interlocutor is baffled.

In our next excerpt (*SPRAY GUN*), Frank and Mustafa are talking about a spray gun. The miscommunication is due to Frank's wrong interpretation of very slow responses as an indicator of noncommunication. Thus, assumed noncommunication can lead to miscommunication.

SPRAY GUN - [Nipponcar]

1 Charlie] what the gun is no good   what
2 Mustafa]   the gun is ah/ they the gun is no good

---

3 Charlie] {sort} were they   okay   are you going
4 Mustafa]   I don't know + 8.0 + yeah   won't stretch

---

5 Charlie] to repair them + huh   did you check with
6 Mustafa]   yeah uh Kim will repair them

---

7 Charlie] Kim + Kim Kim you go check with Kim
8 Mustafa]   I'll I'll got a check with Kim okay

Because of the long wait, Frank follows his question: 'are you going to repair them' with an impatient 'huh'. Then, after waiting four seconds for Mustafa's answer to his final question, he transforms it into a directive, not waiting for Mustafa's delayed assurance. Jefferson (1973) postulates 1.5 seconds as the maximum pause time tolerated, e.g. in American English, and Maynard (1980) argues that a pause longer than that signals a topic change.

A special form of partial non-communication is where two (or more) people are involved in parallel discourse, such as in *PARALLEL WHINGE-ING*, where Frank and Raymond are whingeing independently. Frank begins by starting to make a request concerning construction, while Raymond interprets with a whinge about Gina. Apart from the co-operative identification of the person, each of them rambles on about other workers, about what they said to them, work plans, and so on. Another example of parallel discourse is in *PASSING ON THE COMPLAINT*, where Tim tries to initiate an exchange concerning one of the diners:

this lady always create too many problems.

but Ivan, his superior, ignores this and diverts the conversation to peppercorns. Later Tim manages to gain a response from Ivan about the lady who creates problems.

A successful communication is where the interlocutors co-operate in helping each other understand one another, e.g.:

IRMA: not for us canteen makes last
MARIA: the canteen make the sandwiches

IRMA: time canteen makes   last the canteen make the
MARIA: ah it's not for the muticultural but the students

IRMA: sandwiches when aboriginal group came
(*PRIZE GIVING*, lines 26–30.)

4.7.1   *Identification of communication breakdown*

As communication is a two-way process, communication breakdown can be identified and recognized by:

1. One interlocutor
2. the other
3. both
4. another person who acts as mediator.

A question I would like to consider in this context is: Are there cultural differences in the preparedness to admit that there is communication breakdown (cf. the role of face-saving, in Bremer et al. (1988: 96) and the desire to continue participation in the conversation, accepting the blame or apportioning it to the other person, and how the negotiation or resolution process takes place?

This may vary according to the desire of the speakers to resolve the problem. It may also vary according to whether the interlocutors are from the same cultural region or very different ones. In the example cited in 4.7 above, Giao marks the non-communication with the utterances: 'I beg your pardon what do you want'. This indicates her lack of experience in negotiating meaning (at least in English!)

Each of the examples of negotiation of meaning to be found in 4.3.3 represents a different process. In *NEW LEAVE ARRANGEMENTS*, Anh declares that she does not understand the whole issue and discourse on the new award arrangements on leave and has Aija explain them to her. Anh repeats some of the keywords as back-channelling, but there is evidence of a high degree of non-communication. Seyit and Joe in *SPOILER* co-operate to try and resolve the non-communication but one is left with the impression at the end of the text that the non-communication has not really been resolved. *WE HAVE A COMPANY* is the most co-operative attempt at resolving a communication breakdown as Betty and Daniel are both helping Tim understand what Daniel meant by 'we have a company here' (see 4.3.3).

In most instances, people, regardless of their cultural background, are prepared to admit that there has been non-communication or miscommunication when it comes to lexical and contextual issues. There is rarely any occasion explicitly to apportion blaim. The person who does not understand tends to admit it. The problem is grasping the hidden, culture-based implications of communicative behaviour. These often go unnoticed or are misinterpreted across areal cultures without negotiation of meaning. Longer established Central and Southern European immigrants have commented that the incidence of communication breakdown was a new phenomenon attributable to South-east Asians who do not understand, regardless 'how hard you try'. Some Europeans have cast aspersions on the integrity or trustworthiness of South-east Asians, especially of Vietnamese, because of their own understanding of their communication patterns ('They say yes and then they don't do it'). Between Slobodan and Jennifer (*BAD SOLDERING*), for example, there is two-way communication, but the communication breakdown over the function of 'I want to know the reason' is never really resolved because there is a mismatch between the literal meaning of Slobodan's utterance confirming that he wants to hear the reason and his turn-taking behaviour which does not permit the explanation.

4.7.2 *What makes a person a successful communicator?*

Tom, the Indonesian foreman at Elektro, is a successful communicator. He presents his messages so that they can be decoded successfully in as 'non-culture-specific' and neutral a way as possible. He does not allow Slobodan to appropriate his turn. On the other hand, he lets him communicate all that he needs to. He keeps control of his exchanges, limiting the interactions to their intended goal. An example of a successful interaction is *FINGER PROTECTION*:

FINGER PROTECTION - [Elektro]

1   Tom   ]   ↑Slobodan +2.4+ can you ↑order 'nother ↑pair of ↑this one +2.4+

---

2   Tom   ]   yeah +1.5+
3   Slobo.]   half-finger job   xx0.9xx what you want with that +1.3+ I

---

4   Slobo.]   am going to ↑worry about that +6.2+ original ↑job or somebody leave it

---

5   Tom   ]   original you can see the + + xxxx
6   Slobo.]   xxxx   yeah you can s/ + + ←for + ←winding of

---

7   Tom   ]   this + + the = the other one is + + 's not really {crumpling} on this side

---

8   Tom   ]   →it doesn't protect the finger er er anyway +1.6+
9   Slobo.]   of course but you have

---

10   Tom   ]   →'s a good ↑ question. what is ↑ that are for ←it was
11   Slobo.]   to order it +2.5+

---

12   Tom   ]   Joseph from Richmond +1.3+ the left one is okay because er most of

---

13   Tom   ]   them + use the right hand one + +   ↑yeah sure + you
14   Slobo.]   may I ↑borrow this

---

15   Tom   ]   can because we ↑ hardly use the left one +3.3+
16   Slobo.]   ↑which side. that side is

---

17   Tom   ]   yeah that side's good +2.5+ thanks Slobodan
18   Slobo.]   alright

As has been indicated, communication is more likely to be successful if the hidden implications are understood by the interlocutor. So non-communication is less likely to occur if the cultural assumptions of the speaker are shared by the hearer. Despite Jennifer's attempts to clarify the meaning of Slobodan's 'What is the reason' this matter is not really resolved. Jennifer's attempts to resolve Krysztina's problem are successful by chance. On the other hand, Inge (*CHALLENGING SLOBODAN*), when asked by Slobodan for some parts that should have been delivered that morning, tells him that she has not received the parts by answering his implied questions with reasons:

> <u>because</u> no I haven't anything.
> <u>because</u> I haven't got anything.
> <u>so</u> you don't need them at all today.
> <u>because</u> whatever Liesl got I haven't got anything yet.
> <u>because</u> you have eight twenty five here.
> <u>because</u> it's still there you know.

She understands perfectly what he is after and gives him the appropriate reply, thereby saving face.

This does not mean that no person of South-east Asian background is ever able to negotiate meaning with Slobodan, as we have seen in 4.3.1. Successful communicators are aware of their own and their interlocutors' expectations of communication. They express themselves in as 'culturally neutral' a way as possible and know which questions to ask to resolve potential causes of communication breakdown.

The above sections underline the existence of broad areal cultural communication patterns and expectations based on cultural value systems. This issue will be taken up again in 6.2.

4.7.3 The 'disadvantage' of South-east Asians in inter-cultural communication

Much of the data containing exchanges between Central Europeans or South Asians and South-east Asians demonstrates the disadvantages of the latter in inter-cultural communication in Australia. They perform the most commissives, but, discounting Quoc, they receive few commissives. They perform a large number of directives, but also receive the most directives. On the whole, they take the shortest turns and often observe silence. They are generally not successful in appropriating the turns of others or even maintaining their own turns. However, their turns are most likely to be appropriated by others. Directives and complaints addressed to them tend to be longer and more explicit than those directed by the same interlocutor to members of other groups (cf. e.g. Tim to Daniel and Tim to Marisa, 3.2.1; Slobodan to Jennifer and Slobodan to Inge, 3.1.2). South-east Asians are unlikely to answer back Central

Europeans or South Asians. (The opportunities for answering back Southern Europeans are limited in our corpus.) Where the South-east Asians receive apologies, the manner in which this occurs is sometimes potentially face-threatening to them, while face-saving to the (European or South Asian) speaker. This contrasts with apologies made to European and Latin American women. South-east Asians fare better in the office context than on the factory floor. In both offices, social distance is much less. Both Quoc and Muntha speak English very fluently and competently. The latter is able to assert herself at meetings, although she is still one of the least vocal of the participants. It may be significant that, in our workplaces, only one of the quality circles has a South-east Asian participant, a Vietnamese man who is unusually vocal, but who still talks less than his European colleagues. Where Europeans and Latin Americans communicate regularly with other Europeans (and Latin Americans) and with South-east Asians, they tend to 'out-talk' the Southeast Asians, but indulge in reciprocal turn appropriation and simultaneous conversation with the other Europeans (and Latin Americans). An example is Marta, a talkative Hungarian, whose main work interlocutors are the equally talkative Austrian Annemarie, a less dominant Filipina conversationist, and an almost completely silent Vietnamese woman. (The atypical nature of Filipino discourse patterns in the Southeast Asian areal context will be discussed in 6.2.6.)

Responses to the attitudinal video experiment (see 4.8) would suggest that the above-mentioned communicative behaviour towards South-east Asians is in keeping with their own expectations. (For further discussion of this, see 6.2.7.) This is the way in which they use their cultural values systems to cope with the power structure of the workplace. However, their self-effacing behaviour at least degrades them in the eyes of cultural groups with other communicative styles and values systems.

The 'disadvantage' of the South-east Asians is moderated in so far as, in some respects, their communicative style is closer to that of the dominant 'Anglo' group (which is outside the scope of this study) than those of the Central and Southern Europeans and Spanish-speaking Latin Americans – e.g. in *not* overstating their case and in not extending the length of turns to add long explanations and vindications. Anglo-Celtic Australians, like South-east Asians, often wonder why Southern and Central Europeans and Latin Americans are 'making so much fuss' about something. This is a discourse manifestation of the cultural dimension of uncertainty avoidance in Hofstede's framework.

The dominance of Europeans (in our corpus particularly Croatians, German speakers, Greeks, and Spaniards), Latin Americans, and South Asians in inter-cultural communication in our data could suggest that A and B are the style options that would need to be promoted among South-east Asians. However, there are two problems with this – the relation to cultural values (see Chapter 6 and 7.4) and the possibility that it is ethnicity and culture rather than their manifestation in communicative behaviour that disadvantages them (cf. 4.6.3).

4.8   Discourse patterns and expectations: comparison with video experiment

The video experiment (for details, see 2.6) was intended to find out if informants watching the role-plays identified more strongly with the communicative styles of the people of similar ethnolinguistic back-ground, thus perceiving any communicative conflict from this point of view. According to the data analysis, the expectation would be that, say, Europeans might identify more with Style A and South-east Asians with Style C. A wide variety of ethnolinguistic backgrounds was represented among the respondents – ethnic Chinese, Vietnamese, Laotian, Singa-pore-Malays, Indonesians, and Filipinos (totalling 19) and Germans, Dutch, Serbs, Croats, Poles, Czechs, Russians, Greeks, Italians, Mace-donians, and Spaniards (the Central and Southern European groups totalling 33). Both genders were represented, as were subordinates and superordinates from the workplaces and people with apparently varying levels of English proficiency.

While some respondents identified the communication breakdown:

> he didn't understand what she's talking about. (Polish woman)
> they don't understand each other what they're talking they just argue. (Vietnamese woman)

others did not refer to non- or mis-communication. Specific pragmatic and discourse issues were not mentioned.

The most clear-cut responses were to Video 1, based on FIVE DAYS OFF (see Clyne, Giannicos, and Neil 1994) where 22 out of 33 Europeans implied that the Vietnamese was at fault and 12 out of 19 of the South-east Asians that the European was. Of the 7 Europeans who 'sided' with the Vietnamese, 6 could be described as 'Southern European' (4 Greeks, 1 Italian, and 1 Macedonian). Of the 3 Asians whose responses favoured Style A, 2 were Vietnamese and 1 a Filipino, while an Indonesian, a Thai, a Filipino and 1 of the 9 Vietnamese saw both points of view. All the Greek informants felt that small-talk was appropriate in workplace communication.

In response to Video 2, based on WORK ETHICS, 15 of the 33

Europeans approved of the European's style, 11 Europeans approved of that of the South-east Asian, and 5 showed sympathy in both directions. Of the 19 South-east Asians, 7 identified with the Asian's style, 5 with the European's, and 6 presented sympathetic arguments on both sides. This included both the Indonesians and 2 of the 3 Filipinos. It appears that many Asians believe that an older (white?) male in authority has the right to 'boss' his younger female subordinate around. Even if he may do this in a European way, a slight majority of the Europeans in our sample disapproved of the practice.

Twenty-five of the 33 Europeans identified with the apologetic European in Video 3, based on SELF-REPROACH, and 4 with the Asian woman supervisor who was trying to terminate his turn. Only 3 of the south-east Asians sympathized with her communicative style. There was clearly an identification with the underdog, regardless of that person's ethnicity. The fact that the superordinate was a younger female may have influenced attitudes. Kasper (1994) points out that 'age matters more' to most Asian interlocutors than to most westerners. In any case, there was a violation of the cultural core value of harmony (see 6.2). Central and Southern Europeans' sense of social hierarchy also determined by age, gender and status (and perhaps by race and ethnicity!) is disturbed by the nature of the interactional imbalance in the exchange.

This small-scale study, while further challenging the usefulness of role-play in cross-cultural pragmatic and discourse study, has confirmed areal variation in communication patterns and expectations. The European respondents *tend* to favour Style A, but the Greeks and Poles among them only peripherally. The South-east Asians tend to favour Style C, but the Filipinos, Indonesians, and Malays only peripherally (see below, 4.9). In at least one of the videos, the accentuation of cultural stereotypes in the role-plays may have led to overreaction on the part of the respondents.

There is evidence in the videoed responses to the video of differences in the structuring of the discourse. Some Central or Southern Europeans exhibit contrariness in their responses by presenting a position which is not a direct reply to the question, but which they consider more relevant. They give relatively long responses with explanations or parenthetical amplification (thinking aloud), and sometimes presented in a dialectic way, e.g. from a Polish woman:

> I think he wasn't interested in races you see very much because maybe not everybody is maybe he wasn't or maybe he was interested but he didn't have time for it I think he did understand but that's my opinion you should ask him direct.

or from a Greek:

> all depends how much times happen say if one worker do that all the time then if you come every week late then you get a complain but if it happens once in three months you come late ten minutes I believe it can happen to anyone that's my opinion.

Many of the South-east Asians, especially the Vietnamese, on the other hand, gave a yes or no response, with or without expansion, e.g.:

> yes I think so he understands her because she excuses himself.

4.9   Core and peripheral groups

In 1.3.6, I referred to the work of Galtung (1985) in which he postulated four intellectual styles – Gallic, Nipponic, Saxonic, and Teutonic – which have arisen out of the academic cultures of France, Japan, Britain/the US, and Germany. Some of the neighbouring cultures have been influenced by these to a greater or lesser extent, but have adopted the intellectual styles only in a peripheral way.

The same applies to the tendencies in the communicative styles in inter-cultural workplace communication which I am hypothesizing here on the basis of a limited set of criteria:

Table 4.9 *Communicative styles*

Style A	Style B	Style C
Relatively long turns with downtoners and explanations and 'apparent disclaimers', digressive discourse patterns, increase in speed and volume in order to maintain and appropriate turns, simultaneous speech, mixture of positive and negative politeness.	Relatively long turns (except in particular work situations), much repetition, rhetorical parallelism, bureaucratic style, increase in speed and volume in order to maintain turns but decrease in speed to appropriate them, positive politeness.	Relatively short turns, turn maintenance and appropriation attempted by elongation of words, a decrease in speed, rising intonation, and repetition, negative politeness expressed particularly through deferential speech, compliant with anticipated expectations (including commissives).

Style A (or many features of it) prevails among most of our Continental European respondents, Style B among those from a South Asian background as well as Iranians, and Style C among most of our South-east Asian informants. This transcends ethnic background or linguistic typology of the first language. We are dealing with cultural areas which may be larger than and embrace several *Kommunikationsbünde* of a sort (cf. reference to Neustupný, 1.3.7). There appear to be more variants of A than of B, and it may be that there are a number of independent centres where Style A is employed (e.g. the old Austro-Hungarian Empire, Greece, Spain and its former colonies). Style C is to be found in South-east Asians, especially from Confucian-based cultures, such as Viet-namese and Chinese.

In the past two chapters, I have mentioned Filipinas who take the responsibility for generating inter-cultural conversation just like Southern and Central Europeans and Latin Americans, another Filipina who is able to hold her own when her face is threatened, and an Indonesian who is successful in inter-cultural communication with speakers employing Style A or C. Responses to the video as well as the discourse of these responses confirm that some cultures of a particular area consistently adopt a communicative style, while others employ only some features. The areal cultures can be regarded as being on a continuum. Muslim-influenced Indonesians and Malays (but not Malaysian-Chinese) appear to be on the periphery of Style C, whereas Filipinos could be placed on the periphery of both the Style A and C areas (e.g. using personal questions of Style C (cf. Platt 1989), but with longer turns and the turn maintenance and appopriation conventions of A). Croats are at or near the centre of the (Central) European area employing Style C. There are no doubt characteristics of communicative behaviour where many of the cultural groups within an area diverge. In the present considerations, we are concerned with broad directions, proposed on the basis of a limited set of criteria. As this is an interactive inter-cultural study and not a contrastive one, our data is derived from 'contact' situations. As Neustupný (1985) has pointed out, norms in such situations may differ from those in 'native' communication.

4.10   Closing remarks

An intended message can be conveyed by a combination of the illocutionary and/or perlocutionary force of a series of utterances, turn behaviour and turn length. In the Australian inter-cultural workplace communication which I am examining, the power relations, social distance, and work arrangements in the workplace play an important part in determining the nature of discourse. There are particular tendencies of communicative behaviour which cluster together in speakers from certain parts of the world. The interface between speech acts and turn taking suggests the existence of at least three distinct communicative styles in our corpus, each of which predominates among immigrants from different areas. Some cultures can be more centrally identified with a particular style, others applying only some of the characteristics or even combining features of several styles. Style C, characteristic of most of the South-east Asians in our corpus, seems to disadvantage them in inter-cultural communication according to the norms of the other groups and to some extent those of the 'Anglo' majority. Not only do the South-east Asians often not 'get a go' in dialogues and discussions, they do not always understand the implications of what is said to them. What is more, the Europeans and South Asians with whom they are interacting cannot imagine that or why they are not seeing the implications. These issues will be considered in Chapter 6 in relation to the cultural value systems that give rise to variation in communicative behaviour, and the practical consequences will be considered in Chapter 7.

5   Written discourse across cultures

5.0   The cross-cultural study of written discourse

Although the present study is concerned with spoken discourse, I would like to discuss here some cross-cultural studies of written discourse, including ones which I have undertaken, as they may help to illuminate some relations between discourse and cultural values systems which will be taken up in Chapter 6 and particularly in Section 6.3. I will focus here on studies of coherence rather than of cohesion, in expository, not narrative discourse as it is here that the link with cultural values rather than linguistic structures is strongest. As written discourse is not the focus of the present study, I will restrict myself to some examples of the field.

For shorter, and particularly narrative texts, Givón (1983) has developed a quantitative model for cross-language discourse analysis to measure topic continuity (thematic, action, and topics/participants continuity) in discourse. This method is employed to analyze texts in eight languages of varying types. The measures used are: referential distance (the gap between the previous and current occurrence of the topic, up to 15 clauses); potential interference (the disruptive effect of other references on topic availability and identification, measured in the number of NPs (in 1 to 5 clauses to the left) with an argument comparable to the one under consideration), and persistence (the continued presence of a topic/participant as a semantic argument – in up to 5 successive clauses to the right).

The investigation of written (especially academic) discourse across cultures was initiated by Kaplan (1972), and it is his work that has provided the foundations for contrastive discourse analysis, also known as contrastive rhetoric (see also e.g. Kaplan 1988, Connor and Kaplan 1987). On the basis of English essays written by foreign students in the US, he postulated four kinds of discourse structures that contrasted in different ways with the English ideal of 'linear texts', focussing on paragraphing:

1. Parallel constructions, with the first idea completed in the second part.
2. Circularity, with the topic looked at from different tangents.
3. Freedom to digress and to introduce 'extraneous' material.
4. Similar to 3, but with different lengths, parenthetical amplications of subordinate elements, and no 'rounding off'.

Kaplan at that time (erroneously) linked the discourse types with genetic language types: 1 with 'Semitic', 2 with 'Oriental', 3 with 'Romance', 4 with 'Russian'. In fact, they should have been identified with cultures. 1 is characteristic of Arabic academic discourse, but not e.g. of Maltese academic discourse, which has been influenced by British norms. 2 is typical of Indonesian and Indian as well as Chinese, Japanese and Korean discourse (Pandharipande 1983, Kachru 1988, Hinds 1983a,b, 1984, Eggington 1987), and 3 of Central European discourse, including both German and Italian, as well as Spanish and Latin American (see below), but less of French, while 4 could be an Eastern European variant of 3.

Kaplan's pioneering study has led to much further study in this area – data collection and analysis in both the contrastive and interlanguage frameworks, and attitude testing. In the following brief literature survey, I will consider only top-to-bottom studies, and not ones such as Kroll (1990), focussing on number of words, syntactic variables, and lexical variables. This study of Arabic, Chinese, Spanish, and English compositions finds significant similarities between Spanish and Arabic that would not apply to the broad discourse level.

5.1   German/English

As a preliminary to our actual analysis of academic discourse, a small study was carried out on the expectations of expository discourse patterns in upper secondary education. This was based on an examination of English and German essay-writing manuals and the analysis of one set of school assignments each (in three subjects) from different Australian and German schools, together with marks and teachers' comments (Clyne 1980). The following expectations were deduced for English, but not for German:

1. Essay form is mandatory for most upper-secondary assignments (at least in Britain and Australia). (German answers can be in note form, in short sentences, in an essay, or even in a diagram.)
2. The aim of an essay has to be deduced from the wording of the topic or question. The topic has to be defined at the beginning of the essay.

(German topics, being more general, do not need to be considered so carefully.)
3. 'Relevance' is the most important criterion of a good essay. (There are few limitations on the inclusion of material in a German assignment as it is the extent and correctness of the content that is most important).
4. Repetition is not desirable. (As we will see, linearity is not a cultural requirement of German discourse as it is of English discourse. Thus, recapitulation is necessary to ensure logical development.)

An analysis of four years of final year secondary school examination reports in the state of Victoria (Australia) demonstrates that linearity and 'relevance' (i.e. excluding what is outside the confines of the wording of the topic) are the virtues sought (Clyne 1980), e.g.:

- Clearly many candidates had either a general knowledge of the topic ... or a thorough specific knowledge ... But just having such information is not what is required by most ... essays ... those who write controlled relevant essays will always be appropriately advantaged. (18th Century History 1978: 135)
- Lack of relevance remains the major cause of failure. (Politics 1987: 365)
- Rather than answer in structural terms, many resorted to circular arguments. (Biology 1972: 37)
- The link between marks gained and discourse structure was confirmed in a perusal of 400 History exam papers and examiners' comments. (Clyne 1980: 14–15)

The actual corpus of academic discourse comprised 52 linguistics and sociology texts of which 26 were written in English by native speakers of English who had received their secondary education and the bulk of their tertiary education in an English-speaking country (in this case, Australia, Britain, or the US). The other 26 texts were from native speakers of German who had received their secondary education and all or most of their tertiary education in Germany.[1] Seventeen of the texts were in German, the others in English. Texts were chosen and matched according to the discipline and sub-discipline, type of text (article, book chapter, published conference paper), topic, intention of the text, and the author's gender. (For details of the methodology and sample analyses, see Clyne 1987.)

The findings of the research show (Clyne 1987):

[1] Texts by Austrians and Swiss were examined at a later stage and found to have the same features as those by Germans.

1. Although there are texts by both English- and German-speaking writers which are more or less linear, those by Germans tend to contain more 'digressions'.

'Linearity' vs. 'digressiveness' is measured according to the position of propositions in relation to the macroproposition on which they are dependent. A text is 'slightly digressive' if:

(a) some propositions are dependent on the overarching proposition (macroproposition) of the section of the text in which they are situated;
(b) some propositions do not follow the macroproposition on which they depend; and/or
(c) some segments of the text are inserted inside another topic segment on a different topic (Clyne 1987: 225). (The term 'digression' is intended to be descriptive not judgmental, hence the inverted commas.)

'Digressions' generally fulfil particular functions in German academic texts. In our corpus, 'digressions' enable writers to add a theoretical component in an empirical text, a historical overview, ideological dimension, or simply more content, or engage in a continuing polemic with members of a competing school. As we shall see (below, 1.3.6 *re* Galtung, 6.3.1), these are all crucial aspects of German intellectual style and German culture. The presence of one or more sections labelled *Exkurs* (excursion, 'digression') in most good dissertations in German-speaking universities confirms that linearity is not a prerequisite of academic writing in German.

The texts written by Germans show more subordination at the discourse level (in the hierarchy of propositions) than do those by English speakers. Half the texts by English speakers exhibit both discourse subordination and co-ordination.

2. The Germans' texts exhibit both more textual and more propositional asymmetry than the texts by English-speaking scholars.

'Textual asymmetry' is where some sections of a text are very much longer than others, and 'propositional asymmetry' where there is an imbalance in the length of related propositions branching from the same macroproposition.

3. English-speaking scholars tend to use more advance organizers indicating the path and organization of the text and to place them early in the text. As 'digressions' in English texts are often marked ('Let us now digress to ...'), a text by an English speaker will be more 'predictable' than one by a German. In so far as advance organizers occur at all in German texts, they are often in obscure positions.

4. Key terms are more likely to be defined in a text by an English speaker. Such definitions will be found at or near the start in more texts by English speakers than in texts by German speakers, where the definition process may evolve in the course of the text.

5. Examples, statistics, and quotations are more likely to be embedded in the text by English-speaking scholars while German speakers may present them in an unintegrated way, e.g. at the end, in unexplained tables or footnotes.

A correlation analysis (Clyne and Kreutz 1987) has indicated a bundle of features in texts by English speakers which correlate significantly with linear organization. These can be regarded as the properties of a well-formed English academic text:

Early placement of advance organizers	1.000
Data integration	0.948
Propositional symmetry	0.887
Textual symmetry	0.843

No such concomitance occurs in German, where linearity correlates significantly only with advance organizers (0.985).

5.1.1 *Hedging in texts by English and German-speaking academics*

An analysis of hedging was undertaken on 12 matching pairs of texts randomly selected from our academic discourse corpus and matched according to length, discipline, and type of text (Clyne 1991b). Seven of the texts by German speakers are in German and five in English. The study concerns:

1. Hedged performatives, such as modals (can, may), parenthetical verbs (seem, appear, guess), and passive infinitives (it is to be hoped), e.g.:

Thus it <u>seems</u> unnecessary to discuss a new model here.

Summarizing these figures, it <u>can</u> be stated that...

2. Impersonal constructions, such as impersonal pronouns (one, there, anybody), impersonal intransitive (and perlocutionary) verbs (surprise, satisfy), impersonal phrases (there can be no doubt, it is clear, it is interesting), and reflexive constructions (*es zeigt sich* (it shows itself), *läßt sich erklären* (let itself be explained)), e.g.:

One can assume that there was competition for the better jobs.
There <u>it is obvious</u> that returnees are underprivileged.

Es fragt sich eben, ob nicht ... (No English equivalent. Literally:
'It asks itself if not ...')

3. Agentless passives (Passives without a by), e.g.:

Selection error must be regarded as a defect.

These findings contrast with those of House and Kasper (1981) for
spoken discourse in that the German authors used far more hedging than
their English-speaking peers. The total instances of hedging ranged from
1 to 14 in our texts by English speakers, from 7 to 54 in our German texts
by German speakers, and 19 to 44 in English texts by German speakers.
Texts by Germans contained far more examples of double hedging (more
than one type of hedging in the same proposition, e.g. modals and
agentless passives or subjunctive).

The average number of hedging instances in the texts by English
speakers was 6.25, in those by Germans it was 24 in German texts and
28.5 in English texts, probably due to the authors' uncertainty about
writing in a foreign language. Double hedging occurred an average of 1.7
times in texts by English speakers, 7.8 times in English texts by Germans,
and 6.14 times in German texts by Germans.

The use of hedging in academic discourse needs to be seen in relation
to authority and responsibility (cf. 1.3.8, 6.3.1). But, as with the discourse
structure, we are here in an area of cultural variation which is frequently
not understood as such.

5.1.2 *Survey*

Some of these conclusions on discourse structures were verified in a
questionnaire on the criteria of judging academic texts (Clyne, Hoeks,
and Kreutz 1988). It was administered on 14 (English-speaking)
Australian linguists, 14 German linguists, and 14 (English-speaking)
sociologists. (A group of 14 German sociologists, sampled for the
purpose, had to be abandoned owing to limited response.) The subjects
were also asked to answer comprehension questions and to assess the
difficulty and well-formedness of texts specially written in more typically
'English' and 'German' ways according to the results of our analysis.
Examples of the questions were: 'What do you like best about the text?';
'What do you like least about the text?'; and 'Can you suggest any
changes to improve the text?' This part of the research failed, largely
because extraneous features had been unwittingly introduced into the
text. However, the survey has provided us with information on the
criteria applied by Australian and German scholars to make such
judgments. A check on this was facilitated by a question in the

questionnaire eliciting the criteria of scholarship, e.g. factual information, theoretical framework (content orientation), organization or presentation of argument or information and readability (form orientation). Whereas Australian linguists are more form-oriented in their responses than German linguists, Australian sociologists stand out as the most content-oriented of the three groups. There were, of course, more formal-oriented and more content-oriented individuals in each of the groups.

Linearity is clearly the criterion of good textual construction for the Australians, but not for the Germans. If we include the correlates of linearity (symmetry, data integration, advance organizers, definition), 70.3 % of Australian linguists and 67.7 % of Australian sociologists, but only 41.4 % of German linguists, comment on these. On the other hand, information content features more prominently in the Germans' evaluations than in those of either group of Australians.

Linearity was also judged to be the main criterion of readability by both Australian groups (50.9 % of linguists, 35.2 % of sociologists), but not the German linguists (11.4 %), who were very conscious of communication barriers created by the use of abstract and 'difficult' words.

All these differences in discourse structures and discourse expectations should not be attributed to the languages, but rather to the cultures reproduced by the education system. It is in the evaluation of discourse that people from a dominant language or cultural group are most likely to be intolerant of, or insensitive to, variation. Thus, German-speaking scholars who are being forced to publish in English-medium international journals and to publish their books in English are being disadvantaged in the refereeing process and in reviews by the reaction of English-speaking peers to their 'un-English-' discourse patterns (Clyne 1981, 1991b).

Among criticisms that have been levelled at the above projects are the use of the line as the unit of counting and the lack of information on the number of words (Sachtleber 1990), and the absence of a verifiable presentation of methodological instructions and text corpus (Oldenburg 1992), making replication of the above studies difficult (Sachtleber 1990). Oldenburg (1992) finds that there are no criteria for 'digressiveness' and that text types and subject areas are not sufficiently sharply divided. Gnutzmann and Oldenburg (1991) regret that the texts were taken from different informants and suggest that variation may depend on the level of abstraction. Gnutzmann (1992) rejects without any argument the suggestion that academic texts need to be restructured in translation (Clyne 1981: 65). The rejection of the assumption that networks of texts are the only possible textual analysis (Oldenburg 1992) is puzzling since I never made such a claim.

Many of these criticisms are quite valid. Early attempts in a relatively new field are often methodologically unsophisticated. In this case, there is necessarily a subjective and non-quantifiable element in the analysis of top-to-bottom phenomena in long texts and particularly in determining cut-off points between categories. This is admitted in Clyne (1987: 224) and addressed by a co-operation between the researcher and research assistants with slightly different bilingual/bicultural backgrounds and, where necessary, further opinions elicited from other colleagues. The general criteria for digressiveness were stated (with examples and sample analyses (1987: 225)) and are indicated again in this section. Text types are matched across the languages in each subject area of the corpus. I believe that, as more work is carried out in this field – such as that of Gnutzmann, Oldenburg, and Sachtleber – methods will be refined.

Considering the task of a complete analysis of academic texts in German and English not possible, Gnutzmann and Oldenburg (1991) conduct an analysis of 40 introductions and 40 conclusions from the American linguistics journal, *Language*, and a German one, *Linguistische Berichte*. The introductions in *Language* and *Linguistische Berichte* were highly conventionalized and very similar. However, the conclusions in *Linguistische Berichte* were longer than, and not as 'forceful', as the Anglo-American counterparts. Discourse markers signal a change of perspective in the conclusions in 50% of boundaries between text segments in *Language* and 35% of those in *Linguistische Berichte*. It needs to be stressed that *Linguistische Berichte* started as a disseminator of modern American-dominated linguistic ideas.

Oldenburg (1992) analyzes summaries in a German-language and a comparable English-language journal in each of the subjects of linguistics, economics, and mechanical engineering. Four types of summaries are proposed: summarizing, discursive, concluding, and complex summaries. In mechanical engineering, there are strong similarities between the English and German texts, but, in economics, the differences are substantial with more summarizing summaries in the American journal. In linguistics, summaries are more clearly developed than in the other disciplines. *Language* has more complex summaries than any of the other journals in any discipline, stressing the contribution of one's own results. *Language* and *Linguistische Berichte* show the biggest interlingual differences, e.g. in the relative frequency of the four types of summaries mentioned above. Also, in English, contextualized sentence structures are signalled through a small number of lexical indicators, while, in German, lexical indicators can occur in many situations.

Stahlheber (1992) compares diachronically articles in the journals *Science* and *Die Naturwissenschaften*. She finds that there is far more fluctuation in the syntactic complexity of articles in the German journal than in those in the American one as well as an increase in passive use. On the other hand, *Science* is characterized by a decrease in syntactic complexity from 1919–46 and an increase from 1946–87. Interestingly, Stahlheber attributes increased syntactic complexity and passive use in the German journal to English influence.

5.2   Studies of other European languages

5.2.1   *German/French*

Sachtleber (1990) focusses on three criteria of the adequacy of academic texts – linearity, completion (following an outline) and symmetry, and orientation aids for the reader. The corpus comprises 10 German and 10 French congress papers at an international Romance linguistics conference. (It is not explicitly stated that the 10 papers in French were given by French speakers.) Sachtleber describes the German texts as more linear, and contends that for that reason they do not necessitate orientation aids (advance organizers) as do the French ones. Nevertheless, the German texts contain more instances of a switch in discourse level from the expository to the metalinguistic signals such as reference and commentary.

5.2.2   *German/Norwegian*

Feigs (1991) suggests that German academic discourse is more polemic than its Norwegian equivalent, with more emphasis on reproaching rather than praising colleagues. Drawing heavily on Galtung (1985), he stresses the theoretical nature of German academic discourse in contrast to the balance between theory and documentation in Norwegian. Norwegian academic texts are (even) more indirect than German ones. Unfortunately we are not told anything about the source of Feigs' data.

5.2.3   *Russian*

Punkki and Schröder (1989) examine the style of two Russian academics, the sociologist Andrejenkova and the philosopher Semjonov. While there are some common elements, e.g. markers of authority, the method of citing and extracting, there are major differences – in the degree of linearity (much greater in the philosopher), thematic progression (sociologist) vs. progression through hyperthemes (philosopher), theoretical orientation (philosopher) vs. thesis orientation (sociologist). Although this is not a cross-cultural project, it is part of a larger one, contrasting Finnish, German, and Russian discourse, using common criteria.

5.2.4   *English/Australian/American/Finnish/Dutch/German*

Degenhart and Takala (1988) conducted an analysis of upper-secondary school students' work from Australia, Finland, the Netherlands, and the US. The Australian (92%) and American (89%) essays show a clear preference for linear structure, while the Finnish ones (53%) do not. The Finnish scripts indicate a preference for logical connection, precision, conciseness, and exhaustiveness not 'narrowed to one point'. The Dutch essays use 'digressions as needed'. It will be noted that the Finnish and Dutch written academic discourse patterns are between the English and the German norms.

This 'in-between' position of Finnish in written discourse is confirmed by Korhonen and Kusch's (1989) study of philosophical texts, although here the school of philosophy plays an important role. Finnish Marxists adopt a more abstract passive and generic pattern, like most German philosophers, especially Marxists. Other Finnish philosophers use more passives in Finnish texts, but I and we in English ones.

5.2.5   *Finnish/English/German*

In their comparison of editorials in Finnish, English, and German quality newspapers, Tirkkonen-Condit and Liefländer-Koistinen (1989) find that Finnish newspapers are the most likely by far to publish editorials without a thesis. Where there is one, it is least likely to appear initially in the Finnish papers.

5.3   East and South-east Asian/English, German

If English and German discourse structures diverge considerably, this will be all the more the case where the cultural parameters are very different. The original Kaplan judgment that Oriental discourse is circular has received widespread currency. Hinds (e.g. 1980, 1983a,b,) has described three organizational patterns ('return to baseline theme', the 'tempura model' and *ki-sho-ten-ketsu* 'beginning-development-change of direction-conclusion', based on a classical Chinese rhetorical pattern) in Japanese expository prose which do not occur in English. His model covers the examination of unity ('logical development' and flow of thought), focus (staying on a topic without wandering), and coherence ('sticking together' of major points of writing; use of transition). In many ways, the reasons for Japanese discourse being so different from English discourse are not unlike those for German discourse being different. In Japanese as in German (but in contrast to English), the emphasis is far more on content than on form. Hence, linearity is not an important virtue. Because advance organizers are explicitly not tolerated, the 'return to the baseline theme' is obligatory. Hinds (1980) shows this through the translation of a Japanese newspaper article where the main topic keeps recurring, seen from different perspectives as it is not indicated explicitly as such. As Harder (1984) indicates, Japanese discourse suggests possibilities, while English discourse argues ideas, supporting them more forcefully.

Eggington (1987) contrasts traditional Korean discourse with texts that are modelled on American patterns. The more traditional structure is a 'back to the baseline' one, *ki-sung-choon-kyul*, which is similar to the Japanese *ki-shoo-ten-ketsu*. In a version described by Eggington, a statement is presented, then various parts are developed, one by one, then a number of sub-arguments are developed, one by one.

Kirkpatrick (1992a,b) shows that Chinese letters of request follow a different pattern to their English equivalents in that the former require introductory explanations and justifications before the focus on the actual request. However, there is a great deal of variation in the structure of Chinese academic essays. The traditional *qi cheng zhuan he* (on which the above-mentioned 'opening-joining-turning point-conclusion' structures in Japanese and Korean are based) was partly displaced by the eight-legged *ba gu wen* (the examination style of the Ming and Qing dynasties, 1368–1911) in the public service exam. Kirkpatrick points out that this style has been discredited in the People's Republic of China as an 'imperialist' one, but refutes the claim that there has been a return to the earlier style under a new name (*flaseng- fazhuan- gaochao- jieju*), arguing that all the styles have been changing and adapted over time. In addition, some scholars follow organizational structures similar to Western ('Anglo-American'?) essays. Liu Mingchen (1990) describes the structure of a typical Chinese literary criticism article as *Qi, cheng, zhuan, he, jie* – beginning, transition, turn, synthesis, end. The transition is a point hinted at and put aside as if it is to lie in ambush until the time comes (Liu Mingchen 1990: 40). The turn often comprises 'twists'. The end is a double-layered macrostructural synthesis rounding up various aspects of argument and, at the same time, presenting the critic's expectations. Mohan and Lo (1985), on examining essays written by Chinese students, claim that they exhibit a high degree of linearity. They challenge Kaplan's conclusions about differences between Chinese and English essay-writing patterns and some of the basic assumptions about the culture specific in discourse.

Taylor and Chen (1991) examine the introductions only of 31 academic texts in the *physical* sciences, which tend to be more 'international' and 'Anglo-dominated' than the social sciences and humanities. Eleven were written in English by English speakers, 10 in English by Chinese speakers, and 10 in Chinese by Chinese speakers. The study is based on Swales' (1984) method of discourse analysis. It points to commonalities between the essays on a disciplinary basis and systematic variation due to culture rather than language. The discourse of the Chinese is shorter, less likely to elaborate moves and more likely to use unconventional moves, while many of the texts by the Chinese delete the literature survey. The Chinese discourse tends to be less dialogic than 'western' ('Anglo-American'?) discourse (cf. the relative tendency against open discussion and long turns).

Yong Liang (1991), in a comparison of *reviews* by Chinese and Germans, points to two major differences:

(i) the absence of any categorically negative evaluation in the reviews by Chinese, with any criticisms being expressed ambiguously, in contrast to the critical evaluations in the German reviews; and
(ii) the insertion of a positive appraisal very early in the text.

In an article on communication between Vietnamese and non-Vietnamese, Cam Nguyên (1991: 43) refers incidentally to a Vietnamese discourse pattern designated as '*rao truoc, don sau*' ('considering all implications and answering all possible objections'), i.e. not 'com(ing) straight to the point but looking at various aspects with a bearing on the point'. This agrees with the Chinese, Korean and Japanese patterns mentioned above.

In a comparison of 40 American English and 50 Thai essays, Bickner and Peysantiwong (1988) find that, while the American English essays accept the tasks in the task description, the Thai ones tend to catalogue characteristics, a major coherence device dating back to fifteenth-century poetry. Whereas the English essays end with an identifiable concluding section encompassing a restatement and predictions of future implications, the majority of the Thai essays that actually have conclusions merely restate.

5.4   South Asian/English

Kachru (1983), in a paper constrasting written discourse in Hindi and English, indicates that Hindi expository texts show a greater degree of tolerance for 'digression' in paragraphs than their English counterparts. The digressions link episodes 'in a spiral-like structure' (Kachru 1983: 58). However, Pandharipande (1983), who comments on the digressiveness of Marathi expository prose, describes its paragraph structure as circular, with the conclusion at the beginning and the end and arguments in the middle. Kachru (1988) refers to studies of classical Indian discourse, based on an oral tradition, which suggest either a spiral or a circular structure. A similar structure is attributed by Kapanga (1992: 337) to African (francophone) discourse. As Chinese and Japanese discourse, Indian discourse does not require an explicit statement. In addition, the paragraph does not have to show a unity of topic, and a claim and its justification do not have to be in the same paragraph. While there *are* linear texts, 38% of the opening paragraphs examined by Kachru (1988) in scientific texts are non-linear, as are 40% of the opening paragraphs in her literary criticism texts.

5.5   Arabic

If there is one culture which exhibits a greater preference for formal (rather than content) considerations than the 'Anglo-American', it is the Arabic. This is shown in Kaplan (1972) and strongly supported by Ostler's (1987) study of 21 expository English essays by Saudi Arabian students (in comparison with a corpus derived from English academic publications). They demonstrate a rhythmic balance where one proposition is followed by a parallel one in contrast or similarity – an ancient Semitic rhetorical pattern to be found in the Psalms, the Lord's Prayer, the Beatitudes, and the Koran. Ostler attributes this to the type of subordination in Arabic. Kaplan (1988) suggests that the Arabic texts' preference for Koranic style symbolizes that the text represents the truth. Kaplan's position is challenged by Sa'adeddin (1989), who attributes 'repetition' and 'redundancy' to aurally developed Arabic discourse. This he distinguishes from visually developed discourse – whose structures are sometimes transferred to written Arabic texts and to English texts written by Arabic speakers. Visually developed discourse has similar norms to English written discourse.

5.6   (Chilean) Spanish, Vietnamese/(English)

Farrell (1994) has been analyzing ten essays each from a number of subjects of four upper-secondary school students in Melbourne, two Chilean and two Vietnamese (one male and one female from each group). The essays of the Chileans are more abstract, digressive, and content-oriented, exhibiting more discourse subordination, and those of one of the Vietnamese more concrete, linear, form-oriented and co-ordinative, with the other also tending in that direction. The teachers marking the essays are guided by the Anglo-Australian norms which are between those of the two cultural groups under investigation. The Chileans' essays are often dismissed as largely irrelevant.

5.7   Israeli-born/Western and Eastern European/Asia Minor immigrants in Israel

In her study of letters received by the Israeli customs office, Danet (1970) investigates the appeal strategies of different cultural (and professional) groups. The Israeli-born choose the 'most bureaucratic' patterns – appeal to impersonal norms and (at least in brief letters) to the officials' altruism. This decreases the more 'western' the origin of the writer. The higher the writer's professional status, the more likely it is that they will appeal to an impersonal norm. East and West European immigrants will tend to make requests based on professional needs and those from Asia Minor on the grounds of family obligations.

5.8   South Asian/Middle Eastern

An analysis of 20 randomly selected letters from each of two regions, South Asia (India, Pakistan, Bangladesh, Sri Lanka) and the Middle East (Egypt, Syria, Jordan, Kuwait, Lebanon, Libya, Oman, Morocco, Saudi Arabia) requesting entrance information from an Australian university (Clyne 1991c) yielded contrastive information on discourse sequencing and request strategies. The letters generally demonstrate a high degree of creativity. Nearly all of them gave an introduction and an expression of interest before coming to the actual request, like the letters of request examined by Kirkpatrick (5.3, above).

The South Asian letters contain expressions of deference, e.g.:

I beg to state.
I have the honour to intimate.
respected Sir.

> Your Honour.
> your esteemed university.

which are not considered appropriate in Australian English. The author's own face is boosted by family, academic, and financial status descriptions, where the effects of both the colonial class system and the Indian caste system may be observed,[2] e.g.:

> My family background too is excellent.
> I possess very good academic career.
> I am well able to finance myself and to fulfil all and any sorts of required expenditure.

Vocatives of address (e.g. Respected Sir, Please Sir) introduce every segment or request in some letters.

The Middle Eastern sample shows more individual variability than that from the Indian sub-continent. Although most of them are able to address the registrar, two omitted the head altogether or devised a personal opening routine, e.g.:

> I hope that you are in good health.
> Good morrning (sic) or after Good Night.

In some cases this led to a mixing of formal and informal registers, e.g.:

> – Dear Sir:
> Hello, hope you are doing well.
> – Dear Sir,
> I hope you are well and enjoying your self.

Expressions of deference are similar to those from the South Asian students. Among the routines supporting their request for information are desperate appeals for pity:

> – My life is now in danger, but to give up my studies I loose my future ... So I'm turning to you in my plight. (Lebanese)
> – I worked as a broiler mgr for 5000000 chiks 1984–1985 in UNITED ARAB EMARETS. (Syrian)

The parallel structure described in Kaplan (1972) and Ostler (1987) and attributed by Sa'adeddin (1989) to 'aurally developed discourse' is to be found in some of the letters, e.g.:

My Dear respecter Master x University Good morrning or after good night. [Greeting]

[2] In an earlier study of letters to the Australian immigration authorities (Clyne 1979), self-eulogy was a characteristic of some of the Asians' letters, but not of those of the European writers.

I hope to complete my university studies. I begged to accepte my application in your university. [Introduction and request]
I gained beshelor (Lecence of Arts and Education). My Department is Arabic Language. [Elaboration of introduction]. (Clyne 1991c: 214)

The letter is opened with the Islamic greeting:

The Name of Allah The Benefecent, the Mirciful.

5.9   Closing remarks

Clearly the temporal nature of spoken discourse such as our workplace corpus contrasts sharply with the academic texts produced for more permanent consumption (cf. 1.0). However, there are a number of commonalities which are important for the understanding of inter-cultural communication. Firstly, in both types of discourse, what is significant in the relevant cultural values system of the group and the individual influences the way in which they communicate in a first or a second language. Secondly, the impact of the cultural values system on discourse patterns transcends individual cultures. We have seen in Chapter 4 how this works for spoken discourse. There are also areal cultures which share features such as 'back to baseline' patterns, a requirement of linearity, parallelism or functions for 'digressions', general concreteness or abstractness, symmetry, or an emphasis on form or content. Thirdly, discourse patterns are concomitant with discourse expectations. These are transmitted through the education system. Finally, intolerance of culture-bound pragmatic and discourse patterns is far greater than a rejection of foreignness markers at the phonological or grammatical levels. It is striking how difficult it is for people to apply cultural relativity to the variation in discourse and not be judgmental.

These issues relating to cultural values will be dealt with in detail in Chapter 6 as we explore the possible basis of a linguistics of inter-cultural communication.

6 Towards a linguistics of inter-cultural communication

6.0 Opening remarks

In Chapters 3, 4, and 5, I reported on data concerning areal variation in the use and expectations of discourse patterns (speech acts and their sequencing in complex interactions, turn taking, organization of discourse). It appears that this is attributable to cultural differences, with the styles of specific cultural groups being more or less typical of areal styles A, B, and C. This applies to written, as well as to spoken (workplace), discourse data which provide the focus of this monograph. In this chapter, I will first examine some of the discourse features in relation to the cultural values systems of their cultural groups, based on the work of others, utilizing especially the framework of Hofstede (1984, 1991). It will be recalled from 1.3.8, that Hofstede's four parameters are – power distance, individualism (vs. collectivism), masculinity (vs. femininity), and uncertainty avoidance. Then I will suggest some parameters determining cultural values in discourse itself. I would like to stress that this is intended not to create or reinforce stereotypes in the evaluative sense but to explain the tendencies in our data in each culture's own terms. Finally I shall 'revisit' the Gricean maxims and attempt some revisions of them in the light of our data and of the parameters proposed and the cultural values discussed. Some other models (e.g. Brown and Levinson) will also be included in the discussion.

In this chapter, I will also attempt to integrate findings from the project on inter-cultural communication in the workplace with ones from my own and others' work on academic discourse (Chapter 5). The commonality is in the relation between discourse patterns and cultural values systems. One of the differences is that between the predominantly 'contrastive' dimension in the academic discourse corpus and the 'interactive' dimension of the workplace data. Another difference lies in the nature of the corpora – one limited in domain and context, but rather comparable, the other vast and quite heterogeneous. However, the cross-fertilization of insights from the analysis of both sets of data will

176

facilitate the proposal of the discourse-cultural parameters which will form the basis of my concept of a linguistics of inter-cultural communication.

6.1   Cultural boundaries

It is extremely difficult to draw boundaries between cultures. To what extent are they unified or divided by language, 'ethnicity' (in itself an ill-definable concept, cf. Fishman et al. 1985: 70, Vallée 1975: 167, Glazer and Moynihan 1975, especially Isaacs 1975), class, religion, and region? Are North German Protestants representative of the same culture as Bavarian Catholics or, indeed, Swabian Protestants? Do Lebanese Muslims and Lebanese Maronites belong to the same culture? Do Tuscans and Calabrians? Working-class Lancastrians and upper middle-class people from Surrey? Recent political developments indicate national self-identities with a long historical memory in the former Soviet Union, Yugoslavia, and Czechoslovakia.

On the other hand, through the formation of *Kommunikationsbünde*[1] (see Neustupný 1969, 1978 and above, 1.3.7), cultural differences between contiguous groups (including those belonging to larger polities) are often broken down or diluted. The communicative styles I am describing are based on cultural areas broader than *Kommunikationsbünde* – European (sometimes subdivided into Central and Southern European as there is hardly any data from Northern Europeans in the corpus), South Asian, and South-east Asian (see 2.3). There are, of course, major differences as well as smaller variations within these areas, some of which will be discussed, and most of which cannot be dealt with in this study due to limited data. Within the broader cultural areas, I will follow Hofstede (1984, 1991) and take 'national cultures' as the starting-point.

As will be recalled from 2.3, the European groups represented here are, in the main, those from the Catholic South and Centre. Included are also Greeks and Macedonians, who are Orthodox, and Maltese, who had in succession been conquered by eight European and Middle Eastern nations and whose culture has been substantially influenced by both the Italians and the British (cf. Cauchi 1990: 1–3). Where there is data from Turks or Arabs, this has been indicated as a separate category.

The cultures of South-east Asia most represented in the corpus – Chinese from Malaysia, Singapore, Cambodia and Vietnam, and ethnic

---

[1] I have been unsuccessful in finding an adequate translation. It is perhaps not surprising that *Sprachbund* and *Sprechbund* were employed as 'loanwords' from German.

Vietnamese – are Confucian-based, whatever adstrata may have influenced them, e.g. English or French (Christian) through colonialism and the education system. But among the South-east Asians we also have represented Malay, Indonesian, and Filipino cultures. The first two are influenced by Islam and by the former European colonizing power (Britain and the Netherlands respectively). Mayers (1984: 11) writes of the Philippines: 'Geography has made the Philippines an Asian country, but history has made it a unique blend of the East and West, a structure has emerged which is uniquely Filipino.' The commonalities between the communication patterns of the groups designated as 'South Asian' will be deduced from Chapters 3, 4, and 5. This is despite the inclusion of a Fijian Indian in the category. As Hofstede (1984: 228) has shown for Belgium and Switzerland, different ethnolinguistic groups within one nation may share one value system or have divergent ones. Although the North Indians came to Fiji mainly between 1876 and 1916 (the South Indians starting to arrive in 1903), Indians have maintained a separate existence from the Fijians (Siegel 1987). This is attributed by Siegel (1987: 110) to the 'continued vitality' of Hindi to 'continued ethnic divisions within the country'. On the other hand, there are commonalities in communication patterns between the Burghers (and Anglo-Indians) and the others from the South Asian region. The Burghers, largely the Christian descendants of Portuguese and Dutch in Sri Lanka (formerly Ceylon) were, to a large extent, integrated into the multicultural population of that island. While they were among the more western-oriented sections of the population, often regarding themselves as Europeans, they could be found in different strata. They were well represented in the elites – professionals and public servants – before Independence, they were also represented among the poorer sections (De Silva et al. 1973).

As has been intimated in Chapter 4, each cultural area has core and peripheral areas which can be designated according to discourse and pragmatic indices as well as the cultural values systems mediating them.

6.2   Cultural values systems – sociocultural interactional parameters as an explanation of communication patterns

Let us now consider some features of the various cultural values systems as described in anthropological/ethnographic studies and surveys which may throw some light on interactions discussed in Chapters 3 and 4. The discussion will be based on a small number of informants and texts which give clear-cut illustrations of more general tendencies.

6.2.1   *Polish and Malaysian-Chinese – relationships* (*SELF-REPROACH*)

According to Wedel (1986: 36), 'Poles use social networks to solve their everyday problems to accomplish day-to-day tasks ranging from buying batteries to resolving bureaucratic impasses to bailing out arrested friends or family members.' Almost all successful business relationships are based on personal ones. There is a verb *zatawic*, 'to arrange, settle, wrangle' which expresses the Polish way of achieving this. This practice has its parallels in other Central European cultures, e.g. Hungarian, Austrian, Croatian (*sich etwas richten*, Austrian German, *kijárni* Hungarian, *srediti*, Serbian and Croatian) (Leslie Bodi and Peter Hill, personal communications). In her apology interaction with Jennifer, Krysztina was aiming at receiving an assurance of Jennifer's patronage and support.

This is in many ways quite different to the Chinese concept of *guanxi* (Brick 1991: 127), 'the network of mutual obligations that bind people together … founded on family ties, ties of shared experience and ties of friendship'. *Guanxi* arrangement is a more permanent one, often extending over generations. (Malaysian-Chinese whom I questioned about this were not aware of the term, but knew the concept.)

Brick (1991: 120) comments that, in Chinese, the apology is often conveyed through body language, e.g. smile, bowing, or even silence, instead of 'verbally', and that the Chinese are surprised by the amount of apologizing that takes place among Australians of British and European descent to whom sin and guilt, rather than relationships, are the basis of social control (cf. Brick 1991: 127). The distinction is sometimes made between 'shame' and 'guilt' cultures (e.g. Hofstede 1991: 60). The relative absence of the use of apologies in Chinese and other Asian cultures (South-east and South Asian), which is confirmed in our corpus (3.4.1) is also related to their collectivist values. In view of all this, it is very likely that a Chinese speaker does not understand what the surface intention of Krysztina's interaction is. Perhaps the South-east Asian–Chinese equivalent would occur in a more 'established' relationship in which no direct communication is required. In that case, Jennifer would not have recognized this as its equivalent.

Krysztina's apology is, however, evidence of a high level of uncertainty avoidance; she is exhibiting pessimism and a fear of failure, e.g.

> it was my fault alright.
> probably she thinks I'm bad because she wants that job.
> he said oh you should leave that job.

This makes it all the more difficult for her message to be understood by Jennifer whose culture, according to Hofstede, has a low uncertainty avoidance. The communication breakdown leads to an even longer apology from a person employing Style A in interaction with a person employing Style C.

6.2.2 Austrian and Vietnamese – phatic introduction (FIVE DAYS OFF, BROKEN PARTS)

Hofstede (1984: 157), referring to the Austrian combination of small power distance and medium individuality, indicates that, in Austria, political superstructures prevail without this threatening 'easy-going' personal relationship between superiors and individuals sometimes interpreted as Austrian 'charm'. On the other hand, Austrians show a fairly high Uncertainty Avoidance Index which is demonstrated in a certain extrovertness such as self-irony and talking your way politely out of stress situations. This is difficult to grasp by Vietnamese women. If their level of uncertainty avoidance and individuality is shared with the surrounding cultures which are included in Hofstede (1984: 159), the Vietnamese value system combines high power distance with low individuality index. 'Confucian dynamism' (Hofstede 1991: 164–5) entails, among other things, 'stability of society based on unequal relationships between people'. This may explain why they cannot understand the necessity of the Austrian leading hand's 'phatic communication' as the politic introduction to the 'work communication'.

6.2.3 Croatian and Malaysian-Chinese, Singapore-Malay, Vietnamese – giving and accepting expressions of authority (BAD SOLDERING, WAITING TIME, WORK ETHICS)

According to Hofstede, 'Yugoslavs' combine large power distance, low individuality, and high uncertainty avoidance. This is confirmed in our data from Croatians. The prime examples are Slobodan's exchanges with South-east Asian women. His communication patterns, e.g.:

> I don't understand the one things peoples are not ashamed to sitting   doing nothing.
> if somebody doesn't like the job then try to escape from a job because doing it wrong no hope about that.

indicate a strong collective work ethic based on loyalty to the job as well as authoritarianism. They also reflect a high level of anxiety and mentality which requires rules for everything. In stressing the role of Catholicism in a strong Uncertainty Avoidance Index and a low Individuality Index, Hofstede (1984: 137, 172) draws on the Max Weber (1904/5/1930) thesis that Protestantism, especially Calvinism, gave rise to the culture of capitalism and individualism in Northern European-based national cultures. I would like to draw attention to Slobodan's pre-Australian experience in German industry. While he has clearly been influenced by the ethos of self-discipline and the service of capitalism, this has been embedded in a Catholic collective ethic which contrasts to 'pessimistically inclined individualism' (Weber 1930: 105). The complaints (3.1, see also the above examples) and the apologies in *BAD SOLDERING*, e.g.:

> not much sorry about it.
> if we blame you for things what you didn't done we apologize but anyway it would happen.

demonstrate that keeping face depends on his power dominance. This may also be seen in the Croatian women, Irma and Boba (to a lesser extent in the latter because of the collegial work relations with Quoc). A high level of anxiety is also reflected in Irma's and Boba's communication patterns, e.g. (*EVERYTHING WENT WRONG* where Boba is devising precautions against evening staff stealing her pens):

> even the er people from the evening they just took my black pen all the time and because of that I'm not taking them out any more I'm gunna sort this problem I'm gunna have a pen with a string I will stick.

In *THE FAX*, Boba's 'collective' spirit and negative politeness, saving Quoc's face, prevent her from refusing to send the fax, while her own face saving and large power distance orientation prevents her from collecting the incoming fax. Her cultural tendency towards uncertainty avoidance causes her to make a major issue out of this and to clarify the bounds of her co-operation. I have referred in a number of sections (3.1.2, 3.2.4, 3.3.1) to the use of the first person plural in directives and complaints as well as in self-directive commissives.

Hofstede's placement of 'Yugoslavs' in the low masculinity category may be justified in our corpus by the large amount of negotiation that the Croatians are involved in. But it is contradicted by the relatively little opportunity that they give their subordinates or colleagues to present their view within the negotiation process due to their own long turns. This applies particularly to Slobodan, who dominates all discourse, more so than to Irma and Boba, but our data does not suggest that the Croatians behave very differently in this regard to other Central Europeans. (Our corpus does not allow us to say anything about Serbs or Bosnian Muslims, for example.)

That the 'South-east Asians' allow themselves to be dominated may be partly due to the fact that they share with 'Yugoslavs' low individuality/high collectivity and large power distance (Hofstede 1984). Brick (1991: 131, 138) refers to the Chinese respect for authority. Hofstede (1991: 40) traces to Confucius the South-east/East Asian cultural acceptance of inequality and feeling that 'the use of power should be maintained by a sense of obligation' (but see also Harmony, 6.2.7). However, political and economic exigencies have brought about some changes within certain cultural constraints. For instance, Chan (1992) has shown that, in Asian societies such as Singapore, Taiwan, and South Korea, social redistribution and economic development have led to human rights, the eradication of poverty and want, and increasing self-esteem and empowerment, with the subsequent evolution of a more open and participatory society.

The South-east Asians cannot see why Slobodan is so anxious. 'The open expression of strong emotions', writes Brick (1991: 113), 'is not encouraged in Chinese culture'. Slobodan's rights-based Central European (and Australian) moral system contrasts with the Chinese, charity-based one (Brick 1991: 132). He keeps on rehearsing the rules which he wants to reinforce. As was mentioned also in 6.2.1, the Singaporean–Hong Kong Chinese low Uncertainty Avoidance Index (Hofstede 1984) makes it difficult for them (and people from similar cultural backgrounds) to grasp why the Central European is creating so much fuss and anxiety.

Uncertainty avoidance is also reflected in the need for confirmation by Croatians (3.2.1, 4.5) which, however, does lead to clarification (4.3.1).

6.2.4   Central European Catholicism (SELF-REPROACH)

I have referred above (6.2.3) to Hofstede's link between three of his parameters (high Uncertainty Avoidance Index, fairly low Individuality Index, high Power Distance Index) and the Catholic ethos. Weber (1930: 40) contrasts Catholic 'otherworldliness' requiring security, and Protestant/Calvinist 'worldliness', desiring risk and enjoyment. In the Catholic ethos, the Church as a collective and the priest as God's representative and the Icon of Christ provides this security through the sacraments. For instance, in the sacrament of Reconciliation (Confession), the penitent needs only to confess his (her) sins for them to be freed of guilt and its consequences, through the words of Absolution pronounced by the priest. Hofstede (1991: 32) regards confession of sins as a practice which fits the strong uncertainty avoidance cultural pattern and relates it to the western concept of Truth – Confession is a way of preserving a rule which cannot be kept. In *SELF-REPROACH*, the notion of Confession is transferred to the secular domain of the workplace where the immediate superior is the corresponding authority figure who is seen to be able to 'free' the person of guilt on behalf of the collective of the company. As Jennifer is not familiar with the religious situation or its transfer, she takes a long time to stumble on the appropriate words.

6.2.5 South Asian (*BAD SERVING, MULTISKILLING, FEELING BETTER, BRIEFING ON CHANGES,* and others).

As may be seen in 3.1.1, Tim reflects the low individuality attributed by Hofstede to Indians in so far as he creates a 'collective' around him and ensures that all members of it share the responsibility of enforcing the regulations on the hostel diners. This behaviour is also a manifestation of the power distance in South Asians, also evident in Khalil's, Dulip's, Mick's and Raymond's long turns (e.g. *BRIEFING ON CHANGES, DYEING AND LOADING, SICK LEAVE, MULTISKILLING, FEELING BETTER*). Another reflection of the power distance is the bureaucratic tone. The Burghers were overrepresented in the public service elite in the old Ceylon (De Silva et al. 1973). Indians often follow legal careers in countries such as Malaysia, Singapore, and Fiji. South Asian instances of repetition and reformulation are largely strategies of uncertainty avoidance, which is fairly high in the one South Asian group (Pakistanis) on whom Hofstede has statistics.

6.2.6 Filipinas between East and West – small talk (*PERSONAL QUESTIONS, BAD SOLDERING*)

As is aptly pointed out in the Mayers citation (5.1), Philippines culture is very much at the crossroads, where first Chinese, then Spanish and finally American influence on the basically Malay culture has created a sort of 'hybrid' peripheral communication style. Hofstede's analysis – very large power distance, low individuality, and low uncertainty avoidance – is reflected in deference to the boss (4.5), but articulate chatty conversation with equals (e.g. *PERSONAL QUESTIONS*, 3.5). The deference is exhausted, however, when a Filipino/a's face is threatened severely, as when Slobodan wrongly accuses Ricarda (*BAD SOLDERING*). Impulsive, Latin-American type initiative-taking is combined with a barrage of personal questions in the South-east Asian style (cf. Platt 1989). Hence the positive response from the Vietnamese interlocutor in *PERSONAL QUESTIONS* when a European might be offended.

Incidentally, adaptability to foreign influences has also somewhat moderated the (still present) South-east Asian tendencies towards high masculinity, high power distance, and low uncertainty avoidance in Malays and Indonesians (Hofstede 1991). This may be what gives them the 'peripheral' discourse style that makes them effective inter-cultural communicators.

6.2.7   *Harmony: Vietnamese but also ethnic Chinese and South-east Asians generally, interacting with Central Europeans. (GENDER ERROR, TAKING ON CELIA, FIVE DAYS OFF, BROKEN PARTS, and others)*

The Confucian-based notion of harmony is one of the main Chinese and Vietnamese manifestations of the collective ideal (low Individualism Index) (cf. Brick 1990: 131–2, Hsu 1972). Cam Nguyên (1991) argues that the Vietnamese values of preserving harmony and concern for face saving (one's own and the others') mean that the interlocutors' expectations are the basis for the choice of utterance content. She also attributes to this the Vietnamese preference of withdrawal over conflict resolution, for assertiveness indicates a lack of respect. This can help us explain the non-involvement of Vietnamese in several of the encounters in which they were present, and a contribution limited to back-channelling or a few words in nine encounters, what I have described as the 'disadvantage of the South-east Asians' (4.6.3). It can also explain perhaps the very limited representation of South-east Asians in general, and Vietnamese in particular, in quality control groups in the workplaces studied. In Slobodan's exchange with Jennifer and Hung (*TAKING ON CELIA*), totalling 8 minutes 30 seconds, the latter talks for only 43 seconds.

It is with the core value of harmony that we can associate what Cam Nguyên calls the Vietnamese 'tolerance for ambiguity' (1991: 43). She writes: '"What do you mean?" and other requests for clarification and elaboration are rare except among very close friends and relatives who enjoy a high level of trust – otherwise, one tries to read between the lines or interpret another person's sayings as best one can rather than [engage in clarification of meaning]' (Cam Nguyên 1991: 43). The only exceptions in the corpus are Anh's exchange with Aija (*NEW LEAVE ARRANGEMENTS*) and perhaps the ill-fated encounter between Giao and Liesl (*BROKEN PARTS*). This indicates a weakness in Hofstede's model (1991: 91). He establishes a masculinity–femininity dichotomy between resolution of conflict by compromise and resolution by 'fighting them out'. The third compromise – not contributing to conflict resolution at all – is disregarded. 'Tolerance for ambiguity' lies at the centre of the 'circular' discourse structure (cf. 5.3) which only 'hints at' the main

Table 6.2.8 *Summary of contrasts*

Area	Uncertainty avoidance	Power distance	Individualism
Central European	high	high	low
BUT Austrian:	high	low/mid	mid
Southern European/ Latin American	high	mid to high	low (Ital.)/ high (Span.)
South Asian	high	high	low
South-east Asian	low	high	low

point and keeps on coming back to it to elaborate on it. 'Tolerance for ambiguity' probably also relates to the 'indirectness' tendency in the pragmatics of some East and South-east Asian languages (see e.g. Ide 1989).

The harmony value is also reflected in the turn-taking procedures of Vietnamese, ethnic Chinese, and generally South-east Asians who do not 'fight' to maintain their turns and certainly do not increase the speed to do so. They also generally back down rather than engage in simultaneous speech. The core value of harmony contrasts with the Western European/Middle Eastern concept of 'truth' and is something ambiguous rather than absolute in most South-east Asian cultures.

The non-assertiveness of Vietnamese is all the more marked among the women, in what is a culture with a high level of masculinity, where there were, at least until very recently, clearly marked gender roles. Nguyên Xuân Thu (1990) lists the four desirable qualities of women in Vietnamese culture as: *công* (proper work), *dung* (proper demeanour), *ngôn* (proper speech), and *hanh* (proper manners). This, of course, does not mean that these are not virtues for the whole of the culture. It will be noted that the effect on discourse of the high level of collectivity (low Individuality Index) in South-east Asians is totally different to that in Southern and Central Europeans (Hofstede 1984). It is the main South-east Asian manifestation of collectivity, the core value of harmony, that is responsible for the near absence of complaints by South-east Asians in our corpus.

6.2.8   *Summary of contrasts*

The above contrasts between the broader cultural areas may be summarized in Hofstede's terms (1.3.8) as in Table 6.2.8.
(The Austrian values combination supports the indications that Austrian discourse patterns are on the 'periphery' of Style A as well as a special

cultural case. This can be attributed to Austria's history as both a part of the German-language and cultural area and the centre of a multicultural, multilingual Central European area.) The Masculinity Index was not very useful in relation to our data.

Some manifestations of the above – brief summary

Central European –	fear, 'wrangle',
	'fuss', explanations – long turns
	authoritarianism,
	requiring security – waiting for response,
	confirmation
South Asian –	bureaucratic tone
	parallelism
	long turns
South-east Asian –	harmony – few complaints, commissives,
	little negotiation of meaning, conflict
	resolution
	tolerance of silence,
	short turns

It would appear that a number of different configurations of values dimensions can account for partly similar discourse patterns. Uncertainty avoidance is probably the most important of the dimensions influencing communicative style. Hofstede (1991: 77) points out that any convergence between national cultures tends to be in the individuality/collectivity dimension.

6.3   Discourse/cultural parameters

Elsewhere (Clyne 1981) I have proposed four cultural parameters to help account for differences in the structure of written discourse. I believe that they will also throw some light on cultural variation in spoken discourse. A fifth cultural parameter is proposed here. The data base for these assertions is derived from written academic discourse and from meetings in Australia (see also Chapter 5).

6.3.1   *Form vs. content*

All cultures could be expected to apply a combination of formal and content criteria to determine the structure and progression of a piece of discourse. However, some cultures, such as English-based ones, more strongly foreground form while others, such as Central European ones,

are more content-oriented. Formality is exemplified in the rigid Westminster conventions for the running of meetings not only in parliament
but also, for instance, in school parents' associations and councils, trade
unions, church synods, and stamp clubs in most English-speaking
countries. I have already referred (5.1) to the tendency for formal aspects
to play an important role in the structuring and evaluation of academic
discourse in English-speaking countries, and for a narrow notion of
'relevance' based on formal questions to influence secondary school
assessment in English-speaking countries. Similarly, the rules for the
presentation of medical protocols may override in importance the actual
information conveyed (Clyne and Platt 1990). Deviations from the
formal norm detract from the assessment of the content.

People from cultures with a content orientation may have difficulty in
mastering the discourse rules of a language with a formal cultural
orientation, because such rules do not play a significant role in their
culture or because they consider the content of their message to be of
overriding importance. Content orientation often appears to be concomitant with a cultural idealization of knowledge and the authority of
the academic or intellectual (cf. Galtung 1985) and with an education
system oriented towards the cultivation of a cultural elite. German is a
prime example (Nicholas 1983: 213–14, also Galtung 1985 in relation to
intellectual styles). This, in turn, influences the form of academic
writing. Spillner (1982: 48) remarks, from a German point of view, that
'representations of scholarly matters which are comprehensible to lay
people on the whole neither promote careers nor do they strengthen one's
esteem among colleagues' (my translation). It has been pointed out to me
(Gisela Harras, personal communication) that the English compliment
that one's academic text is 'easy to follow' could be interpreted as an
insult in German. Hofstede (1991: 23) cites the facetious remarks of the
German social psychologist Stroebe (1976): 'German students are
brought up in the belief that anything which is easy enough for them to
understand is dubious and probably unsuccessful'. Also, some academics
consider simplicity of style and discourse structures and the use of
advance organizers to be 'talking down' to a competent and informed
reader. In contrast, the Anglo-Saxon education systems place emphasis
on pragmatic abilities, in particular thought structures and strategies of
expression. Even though Japanese education is more universal and
democratic than its German and French counterparts (cf. also Galtung
1985), it still stresses the authority of the learned person within the
complex hierarchial system. Similarities between the German and
Japanese values in relation to academic sub-culture may be related to the
pre-Second World War German influence in Japan. As in German (and

generally in Central European) culture, in Japanese too, there is reader responsibility, i.e. the onus falls on the reader to make the effort to understand the text produced by the knowledgeable, and therefore authoritative, person (cf. Kaplan 1988). This means not making concessions to limiting definitions of what is relevant or to what a less educated person already knows. Kaplan's (1988: 291) observation that Chinese academic discourse was in transition from reader to author responsibility can be explained by a change from the elitist Confucian-Mandarin to a more egalitarian education system (cf. Đô Quý Toàn 1989). English-based cultures practise author responsibility, i.e. it is the author who has to make the effort to make the text understandable. This can mean limiting your content/message. Elitism does not always go hand in hand with a content orientation. An elitist culture, Arabic, has a formal orientation, as I have already pointed out (see above, 5.6). Crismore (1989: 100), influenced by Halliday (1978), projects three dominance relationships between author, reader, and world – each with one of these three in the dominant role. In German academic discourse, from the data discussed above, I would argue that both the author and the world (*die Sache*) need to be at the top, with the reader at the apex of the triangle at the bottom, while the English (and American and Australian) would have the author at the apex at the top.

Turn-taking strategies can be attributed to the form–content dichotomy. The turn maintenance and appropriation procedures characteristic of Central and Southern Europeans (to some extent also of South Asians) with a tempo increase or simultaneous speech indicate that the speaker wants to be able to say all that they need to say, i.e. content. This contrasts with the slower speech (including elongation) of South-east Asians and the repetition in South-east Asians and South Asians suggests a link between face saving and turn maintenance (and appropriation) *per se* rather than between face saving and getting your content/message across. Simultaneous speech and generally the Style A strategies for turn maintenance and appropriation often reflect contrariness and 'putting your position' (rather than 'text sharing') in conversation (cf. Watts 1991). The more complex interactions focussing on complaints, directives, and apologies characteristic of Europeans and South Asians (but not of South-east Asians) are more content-intensive than simpler ones. However, the rhythmical balance of South Asian-background speakers (e.g. 4.5) reflects a strong form orientation, as does parallelism in the written discourse of Arabic speakers (cf. 5.5). This is confirmed by the eloquence of several of our South Asians in meeting situations and by structures in the students' letters (5.9). It has been pointed out to me (by Dr Burusutama Bilimoria) that formal discourse structures in Indian cultures are used to evaluate whether the speaker is worth paying attention to.

However, Nguyên Phuong Linh (1990), commenting on the absence of a conventionalized thank you routine in Vietnamese, attributes this to the content orientation of Vietnamese, here reflecting the Buddhist philosophy that good works will be rewarded: 'The content is more important than the form' (Nguyên Phuong Linh 1990: 43) (cf. complimenting, see Kasper 1994). This suggests that different cultures have varying indices of stressing the more formal or the more content-based aspects through discourse.

6.3.2   Verbal vs. literate

It is well established that some cultures have long oral traditions, but have not yet developed a culture of the written language. However, even in highly literate cultures, there are those who elaborate and instil in the younger generation more rules for the written or the spoken language. In some education systems, such as the British and Australian ones, most upper-school examination requirements are through the written language and, in particular, through the essay form. In others, such as Dutch, Finnish, and Czech, most upper-school examinations are oral and factually oriented. There are certain functions, such as dealing with bureaucracies, which some related cultures will perform personally, over the telephone or in writing (Clyne 1979, Carroll 1987). Even within one pluricentric language, different national (or regional) cultures will stress the spoken or the written language as the main medium of effective communication to practise with the younger generation (cf. American – spoken, British/Australian – written, at least in government schools). An emphasis on articulateness in spoken discourse is reflected in meetings – note e.g. the effectiveness of Indians and Sri Lankans in meeting situations.

6.3.3   Rhythm of discourse

As has already been discussed in Chapter 5, the rhythm of discourse may be more or less differently structured, in different cultures. For instance, a contrastive study of formal meetings in Australia (Clyne and Manton 1978) showed that English meetings tended to constrain the discourse rhythm – e.g. by moving that 'the motion now be put' or by referring an item to a committee – while the meetings of Italian, German, and Dutch ethnic groups generally did not. In Chapter 4, I draw attention to the tendency for the turns of Central and Southern Europeans and South Asians to be longer than those of South-east Asians. As has already been pointed out (4.5), this is related to the Europeans' and South Asians' need to explain out of 'positive politeness' – to take away the bad taste of face-threatening acts of directives and complaints and the South-east Asians' need, within Brown and Levinson's concept of 'negative politeness', to say as little as possible about 'bad things'. This also tallies with Yong Liang's (1991) conclusion that the Chinese tend to insert positive appraisal early in academic reviews and avoid making negative criticisms. In fact, verbosity is not praised in Chinese or Vietnamese cultures. Note Kirkpatrick's findings (5.3) that Chinese written discourse is shorter and 'less dialogic' than 'western' (e.g. Australian English) equivalents. Nguyên Phuong Linh (1990: 44) cites Confucius's declaration: 'The beautiful words are untrue.' Linh expresses the Vietnamese position: 'A wise person does not use much verbal language ...' 'Speaking like a parrot', to the Vietnamese, means words without real content or with internal emptiness. Characteristically, the Vietnamese participants in many of our exchanges are completely, or almost completely, silent. While Germans and Italians, for instance, tend to think aloud and fill in silences, Turks, for example, contemplate for longer periods and then provide a response or an input.

In 5.1, I referred to earlier work on German and English academic discourse which indicated that symmetry is part of the English 'normative package', but of less significance in German. Cam Nguyên (1991) contends that, in Vietnamese discourse ('considering all implications and answering all possible objections'), the size of the stretch of speech indicates its importance, as well as the importance of the interlocutor. The Arabic discourse pattern based on parallels demonstrates the significance of rhythm in the written discourse of some cultures. The spoken discourse of people from Indian and Sri Lankan background in our sample is characterized by repetition, partly in rhetorical patterns, sometimes reminiscent of Indian religious texts, especially mantras.

6.3.4   Directionality

In the sub-sections of Chapters 5, I summarized various findings on cultural variation in the organization of discourse (especially written discourse). English-based cultures seem to be unique in their emphasis on linearity. This is reflected not only in written (especially academic) discourse, but in many aspects of culture ranging from queueing to Westminster meeting procedures in which only one motion can be before the chair at a time, and the amendment becomes the motion so that the meeting can proceed in a linear way (Clyne and Manton 1979). Where a culture has not adopted a linear emphasis, there can appear to be a tendency towards 'digressiveness' or 'circularity'. However, these apparent tendencies are more likely to result from a strong content orientation which detracts from the importance of linearity. 'Digressiveness' may mean little more than 'comprehensiveness'; 'circularity' may be an interpretation of 'implicitness' rather than 'explicitness'.

6.3.5   *Abstractness – concreteness*

The level of abstractness or concreteness is not of very direct significance to this study. However, it plays a part, for example, in Farrell's (1994) comparisons of essays written by Latin American and Vietnamese upper-secondary students in Melbourne (cf. 5.7). Through an analysis of Vietnamese idiomatic expressions and semantic fields, Võ Phiêń (1989) characterizes Vietnamese culture as having a concrete tendency. Phiêń argues that in communication there is a greater emphasis on senses (feeling) rather than reason in Vietnamese. This contrasts with Central European and Latin American abstraction. Note the stress on abstraction in Galtung's description of Teutonic – but also Gallic – intellectual style. The abstraction tendency is reflected in the hedging procedures mentioned in our analysis of German academic texts.

6.4   Language in action and politeness

From Chapter 3, it will be evident that, in South-east Asian Chinese and Vietnamese cultures, it is important to express a commitment linguistically if it appears that the other person (especially if (s)he is the superordinate) expects or desires it (see also 4.7.3, 6.2.7). At least in the case of Vietnamese, this politeness routine is expressed not only through verbal communication, but also through paralinguistic phenomena, such as gestures (personal communication, Nguyên Xuân Thu). The politeness is determined not so much by the future action to which a commitment has been made but rather by the commissive. In European (including 'Anglo') cultures, the commissive *and* future action are meshed and combine as a requirement of being polite. This has two important implications:

(i)   Different expectations may lead not only to inter-cultural communication breakdown, but also to inter-cultural communication conflict, stereotypes, and prejudice; and

(ii) Austin's notion of 'felicity conditions' and the Gricean truth maxim do not apply in the South-east Asian context.

In some cases, there is an attempt to integrate into the verbal commitment a rider that the commissive will not be honoured in the present time-

frame. This is a concession to the Anglo/European significance of truth in a language/culture contact situation, e.g.:
(In response to a request to do the meat, *CAN I HAVE A LOOK*?) Lee says:

> <u>Okay</u> but <u>now</u> we have to clean all the trays. (i.e. commitment to do the meat when she does not intend to do it now)

(In response to a request to move Celia to her section; *TAKING ON CELIA*):

> <u>That's no problem but</u> we don't have many jobs. (Jennifer)

She then twice gives the assurance for the future (i.e. commitment to take Celia when she does not intend to do so now).

6.5   Grice revisited

In 1.3.2, I referred to a controversy on whether Grice's Cooperative Principle needs to be applied differently across cultures or whether it is actually culture-bound or 'monocentric'. In the description and analysis of our corpus, I have found that several of the maxims are not always observed in discourse contributions that are, nevertheless, clearly appropriate in the culture of the speaker. In the following section, I will comment on these and then attempt a reformulation that is, I believe, within the spirit of Grice's intentions. Let us consider the various maxims in order to assess their universal suitability.

In the 'Quantity' category – which relates to the quantity of information to be provided, the first maxim:

> Make your contribution as informative as is required (for the current purposes of the exchange) –

does not seem to present a problem. However, Grice himself appears to feel uneasy (p. 46) about the second:

> Do not make your contribution more informative than is required.

Actually, in content-oriented cultures, both Continental European and East/South-east Asian, the more knowledge provided, the better. Restricting information in the interests of ready comprehension, for instance, may be quite unacceptable. This has been discussed in the section on written discourse, especially in academic contexts in a number of cultures. However, we must not lose sight of Grice's intended concentration on conversation. As I have tried to show in Chapter 4, what 'is required' is subject to much cultural variation.

As has been mentioned above (e.g. 6.2.7, 6.4), the European notion of 'truth' as an absolute is not essential in at least South-east Asian Chinese and Vietnamese cultures. So the Supermaxim of Quality, 'Try to make your contribution one that is true', has little meaning in that cultural context. Certainly in any competition with harmony, charity or respect, 'truth' not only need not, but should not, be a criterion. (The second maxim, 'Do not say that for which you lack adequate evidence', evidently derived from the legal and academic domains, probably does not even apply in many ordinary conversation settings among 'Anglo' inter- locutors.) However, as I have indicated (6.5), in the Australian language/ cultural contact situation, some South-east Asians will simultaneously satisfy their own cultural norms and the truth requirements of the dominant group. The 'Relation' maxim – 'Be relevant' – can, as Grice himself (p.46) suggests, be interpreted according to different kinds and focusses of relevance. In 5.1, and above in 6.3.1, I have shown that, in 'Anglo' discourse but not in content-oriented traditions, relevance is closely linked with linearity, and to some extent with symmetry. This applies to spoken as well as to written discourse. I fear that, if the relevance maxim is kept very open, it may become rather useless. (But cf. Sperber and Wilson 1986.)

The category of 'Manner' – with the Supermaxim 'Be perspicuous' – has four maxims – 'Avoid obscurity', 'Avoid ambiguity', 'Be brief', 'Be orderly'. All of these are culturally limiting. As we have seen, there are contexts in which 'obscurity of expression' is quite appropriate in certain cultures, e.g. in academic discourse in a culture with an author orientation or in spoken discourse, where the culture dictates 'implicitness' for face reasons (see 6.2.7). 'Ambiguity' may be very appropriate in inter- cultural communication in which two (or more) sets of maxims based on two (or more) values systems need to be observed. Bodi (1985) shows how ambivalence has become an identity marker for Austrians. Konrád (1985) projects as characteristics of Central Europeans their convoluted thought patterns, the flexibility with which they take pleasure in diversity, and their ability to handle internal paradoxes flexibly. In some cultures it facilitates negative politeness because it gives the interlocutor maximum freedom to respond. I have referred (6.2.7) to the Vietnamese 'tolerance for ambiguity'. In the section on turn length (4.5) as well as the section on rhythm of discourse (6.3.3), I refer to evidence for brevity being subject to cultural variation and being avoided by Central Europeans to boost one's own face and that of the other. 'Orderliness' in discourse is a concept of form-oriented cultures as is indicated by the survey of criteria of good academic writing in English and German and the structure of some of the complex interactions.

Since Grice is interested in showing how conversation proceeds, and not in imposing cultural hegemony, it would be in the spirit of his Cooperative Principle to extend it to make it more universal, as it had originally been intended (see Allan 1991). I would propose the following 'revised' maxims:

Quantity: A single maxim – 'Make your contribution as informative as is required for the purpose of the discourse, within the bounds of the discourse parameters of the given culture.'

Quality: Supermaxim – 'Try to make your contribution one for which you can take responsibility within your own cultural norms.'

Maxims   (1) 'Do not say what you believe to be in opposition to your cultural norms of truth, harmony, charity, and/or respect.'

(2) Do not say that for which you lack adequate evidence.' (DUBIOUS, see above.)

Manner: The supermaxim can be retained in its original form – 'Be perspicacious.'

Maxims   (1) 'Do not make it any more difficult to understand than may be dictated by questions of face and authority.'

(2) 'Avoid ambiguity unless it is in the interests of politeness or of maintaining a dignity-driven cultural core value, such as harmony, charity or respect.' (But see above.)

(3) 'Make your contribution the appropriate length required by the nature and purpose of the exchange and the discourse parameters of your culture.'

(4) 'Structure your discourse according to the requirements of your culture.'

These 'revised' maxims will hopefully be adaptable for use within any culture. However, they do not altogether suit the needs of *inter*-cultural communication. Should the speaker's or the hearer's culture be the determiner of communication patterns? I would argue that, except for biculturals, it will usually be the original culture that will govern these patterns in inter-cultural communication, but that there will be an increasing convergence towards the 'dominant' norm which, in the case of our informants, is not the language of the interlocutor from another non-dominant culture. This point will be taken up in Chapter 7. Successful inter-cultural communication is achieved by making the communicative intent very clear and, where possible, being aware of the interlocutor's cultural expectations. To those ends, it would be desirable to change the second maxim of Manner to:

> 'Make clear your communicative intent unless this is against the interests of politeness or of maintaining a dignity-driven cultural core value, such as harmony, charity or respect.'

and to add a fifth maxim of Manner:

> 'In your contribution, take into account anything you know or can predict about the interlocutor's communication expectations.'

Sperber and Wilson (1986: 35) rate as one of Grice's main contributions to pragmatics showing 'how, in the event of... an apparent violation of the Cooperative Principle and maxims, hearers are expected to make any additional assumptions needed to dispose of the violation'. Since the Cooperative Principle as postulated originally is not really universal, the additional assumptions will be required to prevent a communication breakdown.

6.6   Some remarks on other theoretical frameworks

From the above discussion of Grice, it will be evident that Searle's sincerity condition – 'Pr(oposition) is to be uttered only if S intends to do A' – (Searle 1969: 63) does not apply to those South-east Asian cultures where the cultural core value, harmony, precludes this.

Brown and Levinson's framework (1978, 1987) does, from the point of view of our data, provide an adequate general theoretical basis for a model of social interaction because it makes provision for cultural impositions. However, it is specifically concerned with politeness, and also it does not help us understand why one strategy may be used in preference to another under particular conditions. From a more specific point of view, Janney and Arndt (1993: 38) suggest that Brown and Levinson's model is in need of extension, taking into account non-western (especially Asian) cultures. Our corpus indicates that positive and negative face and positive and negative politeness exist across many cultures. Nevertheless, one or the other may be preferable in general, or become mandatory in a particular set of circumstances because of the appropriate cultural value system. Low individuality and/or harmony, modesty and restraint as core values promote negative politeness in socially marked situations. Cultures with a high uncertainty avoidance and power distance are conducive to positive politeness.

Leech's Modesty Maxim is challenged by the letters written by students from South Asia and the Middle East (5.9). While Leech does mention cultural variation, he contends that this results in differences in strategies. If modesty is alien to a culture, one cannot expect a Modesty Maxim.

The criticism levelled by Wierzbicka (e.g. 1991) against traditional pragmatics has been shown to be valid. She has made a very important contribution to the field by rejecting monolingual universals or static global comparisons in favour of culture-specific values. She has set a precedent for describing phenomena of a culture in the terms used by that culture, and I have attempted to follow that precedent. However, the close relation between pragmatics and discourse requires more un-ravelling in inter-cultural communication than a particular represen-tation in lexical semantics can achieve.

Our corpus confirms the complexity of communication which is not expressed in the textbook single-utterance speech acts sometimes invented at office desks. There is a close interaction of different speech acts reflecting 'culturally programmed' patterns of action (Ehlich and Rehbein 1986) or schemata (Rumelhart 1975).

6.7   A linguistics of inter-cultural communication?

From the discussion up to now, it will follow that a linguistics of inter-cultural communication to cover both discourse patterns and discourse expectations should proceed from an interdisciplinary base and include the following components, in addition to the more established constituent parts, phonology, morphology and syntax, and (lexico)semantics:

1. A global description of the appropriate discourse-culture(s), ac-cording to the parameters form/content, oral/literate, rhythm, direc-tionality, and concreteness/abstractness (cf. also Kaplan 1988). This is at a high level of generality, one that provides a framework to understand tendencies and preferences in actual discourse. At a lower level, this would include (cf. Clyne 1985a):

> Discourse rules, e.g. rules for the organization of written
>   discourse (letters, essays), of meetings, and for business
>   transactions and professional encounters.

Channel/medium rules, indicating whether communication 'for a particular purpose in a specific situation will take place in face-to-face interaction, over the telephone, in freely constructed or formulaic letters, or through the completion of written forms' (Clyne 1985: 13).

Linguistic creativity rules, governing the use of riddles, limericks, puns and verbal irony in the culture (cf. Chiaro 1992).

2. A global description of interaction-related aspects of the core values of the culture(s), e.g. harmony, charity, respect, modesty, restraint, networks of mutual obligations, role of language in the culture, tolerance for silence and ambiguity, and the Hofstede cultural value dimensions – power distance, individualism/collectivism, uncertainty avoidance, masculinity/femininity.

Different sociocultural and discourse-cultural core values such as these are represented in a range of 'shades' and variations within an area – and even within one *Kommunikationsbund* so that they can lead to communication breakdown, communication conflict, and stereotypical prejudices. Examples are: persuasion by presenting something as in the others' interests may be stronger in Croatians than in, say, Austrians; 'wrangling' through developing personal relationships is present in Austrians and Hungarians as well as in Poles (even to the point of bribing), but less overtly so; academic texts are more digressive in Finnish and Dutch than in English but not as much as in German. This supports Galtung's notion of the 'core' and 'peripheral' areas, as I have argued in Chapter 4.

3. An inter-cultural model of turn-taking – Chapter 4 is a step in that direction – based on areal tendencies.

4. Inter-cultural tendencies in pragmatic usage and rules for the performance of particular speech acts in a given culture or region (cf. Chapter 3). At a lower level, this includes formulaic routines which can be summarized contrastively (e.g. Clyne 1979):

(a) The rule exists in one language but not in the other – e.g. Indonesian *salamat tinggal* by someone leaving to the person staying behind, or the Italian *buon appetito*/Dutch *smakelijk eten* formula to mark the beginning of a meal, which have no English equivalents.

(b) Formulae of completely different structures employed to realize a speech act in different languages – e.g. Excuse me, German *Auf Wiedersehen* for leave-taking at a restaurant table.

(c) Formulae of opposite structures used for a speech act in different languages, e.g. English Is this seat taken?, German *Ist dieser Platz noch frei?* and its equivalents in many other 'Continental European' languages. The likelihood of communication breakdown is promoted where, say, on a train, people not sharing a common language base their nods and head-shakes on a different formula.

(d) Formulae of corresponding structures employed for different speech acts – e.g. How are you (going)? and its translation equivalents. A greeting in Australian English; but an inquiry about the other person's health, which may extract a lengthy and detailed response. However, this difference is often situation-specific.

(e) Formulae of corresponding structures used to realize speech acts with a diametrically opposed intention – e.g. In response to a request to speak to X, English (S)he's on the 'phone is a negative response and (S)he's speaking an affirmative one, while in German, (Er/Sie) ist am Apparat (literally '(s)he's on the 'phone)' is an affirmative response and Er/Sie spricht '(S)he's speaking' a negative one.

The components are complementary so that, for instance, in some cultures, increased length can balance out what some term 'directness' in the interests of politeness.

6.8   Universality and specificity

The cultural area with its communicative style and especially the *Kommunikationsbund* provide a powerful argument for the culture rather than the language determining discourse patterns – there are areal communalities in both the discourse patterns and the values systems underlying them. This is borne out in our corpus (see Chapters 3 and 4) as well as in Hofstede's values research and in the discussion of sociocultural parameters, e.g. for Chinese and Vietnamese (see various sub-sections of 6.2). I refer also to similarities in discourse patterns between the Ceylonese Burghers (with Sri Lankan English as L1), the Sinhalese, and various people from Indian backgrounds. Hungarians, while speaking a Finno-Ugrian language, share communication patterns with Central Europeans employing unrelated Indo-European languages. Austrians have commonalities in discourse culture and sociocultural values with other Central Europeans (e.g. Croats, Hungarians, to a lesser extent Poles) which they do not share with German-speaking Swiss or with Germans other than Bavarians. Note also the similarities which Hofstede (1984: 228–30) has found between the values systems of Dutch- and French-speaking Belgians: high uncertainty avoidance, large power distance, high masculinity. This is not shared with the Dutch who show low uncertainty avoidance, a small power distance, and a low masculinity.

(Hofstede attributes this to the long cultural and political dominance of the French speakers in Belgium.) I have referred, in the literature review of cross-cultural written discourse studies (Chapter 5), to the cultural – rather than linguistic – nature of written discourse variation. For instance, while English-derived cultures do show the same tendencies, similar communicative styles occur in speakers of only partly related cultures in Central and Southern Europe and Latin America. On the other hand, Israelis and Maltese share their academic discourse cultures with Central Europeans and with the British respectively because of the history and nature of their education systems. (cf. also Hofstede's (1984: 215) finding that Austrians and Israelis (many of whom originally migrated from Central Europe) share a high uncertainty avoidance and low power distance).

Diachronic changes in discourse cultures whereby e.g. Dutch and Scandinavians have moved from the periphery of the 'Teutonic' intellectual style to the periphery of the 'Saxonic' one (Galtung 1985) support the cultural rather than linguistic basis of the communication patterns. While discourse cultures are propagated mainly through the education system, the sociocultural values are subject to a much broader socialization process.

Let us return to the question which has kept recurring throughout this monograph: to what extent are discourse patterns determined by universal principles? From 6.5, it will follow that this is so, that people of all backgrounds do try to facilitate successful communication, including successful inter-cultural communication *as long as* it does not contravene their cultural values, which may be harmony, respect, and restraint. In that case, successful communication may, for instance, need to yield to a certain amount of ambiguity, something which some cultures will tolerate and others will not. In 6.5, a preliminary attempt has been made to adapt Grice's maxims to cope with cultural differences. However, any framework purporting to be universal must ensure that the principles are open to the inevitable impact of the values systems of particular cultures on the discourse of groups or individuals, and that the principles are equally sensitive to all cultures and contact between different cultures. For that reason, this field is still in an early stage of development.

It should be stressed that individuals are individuals. While they are conditioned by their culture and that of the environment, discourse patterns will always be influenced by personality factors as is implied in Watts' (1991) work on 'emergent social networks' (cf. 1.3.1). This option is greater in more individualistic cultures than in more collectivist ones. However, the dominance of individualistic values in Australian society can accentuate individual patterns within a contact situation (cf. 7.2.1). It would be interesting to follow this longitudinally in Australians of Vietnamese and other South-east Asian background.

This chapter has drawn on the findings of the inter-cultural workplace study, and also on research into written (mainly academic) discourse. Despite the differences between spoken and written discourse and between contrastive and interactive inter-cultural studies, there are many commonalities in the way cultural values impact on discourse patterns. For instance, a low uncertainty avoidance among South-east Asians leads to a tolerance for ambiguity, therefore little clarification of meaning, to short turns, and 'hinting' resulting in the perception of 'circular discourse'. A high uncertainty avoidance among many European groups leads to longer turns with downtoners, explanations, and apparent disclaimers in spoken discourse, as well as to longer, more 'exhaustive' written texts. A higher power distance in some Europeans leads to author responsibility in written discourse and complex spoken interactions with a content orientation in spoken and written discourse. The rhythm of spoken and written discourse is more symmetrical among Anglos, less symmetrical among most Continental Europeans, parallel among Arabs and South Asians.

6.9   Closing remarks

As soon as language is examined in its broader communicative context, linguistics needs to synthesize its own insights with those of other disciplines. This certainly applies to the linguistics of inter-cultural communication. In this chapter, I endeavoured to draw together components which might show how cultural values systems influence discourse patterns and promote the different communicative styles described in Chapter 4. The research of Hofstede into cultural values systems of many different peoples in contemporary settings is introduced to explain some of the data from inter-cultural encounters discussed in the previous two chapters. Hofstede's parameters, especially uncertainty avoidance and power distance, are useful in grouping the cultural areas we are dealing with. They facilitate an understanding of the variation in communicative behaviour, especially between Europeans and South-east Asians. These parameters are complemented with studies of specific cultures. Very central to the inter-cultural variation is, for instance, the significance of harmony, respect, and restraint in most South-east Asian cultures, and of truth and certainty in many continental European ones. It should be stressed that cultural variation in discourse patterns arising from cultural values systems (particularly in relation to face) affects expectations of communicative behaviour as well as one's own production.

For these reasons, universally intended rules for successful communication, such as Grice's Cooperative Principle, need to be sensitive to cultural variation. The wording of some of Grice's maxims is extended both to accommodate fully the cultural dimension, and to facilitate its application in inter-cultural communication.

7   Some theoretical and practical implications

7.0   Opening remarks

In Chapter 6, I related discourse patterns observed in our corpus of inter-cultural communication to cultural values systems, and attempted to describe some principles of a linguistics of inter-cultural communication. This chapter has an even wider brief. I shall try to bring together various sets of conclusions in the book. This will lead to a discussion of some basic issues concerning language and the interrelation of language and culture. A number of models for language/culture contact will be contrasted, and an attempt will be made to develop a truly 'multicultural' one appropriate to the issues presented in this monograph. The remainder of the chapter will be devoted to consideration of practical implications of this field for communication practice, educational language policy, the management of a multicultural workplace, and the spin-offs in trade and other international communication.

7.1   Synthesis of conclusions so far

The discussion of the corpus drawn from Melbourne workplaces indicates the diversity and complexity of inter-cultural (and probably also intra-cultural) communication. Because of the limited corpus, the conclusions should not be afforded a wider validity than they deserve. The focus on the speech acts – apologies, commissives, complaints and whinges, and directives – shows that they are intertwined in complex interactions often containing several of them. This is obscured by discussion of single-utterance speech acts. It emerges that there is a close interaction between speech act realizations and turn-taking procedures. In some cultures, notably European and South Asian ones, the utterance that has been described as more or less 'direct' becomes more or less 'polite' by gaining in length through additional utterances with other speech acts (e.g. apology, explanation, directive, complaint). This means

that the discussion on 'directness'/'indirectness' in contrastive pragmatics (cf. Blum-Kulka et al. 1989) needs to be seen in relation to turn-
taking procedures which are a factor contributing to illocutionary force.
It also indicates one of the reasons for cultural variation in turn length. I
have attempted (5.5) a revision of the maxims of Grice's Cooperative
Principle to allow for cultural variation from the presupposed norms, and
for communication between people with different cultural norms. This
entails a greater degree of 'relativism', e.g. the addition of: 'within your
own cultural norms' or 'unless it is in the interests of politeness...' The
inter-cultural aspects are handled also by the addition of a new maxim of
manner:

> In your contribution, take into account anything you know or
> can predict about the interlocutor's communication expec-
> tations.

It is not even possible to propose universal maxims concerning
negotiation of meaning, for South-east Asian cultures exhibit a higher
degree of tolerance for ambiguity than European and South Asian ones.
(cf. Hofstede's (1984, 1991) notion of uncertainty avoidance.)

Discourse patterns and expectations can be attributed to cultural
values systems, more particularly to 'sociocultural interactional
parameters' (e.g. truth, harmony, uncertainty avoidance, individuality)
and 'discourse-cultural parameters' (e.g. content orientation, direction-
ality). This applies to both spoken and written discourse.

Each cultural group will use their own discourse patterns to cope with
the power structures of the workplace in order to save their own face in
terms of their own cultural values. Thus, there is cultural variation in the
incidence of particular speech acts in our corpus. Apologies predominate
among Europeans, directives among European men, commissives are
performed largely by South-east Asian women, and complaints by men,
especially from South Asia and Europe. Communication in general is
determined by the power hierarchy and social distance of the workplace,
as well as the type of interdependence between the different units of
production. So, in the office situations and in meetings, there is more
symmetrical communication than in the car factories with their 'sequential work interdependence' (2.3) and the turns are longer than in the
catering unit. The strategies for turn taking are also subject to cultural
variation, and I have proposed different communicative styles, representing the clustering of certain tendencies which are in general
characteristic of particular cultural areas. These cultural areas may
have geographical or historical connections (e.g. Latin America as well as
most of Continental Europe). They may include a number of central or

'core' cultures which combine all the features of the communicative style typical of them (e.g. Croatian, Greek, Spanish) and others – which can be described as 'peripheral' – which share only some of the features of the 'core' groups. Tolerance for silence and for small-talk are also culturally conditioned. The groupings are largely conditioned by the breadth of the sample. Had the corpus contained more data from more informants from a smaller number of closely related cultures, it would have been possible to differentiate between groups sharing broad communicative styles.

People from cultures on the periphery of a cultural area (e.g. Indonesians, Filipinos, Maltese) are often among the good inter-cultural communicators, because their own discourse patterns are more 'open'. Successful inter-cultural communicators are aware of their own and their interlocutor's expectations, express themselves as 'culturally neutral' as possible, keep control of the communication, and keep their own face without threatening that of the other interlocutor(s). People with the same areal cultural style are most likely to understand the (hidden) implications of one another's discourse. It does not necessarily mean that they will give one another a good hearing. For instance, those using Style A are inclined to engage in simultaneous speech. Inter-cultural communication breakdown in our corpus – whether non-communication or miscommunication in Gumperz's (1982) sense – is generally due to pragmatic and discourse issues, and not to matters of morphosyntax, phonology, or the lexicon. Pragmatic and discourse features are far more pervasive, less resistant to change – at least in the first generation (but see below), and far less recognizable by people from other cultural backgrounds as linguistic manifestations of culture.

I have argued, throughout this monograph, in favour of an interactionist view of the relation between language and culture. Discourse is the level of language that is arguably most susceptible to the impact of cultural values. It is the culture that determines the areal networks promoting similarities in discourse patterns and expectations. That is why native speakers of different varieties of a pluricentric language (e.g. American, British, Sri Lankan Burgher English) will employ varying patterns, and discourse patterns will be shared between speakers of unrelated languages (e.g. Croatian, Hungarian). Communicative styles of one's ethnic group may persist, in the national language (here English) even after a complete language shift from the ethnic language has taken place.

7.2   Sociocultural models

Traditional theoretical models of heterogeneous societies (e.g. Gordon 1964, Glazer and Moynihan 1975) distinguish between monistic (assimilationist/anglo-conformist), integrationist, and pluralist attitudes and policies. They assume a dominant group which the others assimilate to, or which they refrain from assimilating to. Tajfel's (1974) theory concerns group boundaries and comparisons the 'minority' makes with the 'majority'. Awareness of cognitive alternatives leads the 'minority' to redefine its existing group attributes. This and Giles' (1977) variant, the accommodation theory, also presuppose a majority or dominant group and a minority, or at least an in-group and an out-group. The Australian discussion, especially the rhetoric surrounding it, focusses on a trichotomy of 'Anglo-(Celtic)', 'Aboriginal' and 'Ethnic' Australians. That this is gross oversimplification is evidenced even in education, media, and translating/interpreting policies. A telephone interpreter service functioning in 90 languages, a state-run television network transmitting in a multitude of languages other than English (with English sub-titles), multilingual radio stations broadcasting in over 60 languages, and the range of languages taught in primary and secondary schools in some Australian states (21) and examined at the end of secondary school (32) indicate a 'multicultural' perspective. Australian community languages have been transplanted from many parts of the world and belong to many different typological and philological groups.

Our study provides evidence that discourse patterns and expectations in a multicultural society such as Australia vary markedly between ethnic groups from different parts of the world. Although our corpus is explicitly on English as a lingua franca, it does indicate that the discourse patterns of 'ethnic' groups vary from each other at least as much as they do from those of the 'dominant group'. Some of the groups, because of their relative cultural proximity to the 'Anglo-Celtic groups' or because of their long-term residence and convergence towards 'Anglo-Celtic' Australians, project themselves as 'surrogate' members of the dominant group. Long-standing European immigrants (Northern and Eastern Europeans and Maltese) have sometimes espoused old assimilationist attitudes. They and some subsequent Southern European as well as British immigrants have difficulty in adapting to the new Australian reality of migrants from Asia with very different discourse patterns and expectations. As Anglo-Australians have moved off the factory floor, the 'ethnic surrogate Anglos' are increasingly acting as gatekeepers in highly diverse multicultural work situations (Erickson and Shultz 1982). It should be noted that all the 'ethnic' groups are converging towards the dominant one far more than they are towards one another. Also, no one 'ethnic' group is exerting a substantial influence on the culture of the nation as a whole – and its communication patterns – but each is making a contribution, by its participation, some more than others. However, the notion of 'out-group' and 'in-groups' is not a suitable basis for examining communication in as multicultural society. A more appropriate model would be one which allowed for a continuum of groups with more or less 'out' or 'in' group features, all interacting with one another, both within the mainstream and outside it. This is shown in the diagram below.

In the absence of empirical studies comparing speakers from particular backgrounds interacting in monocultural and multicultural contexts, it is very difficult to assess the impact of different communicative styles on one another. Four possibilities are:

(a) adoption of 'mainstream' style by the 'other' groups;
(b) maintenance of ethnic communicative styles;
(c) use of two or more styles side by side; and
(d) mutual convergence.

It is my impression that all four tendencies co-occur in Australia (see below, 7.2.1.).

7.2.1   Maintenance of cultural values and communicative styles

There are currently two seemingly conflicting assumptions concerning Australian society often held simultaneously:

(i)   that Australia, being a multicultural nation, embraces a range of different values systems and that this represents an enrichment for Australia; and
(ii) that Australians as a *nation* have their own cultural values system.

The two points of view are reconciled, e.g. by Smolicz (1981), who proposes that there are overarching core values, such as freedom of the individual (see below) that are common to most Australians, held along with the maintenance of some ethnic core values. While there is a fairly rapid language shift to English in most ethnic groups in Australia (cf. e.g. Clyne 1991a), it is possible that cultural values and their manifestations in communicative styles are more tenacious. We do not have evidence for or against this in our data, as it is all drawn from first-generation ethnic-Australians. My own impressions are that many Australians employ two (or more) sets of discourse patterns – e.g. one for home and older members of their ethnic community, the other for the 'mainstream',

MODEL

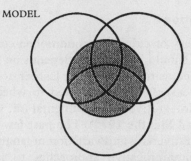

Shaded areas represent 'Mainstream'. Circles represent ethnic
groups interrelating with the 'mainstream', and with each other:
both within the mainstream and outside it. (From Clyne and Ball
1990: 3.)

including younger members of the relevant ethnic community. The
choice of patterns for particular interactants or situations may or may not
coincide with the choice of language. There are biculturals maintaining
a dual identity who can keep the 'systems' apart. Drawing on Östman
(1986), Blommaert and Verschueren (1993) argue that first-generation
Muslim immigrants in the Netherlands communicate implicitly in the
'we' culture while the second generation do so explicitly. This probably
applies quite generally to the children of immigrants in Australia. There
are also biculturals who develop their own 'compromise system'.
Tensions between young people and their parents (and/or grandparents)
are often the result of conflicting values systems and communicative
styles. Miscommunication in mixed marriages – which are the norm
rather than the exception by the second generation in most ethnic
communities in Australia (Price 1988) – is also frequently the result of
the same factors. This applies even between the first and second
generation of the *same* ethnic group.

   Hofstede (1991: 77) believes that 'the deep roots of national cultures
make it likely that ... differences will survive for a long time', but that any
convergence between national cultures would occur in the individualism–collectivism dimension. While Hofstede is writing about international convergence of cultural values, it is likely that the prognosis for
the individual–collective dimension will apply, or is applying to ethnic
communities in Australia (cf. the reference to Smolicz 1981 above). One
of the reasons is that social mobility is an overarching core value,
frequently being the main motive of immigration.

7.3   Educational implications[1]

To what extent an active mastery of culturally conditioned communication patterns in L2 acquirers should be required depends on whether the aim of second language acquisition is for the learner to behave completely like the 'native speaker'. This is related to whether the objectives and motivation are integrative or instrumental (cf. Gardner and Lambert 1972, Gardner and Smythe 1975). The past few decades have seen a greater toleration of diversity and variation in language and culture. The emphasis on communicative approaches to language teaching has introduced more realistic rather than perfectionist expectations, these having detracted from both motivation and communicative output. However, 'foreignness' is still, to a large extent, marked as 'inadequate', in terms of Neustupný's (1978) theory of correction.

Native-like communicative behaviour may entail a change not only in the individuals' cultural values system but also in their psychological make-up. Such a change, achievable by a dramatic voluntary identity shift or through the development of a dual identity, occurs more in younger than older people (cf. Vildomec 1963). There is also a moral dimension – urging or forcing people to conform can be regarded as cultural imperialism or proselytization, assimilation or even suppression.

On the other hand, in an immigrant country such as Australia, with a single national language/lingua franca, access to power (and, to some extent, information) may be limited to those with a fairly high degree of communicative competence in English. Thus some active command of 'Anglo' communication rules, including – in some occupational situations, meeting rules – may be necessary even with instrumental motivation. An equilibrium must be found between the level of active command of discourse patterns required to achieve quality of life, and that which threatens one's own face and identity. This is a decision that can only be taken by adult second language learners themselves on possessing the necessary information. As biculturalism, like bilingualism, brings socioeconomic and psychological advantages to the individual, this, rather than assimilation, should be the ultimate aim of programmes.

What is crucial is for people to be *aware* of variation in discourse patterns and to appreciate their equal validity. There is generally a greater tolerance of grammatical and phonological deviations from native norms than is the case at the pragmatic and discourse levels (cf. also Neustupný 1974: 19), largely due to ignorance. Second language learners

[1]   Some of these points have been made in Clyne (1985b).

also need to be taught to interact in contact situations rather than to pretend that they are native speakers in non-contact situations, as Neustupný argues:

Language teachers of today almost totally ignore consideration of the fact that ... the situations in which [their students] appear will be contact situations ... They should know how native speakers will adapt their behavior, how they are likely to judge foreign speakers' behavior, and how their attitudes can be influenced. (Neustupný 1981: 30)

As Kaplan (1988: 296) points out, referring to essay-writing and to reader/writer responsibility, the teacher must first be aware of cultural differences. I would take this point further. The study on which I have reported relates to English as a lingua franca in workplaces in a multicultural country with English as its national language. But English is used internationally as a lingua franca on a very wide and increasing scale, in many contexts, between people of diverse cultural backgrounds, such as Indians, Germans, Chinese, Lebanese, and Chileans. The same kinds of issues that have been addressed in this monograph are also relevant internationally. There are now about between 300 and 360 million first language users of English today, and at least that many, but perhaps as many as one billion second and foreign language users (Landry 1986, Leitner 1992). In many programmes in English for Speakers of Other Languages, the pragmatic and discourse perspectives are being emphasized. But students are being taught how *native* speakers of English communicate. They are not learning how *non-native* speakers from *other* cultural backgrounds communicate in English – something that may be at least as important for their needs. Moreover, *native speakers* of English need to learn how different cultural groups communicate in English – firstly because their cultural expectations of communication will not necessarily coincide with those of the English native speaker who, in many communication situations, may be in the minority, and secondly because the English native speaker will increasingly be called upon to mediate between different groups communicating in English. However, the monolingual/monocultural tradition of many English-speaking people currently makes them eminently incompetent to do this.

Moreover, English native speakers (here, native speakers of the 'Old Englishes' as opposed to the 'New Englishes', see 2.1) have a responsibility towards an understanding and tolerance of cultural variation. English is both an international language and a national language of numerous nations (Leitner 1992). While non-native speakers of English communicate in the language as a lingua franca in the business, academic, and international transactional domains, they are judged by native speakers of English according to the latter's own norms which are based on *their* cultural values systems. I am, for instance, aware of many articles being rejected by English-language international academic journals because they do not conform to 'Anglo' discourse patterns and of books that are given very negative reviews in such journals for the same reason. 'Clumsy', 'longwindedness', 'confused', and 'chaotic' are among the adjectives used to annihilate the texts of German writers. Note the stereotypes in the following:

- 'For readers not extremely well-versed in German academic prose, the structure of the work limits its readability.' (Wildner-Bassett 1987)
- 'Though W writes in the manner of an Austrian academic, this is a readable volume.' (Salus 1983)
- 'This book is, in brief, rather chaotic... The student... would surely flounder in the murky prose and desultory organization.' (Bills 1979)

None of the four reviews by Central Europeans of the book referred to in the last quotation (Rein 1974, Geye 1974, Leodolter 1974, Prucha 1974) make any judgment of this kind. Just as dispersions cast on the scholarly validity of texts presented according to the other person's cultural discourse patterns are discriminatory, so too are international or multicultural organizations which model their meeting rules according to the discourse structures of one culture. And so are judgments of the reliability and integrity of other people passed according to communication patterns which the 'critics' have not bothered to learn to understand and have simply rejected as 'wrong' or 'deviant'.

I would therefore argue that inter-cultural communication should be an essential component of English as a mother tongue, English as a second language and communication skills courses at school and university. Such programmes can obviously not teach everything about the discourse patterns of a particular culture. Any attempt to do so would most likely end up in merely a series of stereotypes. The most valuable exercise of the programmes might be to equip students with a set of options of discourse patterns and expectations. The students should at least be able to ask questions, the responses to which could contribute to an understanding of the pragmatic or discourse rules and the reasons behind them.

The issue of cross-cultural variation is one which educational authorities and institutions, professional associations, and academic journals need to consider seriously.

7.4   Implications in the multicultural workplace

If there is one domain where training in inter-cultural communication is particularly crucial, it is in multicultural workplaces of the types in which data for this project was collected. In our data, inter-cultural communication breakdown occurs at the discourse and pragmatic levels, rather than being caused by phonological, lexical and morphosyntactic questions. Successful inter-cultural communication has social and economic consequences for both labour and management, since communication breakdown can lead to interpersonal conflict and a drop in productivity due to time lost in negotiation of meaning. There is little evidence of blatant racism. The nearest thing, perhaps, is people talking more politely to people from one group than to those from another. But there are clearly many instances of lack of sensitivity to the cultural needs and styles of people from backgrounds very different from one's own.

It was noted that there are hardly any South-east Asians in employee participation groups in the factories under investigation. And those involved in meetings and meeting situations in any of our workplaces talk far less than most people from other cultural groups (4.4, 4.6.3). This issue is a challenge as there is a need to empower people to realize their potential to the fullest and to facilitate industrial democracy. A less 'democratic' style of chairing meetings appears to be more conducive to participation on the part of people of South-east Asian background (4.4). In 6.2.7, I suggested that it was the cultural values systems stressing harmony and with a low uncertainty avoidance and a high power distance that underlie the short turns and deferential turn-taking procedures of, say, ethnic Chinese and Vietnamese. In this case, we would be forcing alien values on these people if we coerced them to behave in another manner. I believe that a mutual exposure of people from different cultural backgrounds to inter-cultural communication programmes (rather than merely ESL programmes with a communicative approach) could confront interlocutors with the problem of their diverging communicative styles and give them the choice between their own original patterns and variation according to situation. The minimal result should be a better understanding of the issues. Not only non-native speakers of English, but also native speakers need to participate in inter-cultural communication programmes in the workplace. Such programmes should include problem-solving sessions, where, on the basis of empirical data, participants co-operatively compare communicative styles and resolve communication breakdown (cf. Roberts et al. 1992). Where groups of workers are inter-cultural, and include people with a high level of English proficiency (perhaps Australian-educated bilinguals), the opportunities for mutual learning are enhanced. This is likely to help not only workplace communication, but also efforts towards industrial democracy.

In future, 'pooled' and 'sequential' interdependence will be replaced in many industries by semi-autonomous work, team participation, and multi-skilling. All this will require a high level of communicative skills in English, and the ability to communicate and co-operate across cultural boundaries. It is in the car factory which still practised mainly 'pooled' and 'sequential' interdependence that ethnic differentiation in the workers' discourse was strongest. However, that same company displayed a caring consciousness of the ethnic breakdown of the workplace and its implications. Award restructuring (in Australia, under the National Wage Case decision of 12 August 1988) provides for skills upgrading and ensuring that working patterns and arrangements 'enhance flexibility and the efficiency of the industry'. Many workplaces have since introduced 'multiskilling'. In the subsequent negotiations between the trade unions and the employers, survival English has played a significant role. For instance, the metals and telecommunications, health, and railways unions have each demanded ESL courses in work time for those not sufficiently proficient in the language.

The Australian Language and Literacy Policy (1991) sees lack of (basic) English proficiency as a contributing factor in the high level of occupational injuries (costing $300,000 p.a.) and in workers' compensation ($4 billion). Basic English as a second language and English literacy are among the areas in which companies in Australia with a payroll of over $A 200,000 p.a. can fulfil their obligation to spend 1.5% of their annual income on upgrading the skills of employees under the Training Guarantee Act.

While such measures are essential to improve the life and work chances of employees without survival English, it is also necessary to improve inter-cultural communication beyond the 'bare survival' level as has been demonstrated in this project. This is in the interests of a more harmonious, just, and economically viable society. It is in the highest levels of Ehlich's (1986) six-point scale of second language competence (see 1.3.4) that communication breakdown often occurs due to xenisms (foreignness markers) in discourse because native speakers do not expect them. The need for sensitivity to inter-cultural communication is at least as urgent in the professions as on the factory floor. The Melbourne *Age* of 30 November 1991 reports that a Hungarian-born textile teacher who had been denied promotion was awarded $55,000 by the Equal Opportunity Board. According to the report, women teachers from non-English-speaking backgrounds in her department at a college of technical and further education were considered by their colleagues to be 'emotional, highly strung, demanding and overtly conscientious in their work, long-winded and unable to be concise, holding undue regard for academic qualifications as opposed to practical experience...' and the teacher in question had been told that she was 'oversensitive and paranoid'. In view of the discourse patterns of Central Europeans described in Chapters 4 and 5, the importance of a substantial educational programme in inter-cultural communication is evident so that Australia is able to benefit more from its human resources. (It is probable that the treatment of this textile teacher is neither typical nor an isolated instance.) To cite just one more example, studies of communication between Anglo-Australian doctors or lawyers and their patients or clients from other backgrounds (Pauwels 1990, 1991, 1992) demonstrate that the perception of communication problems among English-speaking professionals is often limited to narrowly linguistic problems, excluding discourse and pragmatic issues. Similar cases of communicative norm discrepancy are to be found in Japanese–Australian business encounters (Marriott 1990).

7.5   The international scene

The 'linguistic imperialism' documented in Phillipson (1992) for English involves not only the deliberate spread of the language, but also the cultural domination by the 'core' (e.g. the US and Britain) of the 'periphery' (those nations using English as an international link language or for international purposes) – something which applies also, if to a lesser extent, to other pluricentric languages, such as Arabic and French, which have a number of different centres each with a national variety and different culture-specific norms (cf. the papers in Clyne 1992). The questions discussed in the previous paragraph are also relevant to other multicultural nations which have a single national language, whatever that may be.

Urban Australia has become a microcosm of international communication. As it undergoes even greater demographic change, the variety of communicative styles in contact in the work and non-work domains increases. But European and Asian countries are becoming increasingly interested in each other, and interacting more in a growing range of spheres, especially commercial, technological, and academic. (This will apply also between other regions of the world.) The relationship is no longer one of the west (or the north) 'helping' and dominating the east (or the south). Consequently, the domination of some cultures through rejection of their communicative styles and, by extension, the content of the message, the values system behind it, and, in turn, the speaker or writer, has to be abandoned.

7.6   Closing remarks

This chapter began with a synthesis of the more theoretical conclusions of this study. It proceeded with the consideration of sociocultural models describing the interaction of various groups within a multicultural society, and then to some practical implications. I argue that biculturalism – and therefore an active command of more than one communicative style (their own and a modified version of that of the 'dominant' group, to which other styles are converging) – is desirable. In addition, a passive command of as many styles as possible would be advantageous. As discourse patterns are closely linked with cultural values, including issues of face, it is not desirable to make people abandon those stemming from their own cultural backgrounds. It is, however, necessary for people of all cultural backgrounds to understand and tolerate one another's discourse patterns. These may, in fact, be a key to the understanding of other cultures. This applies in both multicultural societies and international settings, to people from 'dominant' and 'minority' groups. Inter-cultural communication training programmes should be an integral part of regular education as well as workplace training.

The present study has only been able to 'scratch the surface' and the results should be seen as indicative rather than definitive. Further research is required, of greater depth, taking in more data from more specific groups within each area, and more informants from individual groups. It is important to be able to differentiate *Kommunikationsbünde* on the basis of discourse features. The position of cultural groups such as Iranians has to be located through comparison of their discourse with those of adjacent groups. There is also a need for studies of more breadth, encompassing a greater diversity of *Kommunikationsbünde*. We also need analyses of comparable data from monocultural and multicultural settings to assess the influence of the inter-ethnic contact situations on communication patterns. Finally, we require studies of the effects of inter-cultural communication training on the patterns of inter-cultural interaction in the workplace. The task of mapping discourse features across cultures and languages is both exciting and daunting. If pursued in an appropriate spirit, this work may well offer a key to inter-cultural and international understanding. It deserves to become one of the significant areas of linguistics in the early twenty-first century.

Appendix 1

Non-key informants by gender, language, and workplace status

Workplace	Gender	Language (Cultural group)	Status
Amcar	m	Arabic (Syrian)	L
	m	Arabic (Lebanese)	L
	m	Italian	L
	plus nine key informants (see 2.3)		
Nipponcar	f	Italian	L
	f	Vietnamese	L
	plus six key informants (see 2.3)		
Weavers	m	English (Australian)*	H
	m	English (Australian)*	H
	m	Macedonian	M
	m	Macedonian	M
	m	Urdu (Pakistani)	L
	plus five key informants (see 2.3)		
Elektro	m	German	M
	f	Filipino	L
	f	German	L
	f	German	L
	f	Hokkien (Singapore-Chinese)	L
	f	Italian	L
	f	Malay (Singapore-Malay)	L
	f	Polish	L
	m	Vietnamese	L
	f	Vietnamese	L
	f	Vietnamese	L
	f	Vietnamese	L
	plus eight key informants (see 2.3)		
Catering	m	Maltese	M
	m	Spanish (Uruguayan)	M
	m	Hakka (Cambodian-Chinese)	L
	f	Sri Lankan English (Burgher)	L
	m	Sri Lankan English (Burgher)	L
	plus eight key informants (see 2.3)		

Appenxix 1 (*cont.*)

Workplace	Gender	Language (Cultural group)	Status
Employment Office	f	English (Australian)	H
	m	Gaelic (Irish)	H
	m	Maltese, English	H
	f	Cambodian	M
	m	English (Australian)	M
	m	Greek	M
	f	Spanish	M
	m	Teocheow (Vietnamese-Chinese)	M
		no key informants (see 2.3)	
Education Office		*two key informants (see 2.3)*	
Parent group		*two key informants (see 2.3)*	

For the purposes of the analysis, 'European' includes groups from the European continent, excluding Turkey and including Malta. 'South-east Asian' includes Cambodians, Filipinos, Indonesians, Malays, Vietnamese, and ethnic Chinese from that region. 'South Asian' includes Indians and Sri Lankans of all ethnic groups, Pakistanis, and Iranians.
* *Not included in the statistics or description of the corpus.*

Appendix 2

Index of Informants' Pseudonyms, ages and ethnolinguistic background

Name	Company	Sex	Age	Ethnicity	1st Language	2nd Languages
Aija	Nipponcar	female	30	Finnish	Finnish	Swedish, German, English, Greek
Alfonso	Catering	male	40	Uruguayan	Spanish	English
Anh	Nipponcar	female	30	Vietnamese	Vietnamese	Cantonese, English
Betty	Catering	female	35	Burgher	English	Sinhalese
Bill	Weavers	male	55	Maltese	Maltese	English
Blanche	Elektro	female	35	Singaporean-Chinese	Teocheow	Mandarin, Malay, Chinese
Bob	Weavers	male	55	Macedonian	Macedonian	English
Boba	Education Office	female	27	Croatian	Croatian	Serbian, English
Cam	Catering	female	30	Vietnamese	Vietnamese	English
Celia	Elektro	female	35	Singapore-Malay	Malay	Teocheow, Hokkien, English
Charlie	Employment Office	male	40	Maltese	English	Maltese, Dutch
Craig	Employment Office	male	40	Australian	English	–
Daniel	Catering	male	25	Cambodian-Chinese	Hakka	Khmer, Vietnamese, English
Dougall	Weavers	male	35	Australian	English	–
Dulip	Weavers	male	38	Sinhalese	Sinhalese	English
Faith	Elektro	female	30	Fillipino	Tagalog	English, Spanish, Japanese
Farouk	Elektro	male	55	Turkish	Turkish/Armenian	English
Franca	Elektro	female	40	Italian	Italian	English
Frank	Nipponcar	male	40	Maltese	Maltese	English
Gabi	Elektro	female	45	German	German	English
Gary	Weavers	male	35	Australian	English	–
George	Employment Office	male	51	Greek	Greek	English
Giao	Elektro	female	30	Vietnamese	Vietnamese	Cantonese, Mandarin, English

Name	Workplace	Gender	Age	Background	Language	Other Languages
Hoa	Elektro	female	22	Vietnamese	Vietnamese	English
Hung	Elektro	female	30	Vietnamese	Vietnamese	English
Inge	Elektro	female	40	German	German	English
Irma	Parent Group	female	45	Croatian	Serbo-Croatian	Russian, Polish, Hungarian, English
Ivan	Catering	male	50	Croatian	Croatian	English
Jennifer	Elektro	female	35	Malaysian-Chinese	Hokkien	Cantonese, Malay, English
Joe	Amcar	male	35	Syrian	Arabic (Syrian)	English
John	Weavers	male	40	Pakistani	Urdu	English
Khalil	Catering	male	35	Iranian	Farsi	English
Krysztina	Elektro	female	45	Polish	Polish	English
Lee	Catering	male	20	Cambodian-Chinese	Hakka	Khmer, Vietnamese, English
Liesl	Elektro	female	50	Austrian	German	English
Lola	Nipponcar	female	35	Italian	Italian	English
Manuela	Employment Office	female	53	Spanish	Spanish	English
Maria	Parent Group	female	45	Italian	Italian	English
Mario	Amcar	male	50	Italian	Italian	English
Marisa	Catering	female	23	Salvadorian	Spanish	English
Michael	Amcar	male	40	Lebanese	Lebanese	English
Mick	Weavers	male	50	Ukrainian	English	–
Minh	Elektro	male	30	Vietnamese	Vietnamese	English
Muntha	Employment Office	female	31	Cambodian	Khmer	English
Mustafa	Nipponcar	male	25	Turkish	Turkish	English
Patrick	Employment Office	male	59	Irish	Gaelic	English
Peter	Elektro	male	45	German	German	English
Quoc	Education Office	male	33	Vietnamese	Vietnamese	English
Rachel	Employment Office	female	27	Australian	English	–
Raymond	Nipponcar	male	33	Burgher	English	Sinhalese
Ricarda	Elektro	female	30	Filipino	Tagalog	English

220

Name	Company	Sex	Age	Ethnicity	1st Language	2nd Languages
Rose	Nipponcar	female	25	Phillipino	Tagalog	English
Roy	Catering	male	20	Burgher	English	Sinhalese
Sandor	Elektro	male	50	Hungarian	Hungarian	'Czechoslovakian', English
Seyit	Amcar	male	35	Turkish	Turkish	English
Slobodan	Elektro	male	45	Croatian	Croatian	English
Tim	Catering	male	45	Fijian Indian	Hindi	English
Tom	Elektro	male	35	Indonesian	Indonesian	Dutch, English
Tony	Catering	male	30	Maltese	Maltese	English
Tuan	Weavers	male	30	Vietnamese	Vietnamese	English
Tuk	Employment Office	male	42	Vietnamese-Chinese	Teochew	Cantonese, Vietnamese, Mandarin, English
Vin	Weavers	male	55	Italian	Italian	English
Vlad	Weavers	male	37	Macedonian	Macedonian	English

Appendix 3

BAD SOLDERING - [Elektro]

1 Slobo.]   Blanche good morning + 5.0 + ←a <u>ha</u> complain again   afternoon
2 Blanche] morning   no

---

3 Slobo.] shift make the big xxxx xxxx [laughter]
4 Blanche]   no no no no   no no no no no   you put Ricarda on the soldering hand

---

5 Blanche] soldering + 2.3 + I can't sit there and check every/ once she soldered a

---

6 Slobo.]   I put Ricarda there look er + 2.0 +
7 Blanche] couple she'd be alright + 2.3 +   she was

---

8 Slobo.]   Ricarda no = no = ↓yeah. well er that doesn't mean if she was in school
9 Blanche] in the xxxxx school

---

10 Slobo.] that she is expert you know how is it people who are finishing school
11 Blanche]   yeah xxxx xxxxx

---

12 Slobo.]   even   even u/ no no even u = university what
13 Blanche] maybe she doesn't like the job   oh

---

14 Slobo.] if you put them on production they still need a couple of years + to +
15 Blanche] I know

---

16 Slobo.]   become expert and so on   the same things as Blanche
17 Blanche] yeah the problem is they   I can't

---

18   Slobo.]   I can't take someone beside me I've got to check + I haven't got anyone

19   Slobo.]   I am agreed that you cannot sit beside but sometimes er if we check it

20   Slobo.]   and we find it wrong we have to + show care and er...

_____

{a minute later}

_____

21   Slobo.]   ah you know what + the job what she did give her back me check it

_____

22   Slobo.]   no problem about that then I'm going to talk to her + ↓now +
23   Blanche]   yup   mm   > maybe

_____

24   Slobo.]   Blanche that's not that's not/ doesn't
25   Blanche]   she doesn't like the job + 2.1 +   < you know how it is

_____

26   Slobo.]   matter + if somebody doesn't like a job then try to escape from a job

_____

27   Slobo.]   because ←doing it wrong + ←no. + no hope about that.   if people want
28   Blanche]   mm   yeah

_____

29   Slobo.]   have a better job or = or job position or →something like that. they should
30   Blanche]   I know

_____

31   Slobo.]   prove themself on any other work no it's + < if someone doesn't like a
32   Blanche]   that's why   yeah   I just want to work

_____

33   Slobo.]   job they said < oh I'm going to = to make it fair I'm going to = to make a
34   Blanche]   to make it work for you xxxxxxx

_____

35   Slobo.]   scrap and something like that and then you give me some other job

_____

36   Slobo.]   that's not true   if she's not good enough she = she sup =
37   Blanche]   alright + 2.5 +

_____

38   Slobo.]   supposed to go again on the training area and er + 3.0 + Ricarda + +
39   Ricarda]   yes

_____

```
40  Slobo. ]  let's have a talk about the quality of soldering joints + +       yes give
41  Ricarda ]                                                                      yeah
```
_____

```
42  Slobo. ]  me those two there + + Ricarda I understand that you don't have any

43  Slobo. ]  experience with soldering + + you've been on that area for a week week

44  Slobo. ]  and a half + + to be trained on it + + and I know another things that +

45  Slobo. ]  whoever is a-trained for a couple of weeks on soldering cannot become

46  Slobo. ]  expert     and we don't expect that you are expert In these two three
47  Ricarda ]       mm                                      xxxx xxxx xxxxxx xxxx
```
_____

```
48  Slobo. ]  weeks + 2.2 + ←I think is what we would like  happening to concentrate

49  Slobo. ]  your self a little  bit  more + 1.8 + on the job you do + just example

50  Slobo. ]  + 2.5 + it's very unskilled + see this icicle + 1.5 + that's happened

51  Slobo. ]  because you didn't heat it properly + or you did it without any flux

52  Slobo. ]  + 3.2 + and another things          I don't know according to her she
53  Ricarda ]                           ↑this my work
```
_____

```
54  Slobo. ]  said this is
55  Ricarda ]             Franca  ↑is this all my work + 1.6 +
56  Franca  ]                                            that's the one ah you
```
_____

```
57  Slobo. ]                                   yes  is somebody else = is somebody
58  Ricarda ]  gave to me I show you you know xxxx xxxx xxxx xxxx
```
_____

```
59  Slobo. ]  else doing that ↓or what +
60  Ricarda ]                         not xxxx xxxx work is ↑this the one you
```
_____

```
61  Ricarda ]  showed to me
62  Franca  ]              yes but I told you we asked Gianche if someone had to
```
_____

```
63  Ricarda ]                              xxxxxx I didn't do this one  + +
64  Franca  ]  check your work + 2.6 + later + 2.3 +
```
_____

65 Ricarda] and look what you have shown to Blanche all the <u>worst</u> jobs
66 Franca]   {not} one I

_____

67 Ricarda]   I can solder much better than that +2.0+
68 Franca] showed to you those three + +

_____

69 Blanche]   anyone anyone
70 Ricarda]   Franca you're putting me on a treadmill
71 Franca] xxxx xxxx xxxx

_____

72 Slobo.]   ↑look I saw that guy in the afternoon
73 Blanche] else sitting here who did soldering

_____

74 Slobo.] doing something in here. ah   not unless
75 Blanche]   xxxxx xxxxx   anyone sitting here do

_____

76 Slobo.]   ah well
77 Blanche] do soldering +3.5+ well you better make sure who did it

_____

78 Slobo.] she/i = if she never soldered before   she may not do soldering if she
79 Blanche]   yes never soldered

_____

80 Slobo.] never did soldering not at all
81 Franca]   unless she mix with the one with the one you

_____

82 Slobo.]   ←a <u>ha</u> here we are + xxx xxx xxx + w = well anyway + +
83 Franca] gave me

_____

84 Slobo.] Blanche + Blanche it's = it's what happen you don't know →not much

_____

85 Slobo.] sorry about it you have to talk to people otherwise people doesn't know
86 Franca]   no

_____

87 Slobo.] why there they're doing a good =
88 Franca]   that's enough   plenty you gave to me the one I showed to

_____

89 Slobo.]   ↑Blanche
90 Ricarda]   you showed me   not even a board I/ and I even asked you
91 Franca] you +   xxxxx

---

92 Slobo.]   ↑'scuse me
93 Ricarda] I will xxxxxxx   and you said and when I was there things are

---

94 Slobo.]   →Ricarda   how long you are soldering
95 Ricarda] better you can do the hand solderer   yes
96 Franca]   xxxxxx

---

97 Slobo.] on that area + + about + week time +   second week ah ↑←did
98 Ricarda]   this is my

---

99 Slobo.] they find <u>before</u> a solder joints like that on your job +
100 Franca]   no that's why xxxxx

---

101 Slobo.] you didn't now I am sure then that some kind of mistake is done because

---

102 Slobo.] er + 2.4 + this is really ugly
103 Franca]   and I don't try to put you in trouble or

---

104 Slobo.]   see as = as I see look the person who passed the
105 Franca] anything but you I saw xxxx xxxx

---

106 Slobo.] soldering course >can't make it like that + + bit suspicious but anyway

---

107 Slobo.] + + whatever is happened + if we blame you for the things you what

---

108 Slobo.] you didn't done we apologize on it but anyway it would happen   see
109 Franca]   xxxxx

---

110 Slobo.] what I want to   hhm
111 Franca]   the only thing she had twenty done   here and er

---

112 Slobo.] excuse me miss + 3.8 + according to some people here I hear that you

---

113 Slobo.]   did soldering yesterday   ←please don't do soldering. + + the soldering
114 (worker)   yes
_____

115 Slobo.]   is the er job was supposed to be done with the training ah with the

116 Slobo.]   peolple who are trained in soldering + + well we see that some er + +

117 Slobo.]   job is done in here which is really really + 1.5 + unskilful and = and ugly

118 Slobo.]   and et cetera ah that's + not acceptable at all and please don't do a
119 (worker)   xxxxx
_____

120 Slobo.]   soldering + + if you are on waiting time and have nothing to do you see

121 Slobo.]   me or Blanche + and you will get another ↓job + ↑if you interested to

122 Slobo.]   do a soldering ←no problem at all + + we will put you on that area there

123 Slobo.]   on the training + + and you will be trained + + and once when you pass

124 Slobo.]   the course no problem you get the soldering in hand go on with it + +

125 Slobo.]   but please don't do a soldering + any more > ↓thank you + 2.2 +

126 Slobo.]   ↑Blanche I think   I think it's mistake alright   now girls whatever is
127 Blanche]   xxxx xxxx   xxxxxxxxxx
_____

128 Slobo.]   happened
129 Franca]   when   yeah you're right when you = you went away + + she was
_____

130 Blanche]   she's not supposed to sit
131 Ricarda]   xxxxx xxxxxx xxxxx
132 Franca]   sitting there   yeah she was sitting there
_____

133 Slobo.]   I = I just spoke to her alright if she's
134 Blanche]   she's not touching xxxx xxxx
_____

135 Slobo.]   interested to get + + soldering in hand we put her there for a weeks
136 Blanche]   xxxxx xxxxx xxxx
_____

137 Slobo.]   and no problem + + whatever is happened now we see   that some units
138 Blanche]   xxxxx
_____

139 Slobo.] are bad ←girls + + accept it mistake is done please go through + make
140 Blanche]   yeah I know I only want to

---

141 Slobo.] agreement now whoever and er   book the time again   look it's
142 Blanche]   sorry xxxxx   xxxxxx

---

143 Slobo.] xxxxx I'm sorry we ah   apologize for this mistake and that's it okay
144 Blanche] xxxxxx   xxxxxxx xxxxxx
145 Franca]   xxxxxxx xxxxx

---

146 Slobo.] everybody can make mistakes   ah so + +
147 Blanche]   alright so carry on [laughter]

---

148 Slobo.] anyway this fault has to be corrected we may not put it through and

149 Slobo.] please girls ckeck it share it and ckeck it fix it and go on wlth lt well er

150 Slobo.] that's the only way how we can make it

SELF-REPROACH - [Elektro]

1 Jennifer]   yes   Krysztina   yes
2 Krysz.] Jennifer   now I can see you because everything is fixed up so I can

---

3 Jennifer]   yes fixed up what   yeah
4 Krysz.] tell you   I + + yesterday   the incident with Anna +

---

5 Krysz.] I was probably it was my fault alright I don't know whose fault but I

---

6 Jennifer]   why Krysztina just
7 Krysz.] take + my +   yes I blame myself for it
8 Gabi   ]   you blame yourself for it

---

9 Jennifer] for↑get it
10 Krysz.]   it was to make the conn/ the +1.9+   the er transistors
11 Gabi   ]   the transistors

```
12  Jennifer ]                                        ↓oh
13  Krysz.  ] er              ↑alright + +    and that was the reason I don't  want to
14  Gabi    ]    xxxxx transistors
```
_____

```
15  Krysz.  ] give = give Anna the  job + alright + because I find that in the middle of

16  Krysz.  ] the job was accidentally I find oh I said what's going wrong + and after

17  Krysz.  ] all I + check every part I put in but + I didn't know how many had done
```
_____

```
18  Jennifer ] ↓oh
19  Krysz.  ] it     and on the end I just check that and was ←nine wrong + alright
```
_____

```
20  Jennifer ] look Krysztina + for ↑me + is nothing worrying me it's just that if
21  Krysz.  ]                                      xxxxxx xxxxx I thought
```
_____

```
22  Krysz.  ] she was so angry so upset when she said you are worst person + 2.0 +
```
_____

```
23  Jennifer ] ←for ↑me if there's ↑problems  just have to discuss and →sort it out
24  Krysz.  ]                                  it's just = it's just
```
_____

```
25  Jennifer ] that's all
26  Krysz.  ]         xxxxx Hung told me not to tell anyone  it was/ it get/ it was
```
_____

```
27  Jennifer ]                                                oh
28  Krysz.  ] mixed up  and ah + ↑what should I tell her we can't   give xxxx because
```
_____

```
29  Krysz.  ] the components are mixed up alright ↑so I said no you can't take it. and
```
_____

```
30  Jennifer ]                   so you just brought it in by mistake    ←yeah well these
31  Krysz.  ] she's so upset                                yeah
```
_____

```
32  Jennifer ] things happen  these things happen  ↑don't worry Krysztina
33  Krysz.  ]                            yes                  xxxxx xxxxx
```
_____

```
34  Jennifer ]                   hah xxxx ↑don't worry +
35  Krysz.  ] everything is fixed        xxxx            you = you know I'm very
```
_____

36   Jennifer]   mm mmm ←don't worry
37   Krysz.   ] sensitive   xxxxx xxxxx xxxxx
38   Gabi   ]   when I have trouble with Jennifer I tell
39   chorus   ] xxxx xxxx xxxx   xxxxxx xxxxxx

---

40   Krysz.   ]   and I said
41   Gabi   ] her off and she tells me off and then we're right again aren't we (*laughs*)

---

42   Krysz.   ] to my husband you know + that's life and everything and = and he said

---

43   Jennifer]   ↑is your husband back= back from
44   Krysz.   ] oh you should leave that job huh

---

45   Jennifer] Atlantic
46   Krysz.   ]   everytime I just find something out he says ↑you should leave

---

47   Krysz.   ] that job you should stay at home   no I
48   Gabi   ]   ↑so you can't even talk about it at home

---

49   Jennifer]   Krysztina
50   Krysz.   ] can't even talk you know   ↑can't even talk. to anyone + +
51   Gabi   ]   mm   xxxx

---

52   Jennifer] look + ←sometimes people have er   ←I can understand
53   Krysz.   ]   yes but   you don't

---

54   Jennifer]   look I
55   Krysz.   ] even xxxx you know I was so shy that xxx aren't necessary

---

56   Jennifer] understand these things xx xx it just do happen sometimes people just

---

57   Jennifer] overlook ↑yes it's just overlook like they did it's just overlook
                                          but not but not many mistake +

---

58   Jennifer]   oh yes that for sure
59   Krysz..] mistakes anybody can do   I'm= I'm talking about
60   Gabi   ]   xxxxx xxxx xxxxx

---

61 Jennifer]   oh don't worry + just take it + just take it
62 Krysz.   ] the + 1.5 + with xxxxxxx +

---

63 Jennifer] as it comes
64 Gabi   ]   xxxxxxx which one sh/ probably she thinks I'm bad xxxxx

---

65 Jennifer]   oh yeah no worries ↑yes
66 Gabi   ] because that she wants that job

---

some minutes later

---

68 Jennifer]   <u>who</u> which girl + 1.7 + ↑ah
69 Krysz.   ] do want to explain her   do you know yesterday

---

70 Krysz.   ] + + it was their + boards I didn't want to xxxx xxxx the reason was +
71 Krysz.   ] because it was mixed up the components + alright and I want to fix it
72 Krysz.   ] myself because that was my fault + ↑alright. xxxx I got against you or
73 Krysz.   ] + I = I didn't want to give you because I don't like your company so it's

---

74 Jennifer]   ↑oh Krysztina ↓don't
75 Krysz.   ] the only reason I can't give you the boards ↑alright

---

76 Jennifer] worry + 1.5 +   ↑oh →don't
77 Krysz.   ]   ↑yeah but it's = it's so. I feel so. so bad y'know

---

78 Jennifer] worry ↑I'll fix up for you + 1.5 + >no it's nothing. + ←some people is a

---

79 Jennifer] bit sensitive   you know xxxx + ↑<u>good morning Lisa</u>

References

Allan, Keith 1986 *Linguistic meaning*. 2 vols. London: Routledge and Kegan Paul.

1991 Cooperative Principle. In W. Bright (ed.), *Oxford international encyclopaedia of linguistics*. New York: Oxford University Press, 310–11.

1994 Speech act theory – an overview. In R. E. Asher et al. (eds.), *Encyclopaedia of language and linguistics*. Edinburgh: Pergamon and University of Aberdeen Press.

Apitzsch, Gisela and Norbert Dittmar 1987 Contact between German and Turkish adolescents. In Knapp, Enninger, and Knapp-Pothoff, 51–71.

Austin, John L. 1962 *How to do things with words*. Oxford University Press.

1963 Performative – Constative. In C. E. Caton (ed.), *Philosophy and ordinary language*. Urbana: University of Illinois Press, 22–54.

Backa, Susanne 1987 Interkulturelle Probleme in der Beratung – eine Fallstudie. In Redder and Rehbein, 53–68.

Bardovi-Harlig, Kathleen and Beverly Hartford 1990 Congruence in native and nonnative conversations: status balance in the academic advising session. *Language Learning* 40, 467–501.

1992 Natural conversations, institutional talk, and interlanguage pragmatics. Paper read at Pacific Second Language Research Forum, Sydney, July 1992.

Barth, Frederik 1969 *Ethnic groups and boundaries*. Boston: Little, Brown and Co.

Bateson, Gregory 1972 *Steps to an ecology of mind*. New York: Ballantine.

Baumann, Klaus-Dieter and Hartwig Kalverkämpfer (eds.) 1992 *Kontrastive Fachsprachforschung*. Tübingen: Narr.

Bayrataroglu, Arin 1991 Politeness and interactional imbalance. *International Journal of the Sociology of Language* 92, 5–34.

Béal, Christine 1990 It's all in the asking. *Australian Review of Applied Linguistics* Series S, No. 7, 16–32.

1992 Did you have a good weekend? Or Why there is no such thing as a simple question in cross-cultural encounters. *Australian Review of Applied Linguistics* 15, 23–52.

Bernstein, Basil 1962 Social class, linguistic codes and grammatical elements. *Language and Speech* 5, 31–46.

Bickner, Robert and Patcharin Peysantiwong 1988 Cultural variation in reflective writing. In Purves, 160–75.

Bills, Garland D. 1979 Review of Norbert Dittmar, Soziolinguistik. *Language* 55, 454–6.

Blommaert, Jan and Jef Verschueren 1993 The rhetoric of tolerance or what police officers are taught about migrants. *Journal of Intercultural Studies* 13, 49–63.

Blum-Kulka, Shoshana 1989 Playing it safe: the role of conventionality in indirectness. In Blum-Kulka, House, and Kasper, 37–70.

Blum-Kulka, Shoshana and Juliane House 1989 Cross-cultural and situational variation in requesting behavior. In Blum-Kulka, House, and Kasper, 123–54.

Blum-Kulka, Shoshana, Juliane House and Gabriele Kasper (eds.) 1989 *Cross-cultural pragmatics*. Norwood: Ablex.

Bodi, Leslie 1985 Comic ambivalence as an identity marker: the Austrian model. In Pavel Petr, David Roberts, and Philip Thomson (eds.), *Comic relations*. Frankfurt: Lang, 67–78.

Bremer, Katherina et al. 1988 *Achieving understanding*. Vol. 1 of Final Report of European Science Foundation project on Second Language Acquisition by Adult Immigrants. Strasbourg and London: ESF.

1994 *Constructing mutual understanding*. London: Longman.

Brick, Jean 1991 *China: a handbook in inter-cultural communication*. Sydney: National Centre for English Language Teaching and Research.

Brock, Cynthia, Graham Crookes, Richard Day, and Michael Long 1988 The differential effects of corrective feedback in native speaker–nonnative speaker conversation. In Day, 229–36.

Brown, Gillian and George Yule 1983 *Discourse analysis*. Cambridge University Press.

Brown, Penelope and Stephen Levinson 1978 Universals in language usage: politeness phenomena. In Esther Goody (ed.), *Questions and politeness*. Cambridge University Press, 56–289.

1987 *Politeness*. Cambridge University Press.

Bublitz, Wolfram 1988 *Supportive fellow-speakers and cooperative conversations*. Amsterdam: Benjamins.

Button, Graham and John R. E. Lee (eds.) 1987 *Talk and social organization*. Clevedon: Multilingual Matters.

Carroll, Raymonde 1987 *Cultural misunderstanding: the French–American experience*. University of Chicago Press.

Cauchi, Maurice 1990 *Maltese migrants in Australia*. Melbourne: Ethnic Communities Council.

Chan Heng Chee 1992 What comes first? Sunday Review. *Sunday Times*, Singapore, 22 November 1992, p. 6.

Chiaro, Delia 1992 *The language of jokes: analysing language play*. London: Routledge.

Chick, K. 1989 Inter-cultural miscommunication as a source of friction in the workplace and in educational settings in South Africa. In Garcia and Otheguy, 139–60.

Chilton, P. (ed.) 1985 *Language and the nuclear arms debate*. London: Pinter.

Clahsen, Harald, Jürgen Meisel, and Manfred Pienemann 1983 *Deutsch als Zweitsprache: Der Spracherwerb ausländischer Arbeiter*. Tübingen: Narr.

Clyne, Michael 1975 A non-verbal check on acceptability of transference among bilinguals. *ITL Review of Applied Linguistics* 30, 55–64.

1977 Multilingualism and pidginization in Australian industry. *Ethnic Studies* 1, 40–55.

1979 Communicative competences in contact. *ITL Review of Applied Linguistics* 43, 17–38.

1980 Writing, testing and culture. *The Secondary Teacher* 11, 13–16.

1981 Culture and discourse structure. *Journal of Pragmatics* 5, 61–6.

1985a Beyond grammar – some thoughts on communication rules in our multicultural society. In John Pride (ed.), *Cross-cultural encounters*. Melbourne: River Seine, 12–23.

1985b Language teaching for inter-cultural communication: what goals for whom? In Kurt R. Jankowsky (ed.), *Scientific and humanistic dimensions of language*. Festschrift for Robert Lado. Amsterdam: Benjamins, 165–74.

1986 Language and racism. In Andrew Markus and Radha Rasmussen (eds.), *Prejudice in the public arena – racism*. Clayton: Centre for Migrant and Intercultural Studies, 35–44.

1987 Cultural differences in the organization of academic texts: English and German. *Journal of Pragmatics* 11, 211–47.

1991a *Community languages – the Australian experience*. Cambridge University Press.

1991b The sociocultural dimension: the dilemma of the German-speaking scholar. In Schröder, 49–67.

1991c Trying to do things with letters. In I. Malcolm (ed.), *Linguistics in the service of society: essays in honour of Susan Kaldor*. Perth: Edith Cowan University, 207–19.

Clyne, Michael (ed.) 1992 *Pluricentric languages*. Berlin: Mouton de Gruyter.

Clyne, Michael and Martin Ball 1990 English as a lingua franca in Australia, especially in industry: a first progress report. *Australian Review of Applied Linguistics* Series S, No.7, 1–15.

Clyne, Michael, Martin Ball and Deborah Neil 1991 Inter-cultural communication at work in Australia. *Multilingua* 10, 251–73.

Clyne, Michael, Connie Giannicos and Deborah Neil 1994 Cross-cultural responses to cross-cultural communication. *ITL Review of Applied Linguistics* 103–104, 1–17.

Clyne, Michael and Heinz-Josef Kreutz 1987 The nature and function of digression and other discourse structure phenomena in German academic writings. *Working Papers in Migrant and Intercultural Studies* 8.

Clyne, Michael, Jimmy Hoeks and Heinz-Josef Kreutz 1988 Cross-cultural responses to academic discourse patterns. *Folia Linguistica* 22, 457–74.

Clyne, Michael and Susan Manton 1979 Rules for conducting meetings in Australia: an inter-ethnic study. *Ethnic Studies* 3, 25–34.

Clyne, Michael and John Platt 1990 The role of language in cross-cultural communication. In Pauwels, 38–55.

Coates, Jennifer 1986 *Women, men and language*. London: Longman.

Cole, Michael and Sylvia Scribner 1974 *Culture and thought*. New York: Wiley.

Connor, Una and Robert B. Kaplan (eds.) 1987 *Writing across cultures*. Reading, Mass.: Addison-Wesley.

Cordella, Marisa 1991 Spanish speakers apologizing in English: a cross-cultural pragmatic study. *Australian Review of Applied Linguistics* 14, 115–38.

Corder, S. Pit 1981 *Error analysis and interlanguage*. Oxford University Press.

Coulmas, Florian (ed.) 1978 *Conversational routine*. The Hague: Mouton.

Crismore, Avon 1989 *Talking with readers*. Frankfurt: Lang.

Danet, Brenda 1970 Die Sprache der Überredung in der Bürokratie. 'Moderne' und 'traditionelle' Appelle an die israelischen Zollbehörden. In R. Kjolseth and F. Sack (eds.), *Zur Soziologie der Sprache*. Opladen: Westdeutscher Verlag, 315–36.

Day, Richard (ed.) 1988 *Talking to learn: conversation in second language acquisition*. Rowley: Newbury House.

Deen, Jeanine and Roeland Van Hout 1991 Clarification sequences in native non-native interaction. In R. van Hout and E. Huls (eds.), *Artikelen van de 1e sociolinguistische conferentie*. Delft: Eburon, 121–38.

Degenhart, R. Elaine and Sauli Takala 1988 Developing a rating method for stylistic preference. In Purves, 79–107.

De Silva, K. M. (general editor) 1973 *History of Ceylon*. Vol. 3. Colombo: University of Ceylon.

di Pietro, J. Robert 1971 *Language structures in contrast*. Rowley: Newbury House.

Đô Quý Toàn 1989 Notes on education in the traditional culture of Vietnam. *Journal of Vietnamese Studies* 1 (2), 13–16.

Dorval, Bruce (ed.) 1990 *Conversational organization*. (= Vol. 38. *Advances in Discourse Processing*.) Norwood: Ablex.

Edmondson, Willis J. 1981 *Spoken discourse: A model for analysis*. London: Longman.

Edmondson, Willis J., Juliane House, Gabriele Kasper, and John McKeown 1979 *Sprachliche Interaktion in lernzielrelevanten Situationen*. LAUT 51, Series B, Trier.

Eggington, William G. 1987 Written academic discourse in Korean. In Connor and Kaplan, 172–89.

Ehlich, Konrad 1980 Sprache in Institutionen. In H.-P. Althaus, H. Henne, and H. E. Wiegand (eds.), *Lexikon der germanistischen Linguistik*. 2nd edn. Tübingen: Niemeyer, 338–46.

1986 Xenismen und die bleibende Fremdheit des Fremdsprachensprechers. In Ernst W. B. Hess-Lüttich (ed.) *Integrität und Identität*. Tübingen: Narr, 43–54.

1987 Kooperation und sprachliches Handeln. In Frank Liedtke and Rudi Keller (eds.), *Kommunikation und Kooperation*. Tübingen: Niemeyer, 117–32.

1992 On the historicity of politeness. In Watts, Ide, and Ehlich, 71–107.

Ehlich, Konrad and Jochen Rehbein 1972 Zur Konstitution pragmatischer Einheiten in einer Institution: Das Speiserestaurant. In Dieter Wunderlich (ed.), *Linguistische Pragmatik*. Frankfurt: Athenäum, 209–54.

1976 Halbinterpretative Arbeitstranskriptionen (HIAT). *Linguistische Berichte* 45, 21–41.

1986 *Muster und Institution*. Frankfurt: Lang.

Ehnert, Rolf 1988 Komm doch mal vorbei: Überlegungen zu einer 'Kultur-kontrastiven Grammatik'. *Jahrbuch Deutsch als Fremdsprache* 14, 301–12.

Elias, Norbert 1936/1969 *The court society*. Oxford: Blackwell.

Enninger, Werner 1987 What interactants do with non-talk across cultures. In Knapp, Enninger, and Knapp-Pothoff, 269–302.

Erickson, F. and J. Shultz 1982 *The counsellor as gatekeeper*. New York: Academic Press.

Fairclough, Norman 1989 *Language and power*. London: Longman.

Farrell, Lesley 1994 A contrastive study of Chilean and Vietnamese students' writing for the VCE. Ph.D., Monash University.

Feigs, Wolfgang 1991 Textsorten in interkultureller Perspektive – deutsch-norwegische Kontraste. In Roger Mackeldey (ed.), *Festschrift zum 65. Geburtstag von Wolfgang Heinemann*. Leipzig: Universität Leipzig, 44–53.

Ferguson, Charles A. 1971 Absence of copula and the notion of simplicity: a study of normal speech, baby talk, foreigner talk and pidgins. In D. Hymes (ed.), *Pidginization and creolization of languages*. Cambridge University Press, 141–50.

Fishman, Joshua A. 1960 The systematization of the Whorfian hypothesis. *Behavioral Science* 5, 323–79.

Fishman, Joshua A., Michael H. Gertner, Esther G. Lowy, and William G. Milán 1985 *The rise and fall of the ethnic revival: perspectives on language and ethnicity*. Berlin: Mouton.

Fox, Barbara 1987 *Discourse structure and anaphora*. Cambridge University Press.

Fraser, Bruce 1985 On the universality of speech act strategies. In S. George (ed.), *From the linguistic to the social context*. Bologna: CLUEB, 43–9.

1990 Perspectives on politeness. *Journal of Pragmatics* 14, 24–36.

Færch, Claus and Gabriele Kasper (ed.) 1983 *Strategies in inter-cultural communication*. Harlow: Longman.

Galtung, Johan 1985 Struktur, Kultur und intellektueller Stil. In Alois Wierlacher (ed.), *Das Fremde und das Eigene*. Munich: iudicium Verlag, 151–93.

Garcia, Ofelia and Ricardo Otheguy (eds.) 1989 *English across cultures, cultures across English*. Berlin: Mouton de Gruyter.

Gardner, Robert C. and Wallace F. Lambert 1972 *Attitudes and motivation in second language learning*. Rowley: Newbury House.

Gardner, Robert C. and Padric Smythe 1975 Motivation and second language acquisition. *Canadian Modern Language Review* 31, 218–30.

Garfinkel, Harold 1967 *Studies in ethnomethodology*. Englewood Cliffs: Prentice-Hall.

Geye, Ernst-Günther 1974 Review of Norbert Dittmar, '*Soziolinguistik*'. *Muttersprache* 84, 243–4.

Giles, Howard 1977 *Language, ethnicity and intergroup relations*. London: Academic Press.

Givón, Talmy (ed.) 1983 *Topic and continuity in discourse: A quantitative cross-language study*. Amsterdam: Benjamins.

Glazer, Nathan and Daniel Moynihan (eds.) 1975 *Ethnicity*. Cambridge, Mass.: Harvard University Press.

Gnutzmann, Claus 1992 Kontrastive Fachtextlinguistik als Projektaufgabe. In Baumann and Kalverkämpfer, 266–75.

Gnutzmann, Claus and Hermann Oldenburg 1991 Contrastive text linguistics in LSP research. In Schröder, 103–36.

Goffman, Erving 1955 On facework: an analysis of ritual elements in social interaction. *Psychiatry* 18, 213–31.

   1983 Replies and responses. In Erving Goffman (ed.), *Forms of talk*. Philadelphia: University of Pennsylvania Press, 5–77.

Gordon, Milton 1964 *Assimilation in American life.* New York: Oxford University Press.

Grice, P. 1975 Logic and conversation. In Peter Cole and J. Morgan (eds.), *Syntax and semantics 3: speech acts.* New York: Academic Press.

Grießhaber, Wilhelm 1987 *Authentisches und zitierendes Handeln.* Band 1 – *Einstellungsgespräche.* Band 2 – *Rollenspiel im Sprachunterricht.* Frankfurt: Lang.

Gumperz, John J. 1982 *Discourse strategies.* Cambridge University Press.

Gumperz, John J., Tom Jupp, and Celia Roberts 1979 *Crosstalk.* National Centre for Industrial Language Training.

Hafez, Ola Mohamed 1991 Turn-taking in Egyptian Arabic. *Journal of Pragmatics* 15, 59–81.

Halliday, M. A. K. 1973 *Explorations in the functions of language.* London: Edward Arnold.

   1978 *Language as a social semiotic.* London: Edward Arnold.

   1993a New ways of meaning: a challenge to applied linguistics. *Australian Review of Applied Linguistics*: Occasional Paper 13, 1–41.

   1993b Language in a changing world. *Australian Review of Applied Linguistics*: Occasional Paper 13, 62–81.

Halliday, M. A. K. and Ruqaiya Hasan 1976 *Cohesion in English.* London: Longman.

Halmari, Helena 1993 Intercultural business telephone conversations: A case of Finns versus Anglo-Americans. *Applied Linguistics* 14, 408–30.

Harder, B. H. 1984 Cultural attitudes in discourse analysis. *Canadian Journal of Linguistics* 29, 115–30.

Hatch, Evelyn Marcussen 1978 Discourse analysis and second language acquisition. In E. M. Hatch (ed.), *Second language acquisition*. Rowley: Newbury House.

Held, Gudrun 1992 Politeness in linguistic research. In Watts, Ide, and Ehlich, 131–53.

Herder, Johann Gottfried 1877–1913 *Sämtliche Werke.* (ed. B. Suphan.) Berlin: Weidmann.

Heritage, John 1984 The change of state token. In M. Atkinson and J. Heritage (eds.), *Structures of social action.* Cambridge University Press.

Hill, Ben, Sachiko Ide, Shoko Ikuta, Akiko Kawasaki, and Tsunao Ogino 1986 Universals of linguistic politeness: quantitative evidence from Japanese and American English. *Journal of Pragmatics* 10, 347–71.

Hinds, John 1980 Japanese expository prose. *International Journal of Human Communication* 13, 117–58.

   1983a Contrastive rhetoric: Japanese and English. *Text* 3, 183–95.

1983b Contrastive studies of English and Japanese. *Annual Review of Applied Linguistics* 3, 78–84.

Hinnenkamp, Volker 1982 *Foreigner talk und Tarzanisch*. Hamburg: Buske.

1987 Foreigner talk, code-switching and the concept of trouble. In Knapp, Enninger, and Knapp-Pothoff, 137–80.

Hofstede, Geert 1984 *Culture's consequences*. New York: Sage.

1991 *Cultures and organizations*. London: McGraw-Hill.

House, Juliane and Gabriele Kasper 1981 Politeness markers in English and German. In Florian Coulmas (ed.), *Conversational routine*. The Hague: Mouton, 157–85.

Hsu, Francis L. K. 1972 *Americans and Chinese: reflections on two cultures and their people*. New York: American Museum Science Books.

Humboldt, Wilhelm von 1903–18 *Gesammelte Schriften*. 7 vols. (ed. A. Leitzmann.) Berlin: Behrs.

Hymes, Dell H. 1972 On communicative competence. In J. B. Pride and Janet Holmes (eds.), *Sociolinguistics*. Harmondsworth: Penguin, 269–93.

1974 *Foundations of sociolinguistics*. Philadelphia: University of Pennsylvania Press.

Ide, Sachiko 1989 Formal forms and discernment. *Multilingua* 8, 223–48.

Ide, Sachiko, Beverly Hill, Yukiko M. Carnes, Tsunao Ogino and Akiko Kawasaki 1992 The concept of politeness: an empirical study of English and Japanese. In Watts, Ide, and Ehlich, 281–97.

Isaacs, H. R. 1975 Basic group identity. In Glazer and Moynihan, 29–52.

James, Carl 1980 *Contrastive linguistics*. Harlow: Longman.

Janney, Richard W. and Horst Arndt 1993 Universality and relativity in cross-cultural politeness research: a historical perspective. *Multilingua* 12, 13–50.

Jupp, James 1988 Settlement patterns in Melbourne. In James Jupp (ed.), *The Australian People*. Sydney: Angus and Robertson, 942–9.

Jupp, Tom 1982 *The teaching of the national language of the host country to adult immigrants*. Strasbourg: Council of Europe.

Kachru, Yamuna 1983 Contrastive studies of English and Hindi. *Annual Review of Applied Linguistics* 3, 50–77.

1988 Writers in Hindi and English. In Purves, 109–37.

Kallmeyer, Werner and Reinhard Meyer-Hermann 1980 Textlinguistik. In H.-P. Althaus, H. Henne, and H. E. Wiegand 1980 *Lexikon der germanistischen Linguistik*. Tübingen: Narr, 242–58.

Kandiah, Thiru 1991 Extenuatory sociolinguistics. *Multilingua* 10, 345–79.

Kapanga, A. M. 1992 Discourse strategies in Francophone African literary works. *Journal of Multilingual and Multicultural Development* 13, 327–40.

Kaplan, Robert B. 1971 *The anatomy of rhetoric: prolegomena to a functional theory of rhetoric*. Philadelphia: The Center for Curriculum Development.

1972 Cultural thought patterns in inter-cultural education. In K. Croft (ed.), *Readings on English as a second language*. Cambridge, Mass.: Winthrop, 246–62.

1988 Contrastive rhetoric and second language learning: notes toward a theory of contrastive rhetoric. In Purves, 275–304.

Kasper, Gabriele 1981 *Pragmatik in der Interimsprache*. Tübingen: Narr.

1994 Politeness. In R. E. Asher et al. (eds.), *Encyclopaedia of language and linguistics*. Edinburgh: Pergamon and University of Aberdeen Press.

Kasper, Gabriele and Merete Dahl 1991 Research methods in intercultural pragmatics. *Studies in Second Language Acquisition* 13, 215–47.

Keim, Inken and Johannes Schwitalla 1993 Formen der Höflichkeit – Merkmale sozialen Stils. In J. Janota (ed.), *Vielfalt der kulturellen Systeme and Stile*. Tübingen: Niemeyer, 129–45.

Kirkpatrick, Andrew 1992a Chinese composition structure – ancient or modern? Paper given at 9th National Languages Conference, Darwin, July 1992.

1992b Rhetorics in Mandarin. Paper given at Applied Linguistics Association of Australia conference, Sydney, June 1992.

1993 Information sequencing in Mandarin in letters of request. *Anthropological Linguistics* 33, 1–20.

Klein, Wolfgang and Norbert Dittmar 1979 *Developing grammars*. Berlin: Springer.

Kluckhohn, C. 1951 The study of culture. In D. Learner and H. D. Lasswell (eds.), *The policy of sciences*. Stanford University Press.

Kluckhohn, Florence R. and Fred L. Strodtbeck 1961 *Variations in value orientations*. Evanston, Ill.: Row, Peterson and Co.

Knapp, Karlfried, Werner Enninger and Annelie Knapp-Pothoff 1987 *Analyzing inter-cultural communication*. Tübingen: Narr.

Knapp-Pothoff, Annelie 1992 Secondhand politeness. In Watts, Ide, and Ehlich, 203–18.

Kochman, Thomas 1981 *Black and white styles in conflict*. University of Chicago Press.

Konrád, György 1985 Mein Traum von Europa. *Kursbuch* 81. Die andere Hälfte Europas. September 1985.

Korhonen, R. and Martin Kusch 1989 The rhetorical function of the first person in philosophical texts. In Kusch and Schröder, 61–78.

Kress, Gunter and Bob Hodge 1979 *Language and ideology*. London: Longman.

Kroll, Barbara (ed.) 1990 *Second language writing: research insights for the classroom*. New York: Cambridge University Press.

Kufner, Herbert L. 1962 *The grammatical structures of English and German*. University of Chicago Press.

Kusch, Martin and Hartmut Schröder (eds.) 1989 *Text – interpretation – argumentation*. Hamburg: Buske.

Kwarciak, B. J. 1993 The acquisition of linguistic politeness and Brown and Levinson's theory. *Multilingua* 12, 51–68.

Labov, William F. 1970 The study of language in its social context. *Studium Generale* 23, 30–87.

1972 *Sociolinguistic patterns*. Philadelphia: University of Pennsylvania Press.

Lado, Robert 1957 *Linguistics across cultures*. Ann Arbor: University of Michigan Press.

Landry, Walter J. 1986 Comment. In Joshua A. Fishman (ed.), *Language rights and the English language amendment*. (= *International Journal of the Sociology of Language* 60), 129–38.

Leech, Geoffrey 1983 *Principles of pragmatics*. New York: Longman.

Leisi, Ernst 1952 *Der Wortinhalt : Seine Struktur im Deutschen und Englischen.* Heidelberg: Quelle and Meyer.

Leitner, Gerhard 1992 English as a pluricentric language. In Clyne, 117–47.

Lenz, Friedrich 1990 *Der wortkarge Finne und beredte Deutsche? der die Angst des Geschäftsmanns vor dem Muttersprachler.* Helsinki: School of Economics.

Leodolter, Ruth 1974 Review of Norbert Dittmar, '*Soziolinguistik*'. *Die Sprache* 20, 168–9.

Liedtke, Frank and Rudi Keller (eds.) 1987 *Kommunikation und Kooperation.* Tübingen: Niemeyer.

Liu Mingchen 1990 Qi, Cheng, Hé, Jié. *Australian Review of Applied Linguistics* Series S, No.6, 38–69.

Long, Michael 1991 Focus on form: a design feature in language teaching methodology. In Kees de Bot, Ralph Ginsberg, and Claire Kramsen (eds.), *Foreign language research in cross-cultural perspective.* Amsterdam: Benjamins, 39–52.

Lorf, Ira 1987 Sprachliche Verarbeitung von Lerner-Antworten im DaF-Unterricht. In Redder and Rehbein, 85–105.

Lucy, John 1992 *Language diversity and thought : a reformulation of the linguistic relativity hypothesis.* Cambridge University Press.

Magazanik, Michael 1991 Record award to teacher penalised for dedication. *The Age*, Melbourne, 30 November 1991.

Malinowskiu, Bronislaw 1949 (1975) *Eine wissenschaftliche Theorie der Kultur.* Frankfurt: Suhrkamp.

Markel, Norman N. 1975 Coverbal behavior associated with conversation turns. In A. Kendon, R. M. Harris and M. R. Key (eds.), *Organisation of behavior in face-to-face interaction.* The Hague: Mouton, 189–97.

Markus, H. R. and S. Kitayama 1991 Culture and the self: implications for cognition, emotion and motivation. *Psychological Review* 98, 224–53.

Marriott, Helen E. 1990 Intercultural business negotiations. The problem of norm discrepancy. *Australian Review of Applied Linguistics* Series S, No.7, 33–65.

Matheson, Alan 1991 *Migrant workers and Australian trades unions.* Melbourne: A. C. T. U.

Mathiot, Madeleine (ed.) 1979 *Ethnolinguistics : Boas, Sapir and Whorf revisited.* The Hague: Mouton.

Mayers, Marvin K. 1984 *A look at Filipino lifestyles.* Dallas: International Museum of Cultures.

Mohan, Bernard and Winnie Au-Yeung Lo 1985 Academic writing and Chinese studies. *TESOL Quarterly* 19, 515–34.

Moulton, William G. 1962 *The sound systems of English and German.* University of Chicago Press.

Mühlhäusler, Peter 1983 Talking about environmental issues. *Language and Communication* 3, 71–81.

Neu, Joyce 1985 A multivariate sociolinguistic analysis of the speech event negotiation. Unpublished dissertation, University of Southern California.

Neustupný, Jiří V. 1969 On 'interpénétration des systèmes linguistiques' by E. Petrovici. *Actes du xe congrès internat. des linguistes.* Bucharest: Editions de l'Académie. Vol. 1. 57.

1974 Sociolinguistics and the language teacher. *Linguistic Communications* 12, 1–24.

1978 *Post-structural approaches to language.* University of Tokyo Press.

1981 Communication with the Japanese. *The Wheel Extended* 12, 28–30.

1985 Language norms in Australian–Japanese contact situations. In Michael Clyne (ed.), *Australia meeting place of languages.* Canberra: Pacific Linguistics, 161–70.

Newbrook, Mark 1991 Which Englishes? Institutionalised second-language varieties of English in Asia and the implications for educators. Paper delivered at the conference on bilingualism and language development, Brunei, December 1991.

Nguyên, Cam 1991 Barriers to communication between Vietnamese and non-Vietnamese. *Journal of Vietnamese Studies* 1 (4), 40–5.

Nguyên Phuong Linh 1990 Why they rarely say: 'Thank you'. *Journal of Vietnamese Studies* 1 (3), 42–4.

Nguyên Xuân Thu 1990 The Vietnamese family moral code. *Journal of Vietnamese Studies* 1 (3), 32–6.

Nicholas, E. J. 1983 *Issues in education.* London: Harper and Row.

Nordenstam, K. 1992 Male and female conversational style. *International Journal of the Sociology of Language* 94, 75–98.

Ohama, Ruiko 1987 Eine Reklamation. In Redder and Rehbein, 27–51.

Oldenburg, Hermann 1992 *Angewandte Fachtextlinguistik.* Tübingen: Narr.

Olesky, Walter (ed.) 1989 *Contrastive pragmatics.* Amsterdam: Benjamins.

Olshtain, Elite 1989 Apologies across languages. In Blum-Kulka, House, and Kasper, 155–73.

Ostler, Shirley E. 1987 English in parallels: a comparison of English and Arabic prose. In Connor and Kaplan, 169–85.

Östman, Jan-Ula 1986 Pragmatics as implicitness. Unpublished dissertation, University of California, Berkeley.

Pandharipande, Rajeshwari 1983 Contrastive studies of English and Marathi. *Annual Review of Applied Linguistics* 3, 118–36.

Patthey, Ghislaine G. 1991 The language and problem solving in a computer laboratory. Unpublished dissertation, University of Southern California.

Pauwels, Anne (ed.) 1990 *Proceedings of the conference on cross-cultural communication in the health professions.* Monash University: National Centre for Community Languages in the Professions.

(ed.) 1991 *Cross-cultural communication in medical encounters.* Monash University: National Centre for Community Languages in the Professions.

(ed.) 1992 *Cross-cultural communication in legal encounters.* Monash University: National Centre for Community Languages in the Professions.

Phillipson, Robert 1992 *Linguistic imperialism.* Oxford University Press.

Pica, Teresa 1992 Negotiation and interaction in second language acquisition. Keynote address at Pacific Second Language Research Forum, Sydney, July 1992.

Pica, Teresa, Catherine Doughty, and Richard Young 1986 Making input comprehensible: do interactional modifications help? *ITL Review of Applied Linguistics* 72, 1–25.

Pica, Teresa and Michael Long 1988 The linguistic and conversational performance of experienced and inexperienced teachers. In Day.

Platt, John T. 1989 Some types of communicative strategies across cultures: sense and sensitivity. In Garcia and Otheguy, 13–30.

Price, Charles A. 1988 The ethnic character of the Australian people. In J. Jupp, 119–28.

Prucha, Jan 1974 Review of Norbert Dittmar, 'Soziolinguistik'. Linguistics 160, 114–16.

Punkki, Marja and Hartmut Schröder 1989 Argumentative Strukturen in russischsprachigen Texten der Gesellschaftswisschaften. In Kusch and Schröder, 110–24.

Purves, Alan C. (ed.) 1988 Writing across languages and cultures. Newbury Park: Sage.

Redder, Angelika and Jochen Rehbein (eds.) 1987 Arbeiten zur interkulturellen Kommunikation. (= Osnabrücker Beiträge zur Sprachtheorie 38). Osnabrück.

Rehbein, Jochen 1972 Entschuldigungen und Rechtfertigungen. In Wunderlich, 209–54.
    1977 Komplexes Handeln. Stuttgart: Metzler.

Reichman, R. 1990 Communication and mutual engagement. In Dorval, 23–48.

Rein, Kurt 1974 Review of Norbert Dittmar, 'Soziolinguistik'. Germanistik 15, 249.

Richards, Jack, John Platt, and Heidi Weber 1985 Longman's dictionary of applied linguistics. Harlow: Longman.

Roberts, Celia, Evelyn Davies, and Tom Jupp 1992 Language and discrimination. London: Longman.

Roche, Jürgen 1989 Xenolekte. Berlin: Springer.

Rokeach, Milton 1968 Beliefs attitudes and values. San Francisco: Jossey-Bass.

Rumelhart, D. E. 1975 Notes on a schema for stories. In D. G. Bobrow and A. Collins (eds.), Representation and understanding. New York: Academic Press, 211–36.

Sa'adeddin, Mohammed Akram A. M. 1989 Text development and Arabic-English negative interference. Applied Linguistics 10, 36–51.

Sachtleber, Susanne 1990 Linearität vs. Digressivität. Wissenschaftliche Texte im zweisprachigen Vergleich. Folia Linguistica 24, 105–22.

Sacks, Harvey, Emanuel Schegloff, and Gail Jefferson 1974 A simplest systematics for the organization of turn-taking for conversation. Language 50, 696–735.

Sajavaara, Kari 1977 Contrastive linguistics past and present and a communicative approach. Jyväskälä Contrastive Studies 4, 9–30.

Salus, J. H. 1983 Review of Ruth Wodak, 'Das Wort in der Gruppe'. Language 59, 941–2.

Sapir, Edward 1921 Language : an introduction to the study of speech. New York: Harcourt Brace.

Saussure, Ferdinand de 1959 Course in general linguistics. (ed.) Charles Bally and Albert Sechehaye. Translated by Wade Baskin. London: Fontana-Collins.

Schank, Roger C. and Robert P. Abelson 1977 Scripts, plans, goals and understanding. Hillsdale, N.J.: Erlbaum.

Schermerhorn, R. A. 1970 *Comparative ethnic relations : a framework for theory and research*. New York: Random House.

Schiffrin, Deborah 1984 Jewish argument as sociability. *Language in Society* 13, 311–36.

1987 *Discourse markers*. Cambridge University Press.

Schmale, Günter 1987 Reziprozität als Grundlage kooperativen Handelns in Kontaktsituationen zu deutschen und französischen Sprechern. In Liedtke and Keller, 219–42.

Schneider, Klaus P. 1988 *Small talk*. Marburg: Hitzeroth.

Schröder, Hartmut 1989 Kulturunterschiede in der schriflichen Kommunikation und Wege ihrer Erforschung. *Gal Bulletin* 11, 22–33.

(ed.) 1991 *Subject-oriented texts*. Berlin: De Gruyter.

(ed.) 1993 *Fachtextpragmatik*. Tübingen: Narr.

Schumann, John H. 1978 *The pidginization process : a model for second language acquisition*. Rowley: Newbury House.

Scollon, Roy and Suzanne Scollon 1981 *Narrative, literacy and face in interethnic communication*. Norwood: Ablex.

Searle, John R. 1969 *Speech acts*. Cambridge University Press.

Selinker, Larry 1972 Interlanguage. *International Review of Applied Linguistics* 10, 209–31.

Senft, Gunter 1982 *Sprachliche Varietät und Variation im Sprachverhalten Kaiserslauterer Metallarbeiter*. Bern: Lang.

Sharrock, Wes and Bob Anderson 1987 Epilogue: the definition of alternatives: some sources of confusion in interdisciplinary discussion. In Button and Lee, 290–321.

Siegel, Jeffrey 1987 *Language contact in a plantation environment*. Oxford University Press.

Sinclair, John and R. M. Coulthard 1975 *Towards an analysis of discourse*. London: Oxford University Press.

Smolicz, J. J. 1981 Core values and cultural identity. *Ethnic and Racial Studies* 4, 75–90.

Spender, Dale 1980 *Man made language*. London: Routledge and Kegan Paul.

Sperber, Dan and Deirdrie Wilson 1986 *Relevance*. Oxford: Blackwell.

Spillner, Bernd 1982 Formen und Funktionen wissenschaftlichen Sprechens und Schreibens. *Locumer Protokolle* 6, 33–56.

Stahlheber, Eva 1992 Die Fachsorte Zeitschriftenartikel im Deutschen und address/article im Amerikanischen. In Baumann and Kalverkämpfer, 162–89.

Steinmetz, Ariane 1987 Verbalisierungen beim kollektiven Nacherzählen. In Redder and Rehbein, 106–20.

Steinthal, H. 1880 *Gesammelte kleine Schriften*. Vol. 1. Berlin: Dümmler.

Stockwell, R. P. and J. P. Bowen 1965 *The sounds of English and Spanish*. University of Chicago Press.

Stockwell, R. P., J. P. Bowen, and J. W. Martin 1975 *The grammatical structures of English and Spanish*. University of Chicago Press.

Stroebe, Wolfgang 1976 Is social psychology really that complicated? A review of Martin Irle's '*Lehrbuch der Sozialpsychologie*'. *European Journal of Social Psychology* 6, 509–11.

Stubbs, Michael 1983 *Discourse analysis*. Oxford: Blackwell.

Swales, John 1984 Research into the structure of introductions to journal articles and its applications to the teaching of academic writing. In R. Williams, J. Swales, and J. Kirkman (eds.), *Common ground: shared interests in ESP and communication studies*. Oxford: Pergamon, 77–86.

Tajfel, Henri 1974 Social identity and intergroup behavior. *Social Science Information* 13, 65–93.

Tannen, Deborah 1986 *That's not what I meant!* New York: Ballentyne Books.

Taylor, Gordon and Chen Tingguang 1991 Linguistic, cultural and subcultural issues in contrastive discourse analysis: Anglo-American and Chinese texts. *Applied Linguistics* 12, 319–36.

Thomas, Jenny 1983 Cross-cultural pragmatic failure. *Applied Linguistics* 4, 91–112.

Thompson, James A. 1967 *Organization in action*. New York: McGraw-Hill.

Tirkkonen-Condit, Sonja and Luise Liefländer-Koistinen 1989 Argumentation in Finnish. In Kusch and Schröder, 173–81.

Tomić, Olga and Roger Shuy (eds.) 1987 *The interrelation of theoretical and applied linguistics*. New York: Plenum.

Urban, Wilbur M. 1939 *Language and reality*. New York: Macmillan.

Vallée, F. G. 1975 Multi-ethnic societies: The issues of identity and equality. In D. S. Forase and S. Richter (eds.), *Issues in Canadian society*. Toronto: Prentice-Hall, 162–202.

Van Dijk, Teun 1977 *Text and context*. London: Longman.

　1980 *Textwissenschaft*. Munich: DTV.

　1991 *Racism in the press*. London: Routledge.

Verschueren, Jef 1984 Linguistics and crosscultural communication (Review article). *Language in Society* 13, 489–509.

Vildomec, V. 1963 *Multilingualism*. Leiden: Sijthoff.

Võ Phiên 1989 The Vietnamese language and people abroad. *Journal of Vietnamese Studies* 1 (2), 3–12.

Wardhaugh, Ronald 1985 *How communication works*. Oxford: Blackwell.

Watts, Richard J. 1989 Relevance and relational work: linguistic politeness as politic behavior. *Multilingua* 8, 131–66.

　1991 *Power in family discourse*. Berlin: Mouton de Gruyter.

　1992 Linguistic politeness and politic verbal behaviour: reconsidering claims for universality. In Watts, Ide, and Ehlich, 43–69.

Watts, Richard J., Sachiko Ide and Konrad Ehlich (eds.), 1992 *Politeness in language*. Berlin: Mouton de Gruyter.

Weber, Max 1904/1905 *Die protestantische Ethik und der Geist des Kapitalismus*. Archiv für Sozialwissenschaft und Sozialpolitik 20–1. (Translated by Talcott Parsons. *The Protestant Ethics and the Spirit of Capitalism*. London: Unwin, 1930.)

Wedel, Janine 1986 *The Private Poland*. New York: Facts on File.

Weisgerber, Leo 1962 *Grundzüge der inhaltbezogenen Grammatik*. Düsseldorf: Schwann.

Werkgroep Taal Buitenlandse Werknemers 1978 *Nederlands tegen Buitenlanders*. Amsterdam: Instituut voor Algemene Taalkunde.

Werkhofer, Konrad T. 1992 Traditional and modern views: the social consitu-tion and the power of politeness. In Watts, Ide, and Ehlich, 155–199.

Whorf, Benjamin L. 1956 Science and linguistics. In J. B. Carroll (ed.), *Language, thought and reality: selected readings of Benjamin Lee Whorf.* Cambridge, Mass.: Polity Press, 207–19.

Widén, P. 1985 Interkulturelle Verständigung am Beispiel der finnisch-deutschen Kommunikation. *Lebende Sprachen* 85, 167–70.

1988 Fettnäppchen im deutsch-finnischen Handelsverkehr. *Deutsch-finnische Handelskammer* 88, 14–16.

Wierzbicka, Anna 1985 A semantic metalanguage for a cross-cultural comparison of speech acts and speech genres. *Language in Society* 14, 491–514.

1991 *Cross-cultural pragmatics.* Berlin: Mouton de Gruyter.

1993 Intercultural communication in Australia. In Gerhard Schulz (ed.), *The languages of Australia.* Canberra: Australian Academy of the Humanities, 83–103.

Wiesenhütter, Angela 1987 Touristen und Einheimische verabreden sich. In Redder and Rehbein, 135–50.

Wildner-Bassett, Mary E. 1987 Review of W. Schöperle, '*Argumentieren – Bewerten – Manipulieren*'. *Language in Society* 16, 248–51.

1989 Coexisting discourse worlds and the study of pragmatic aspects of learner's interlanguage. In Olesky, 251–75.

Williams, Raymond 1981 *Culture.* Glasgow: Fontana.

Willis, R. 1983 *Learning to labour.* Aldershot: Gower.

Wilson, Steven R., Min-Sun Kim, and Hendrika Meischke 1992 Evaluating Brown and Levinson's politeness theory. *Research on Language and Social Interaction* 25, 215–52.

Wolfson, Nessa 1986 Research methodology and the question of validity. *TESOL Quarterly* 20, 689–99.

Wolfson, Nessa, Thomas Marmor, and Steve Jones 1989 Problems in the comparison of speech acts across cultures. In Blum-Kulka, House, and Kasper, 197–218.

Wunderlich, Dieter (ed.) 1972 *Linguistische Pragmatik.* Frankfurt: Athenäum.

Yli-Renko, Kaarina 1993 Interkulturelle Kommunikation – eine Herausforderung an den Deutschunterricht. Paper presented at the International German Teachers' Conference, Leipzig, August 1993.

Yong Liang 1991 Zu soziokulturellen und textstrukturellen Besonderheiten wissenschaftlicher Rezensionen. *Deutsche Sprache* 1991, 289–311.

Yuill, Bruce F. 1970 *Organization and management.* Sydney: West.

Zimmermann, Klaus 1984 Bemerkungen zur Beschreibung der interaktiven Funktion höflichkeitsmarkierter grammatischer Elemente. In E. Gülich and T. Kotschi (eds.), *Grammatik, Konversation, Interaktion.* Tübingen: Niemeyer, 67–81.

Index of text transcriptions

Name Index

Abelson, R. P., 7
Allan, K., 11, 13, 14, 194
Anderson, B., 9, 10
Arndt, H., 6, 15, 195
Austin, J. L., 2, 10, 11, 16, 49

Backa S., 24
Ball, M., 4, 91, 207
Bardovi-Harlig, K., 17, 18
Bateson, G., 7
Bayrataroglu, A., 14
Béal, C., 21, 22
Bernstein, B., 6
Bickner, R., 171
Bilimoria, B., 188
Bills, G. D., 210
Blommaert, J., 207
Blum-Kulka, S., 6, 17, 20, 21, 139, 203
Bodi, L., 179, 193
Bowen, J. P., 6
Bremer, K., 22, 24, 56, 69, 150
Brick, J., 179, 182, 184
Brock, C., 26
Brown, G., 5
Brown, P., 14, 15, 21, 56, 60, 64, 109,
    139, 141, 144, 176, 190, 195
Bublitz, W., 9, 110
Button, G., 5, 7, 9

Carroll, R., 25, 189
Cauchi, M., 177
Chan Heng Chee, 182
Chen Tingguang, 171
Chiaro, D., 197
Chick, K., 22, 24
Chilton, P., 6
Clahsen, H., 26
Clyne, M. G., 4, 6, 18, 19, 26, 32, 46, 91,
    155, 161, 162, 163, 164, 165, 166,
    167, 173, 174, 175, 186, 187, 189,
    190, 196, 197, 206, 207, 208, 213
Coates, J., 6

Cole, M., 6
Connor, U., 160
Cordella, M., 21
Corder, S. P., 5
Coulmas, F., 16
Coulthard, R. M., 7, 8
Crismore, A., 188

Dahl, M., 17, 18
Danet, B., 173
Davies, E., 18, 27
De Silva, K. M., 178, 183
Deen, J., 26
Degenhart, R. E., 169
di Pietro, J. R., 6
Dittmar, N., 26
Đô Quý Toàn, 188
Dorval, B., 9
Doughty, C., 9

Edmondson, W. J., 5, 20
Eggington, W. G., 170
Ehlich, K., 2, 13, 15, 20, 24, 45, 196, 212
Elias, N., 15
Enninger, W., 25
Erikson, F., 205

Fairclough, N., 22
Farrell, L., 173, 191
Feigs, W., 168
Ferguson, C. A., 26
Fishman, J. A., 6, 177
Fox, B., 8
Fraser, B., 15, 16
Færch, C., 5, 9, 27, 33

Galtung, J., 28, 157, 163, 168, 187, 191,
    197
Gardner, R. C., 208
Geye, E.-G., 210
Giannicos, C., 18, 46, 155

246

Index of Subjects